Y0-CUZ-491

M782.42083 Bricu.L Leslie

Bricusse, Leslie.

The Leslie Bricusse
children's songbook /
c1992.

DATE DUE	
JAN 8 - 2004	
NOV 1 8 2004	
OCT 1 3 2005	
FEB 4 - 2006	
NOV 2 8 2006	

The Leslie Bricusse Children's Songbook

Illustrated by Evie Bricusse

Compiled by Len Handler
Production Manager: Daniel Rosenbaum
Art Direction: Kerstin Fairbend
Director Of Music: Mark Phillips

All photos courtesy of Leslie Bricusse unless otherwise specified.

ISBN:0-89524-693-7

Copyright © 1992 Cherry Lane Music Company, Inc.
International Copyright Secured All Rights Reserved

All rights reserved. No part of this publication may be reproduced, stored in a database or retrieval system, or transmitted in any form or by any means, electronic, mechanical, photocopying, recording or otherwise, without the prior written permission of the publisher. Inquiries should be addressed to:
Print Licensing Division, Cherry Lane Music Company, Inc., P.O. Box 430, Port Chester, NY 10573

Care has been taken to trace the ownership of any copyrighted material contained in this text. The publishers welcome any information that will enable them to rectify, in subsequent editions, any incorrect or omitted reference or credit.

EVANSTON PUBLIC LIBRARY
1703 ORRINGTON AVENUE
EVANSTON, ILLINOIS 60201

FOREWORD

Between a bunch of schoolkids singing "The ABC Song" in Anthony Newley's *Stop The World—I Want To Get Off* in 1961, and another bunch of schoolkids singing "We Don't Wanna Grow Up" in Steven Spielberg's magical revisit to the Peter Pan story exactly 30 years later, I have been lucky enough to write songs for no less than 20 children's movies and stage shows—a wondrous musical roller coaster fantasy ride that has taken me from Rex Harrison as "Doctor Dolittle," talking to the animals, to Gene Wilder as "Willy Wonka," showing Charlie Bucket and the other lucky Golden Ticket winners the world of pure imagination that is his amazing Chocolate Factory...from Peter O'Toole as "Mr. Chips," staring at generation after generation of hopelessly unruly English schoolboys and wondering what these hideous little monsters can possibly hope to become if they ever grow up, to Mia Farrow as "Peter Pan," flying and battling to the death with Danny Kaye as the evil Captain Hook in 1976, and Robin Williams as an older Peter Pan, dazzlingly aided by Julia Roberts as Tinkerbell, flying again and battling anew with Dustin Hoffman as an even more evil "Hook" in 1991...from Albert Finney as the miserly "Scrooge," of Charles Dickens' *Christmas Carol*, magically transformed into Santa Claus, to Santa Claus himself in *Santa Claus: The Movie*...from the infant Drew Barrymore, as Lisa, catapulted from her routine little life in Cincinnati into the endless wonders and dangers of existence among the "Babes In Toyland," to Macaulay Culkin, as Kevin, outwitting the world's two all-time bungling burglars as he spends a slightly unexpected house-defending Christmas at "Home Alone"...from a homeless Tom the Cat and Jerry the Mouse seeking a new life and facing endless dramas and setbacks in a hostile animated world in *Tom and Jerry—The Movie*, to Julie Andrews singing and narrating to a bunch of wide-eyed and horrified children the terrifying tale of "Santa's Last Ride"...and on and on and on, through many other exciting journeys and adventures that only a happy, ongoing association with the unending joys of childhood can possibly provide.

Adam and Leslie Bricusse, 1967 Photo courtesy of Richard Donner

I've never been quite sure exactly when or how this lovely and rewarding part of my life began. I know I first became seriously involved in my children's projects when my son Adam was two and three and four years old, around "Doctor Dolittle" time, because I so loved amusing him,—and I was amusing myself at least as much at the same time, I saw no harm in continuing the process—a decision I have never regretted, for to this day I am at my happiest when I am working on any project for or about children.

And as the illustrations in this book so amply demonstrate, my darling wife Evie's remarkable talent to depict visually the magical world of childhood fantasy has always fascinated and delighted me—her imagination so wonderfully inventive and pure and innocent, her touch so delicate and charming and uniquely original. Her paintings are truly a mirror of her soul, for Evie inhabits a genuinely beautiful world of her own creation that the rest of us can only envy.

It is a happy comment on an often unhappy world that at this moment in time there is an ever-increasing demand for more and more projects for children and family audiences to appeal to the sunnier side of man's sometimes too-dark soul.

In the 1990's, I predict and I pray that for every Barbarian, Destroyer, Terminator, Rocky and Rambo, there will also be a Peter Pan, a Hook, a Home Alone, a Tom and a Jerry. For every mortal blow, a belly laugh, and for every act of cruelty and anger, a song of love and laughter and happiness and hope. Let's start with these....

Leslie Bricusse
St. Paul de Vence
France
June, 1991

LESLIE BRICUSSE

Leslie Bricusse was born in London and educated at University College School and Caius College, Cambridge. His stage musicals include *Stop the World—I Want To Get Off, Harvey!, The Roar of the Greasepaint—The Smell of the Crowd, Pickwick, The Good Old Bad Old Days, One Shining Moment & Sherlock Holmes—The Musical*. He has written songs and/or screenplays for such films as *Dr. Dolittle, Scrooge, Willy Wonka & the Chocolate Factory, Goodbye, Mr. Chips* and *Victor/Victoria* and collaborated with such musical talents as Anthony Newley, Henry Mancini, John Williams, John Barry, Jerry Goldsmith, Jule Styne, Alan Jay Lerner and Andre Previn. His better known songs include "What Kind of Fool Am I," Once in a Lifetime," Gonna Build a Mountain," Who Can I Turn To?," "The Joker," "If I Ruled the World," "When I Look in Your Eyes," "Goldfinger," the Love Theme from *Superman* ("Can You Read My Mind?"), You Only Live Twice," "Le Jazz Hot," On a Wonderful Day Like Today," "Two for the Road," and "The Candy Man." He has been nominated for eight Academy Awards, six Grammys, four Tonys and won two Oscars, a Grammy and seven Ivor Novello Awards (the British equivalent of a Grammy cum Tony). He is currently working on a Broadway version of *Victor/Victoria* in collaboration with Blake Edwards and Henry Mancini. In 1989 he received the Jimmy Kennedy Award for consistent excellency in British songwriting, and was inducted into the American Songwriter's Hall of Fame.

EVIE BRICUSSE

Under the stage name of Yvonne Romain, Evie Bricusse has played featured and starring roles in more than 40 motion pictures, movies for television and top TV series.

Her films include *Dr. Syn, The Frightened City, Night Creatures, Smokescreen, Double Trouble, The Swinger, Devil Doll, Circus of Horrors, The Curse of the Werewolf, The Last of Sheila, Action of the Tiger, Village of Daughters, The Brigand of Kandahar, Murder Reported, Doctor from Seven Dials, Robbery Under Arms, Seven Thunders, The Silent Enemy* and *The Baby and the Battleship*.

Movies for television include *On the Spot, Miss Olive, The Innocent, Clash of Arms, Don Juan*, and *A Gust of Wind*.

TV series include *The Avengers, Danger Man, T.H.E. Cat, Robin Hood, Lancelot, Dial 999, Miss Adventure, The Third Man, International Detective, The Buccaneer, Martin Kane, O.S.S., Dick and the Duchess, Top Secret* and *Douglas Fairbanks Theatre*.

Her leading men have included Sean Connery, Roger Moore, Elvis Presley, Oliver Reed, Peter Cushing, Christopher Lee, Tony Franciosa, Herbert Lom, Patrick McNee, Robert Loggia and John Gregson.

She is married to Academy Award-winning composer and lyricist Leslie Bricusse. Her hobbies are international cuisine, interior decorating and collaborating on children's books, such as this one, which she illustrates and her husband writes. She lives in France, California and Mexico.

Goodbye, Mr. Chips © 1969 Turner Entertainment Co. All Rights Reserved

Dr. Dolittle © 1967 Twentieth Century Fox Film Corporation All Rights Reserved

Contents

■ **MUSIC FROM THE MOVIES**

    Reflections by Leslie Bricusse   1

◆ **Doctor Dolittle**

Talk To The Animals	5
Doctor Dolittle	12
Beautiful Things	14
I've Never Seen Anything Like It	18
Fabulous Places	22
My Friend The Doctor	27

◆ **Goodbye, Mr. Chips**

Schooldays	34
Fill The World With Love	40
When I Am Older	44
A Day Has A Hundred Pockets	52
That's A Boy!	56
Where Did My Childhood Go?	66

◆ **Scrooge**

A Christmas Carol	71

Babes In Toyland © Copyright Orion Television Entertainment. All Rights Reserved

Scrooge © MCMLXX Cinema Center Films, Inc. All Rights Reserved

The Beautiful Day	74	Oompa-Loompa Doompadee-Doo	105
Christmas Children	76	Cheer Up, Charlie	108
Thank You Very Much	80	I've Got A Golden Ticket	112
Father Christmas	84	Pure Imagination	116
I Like Life	87	◆ **Santa Claus: The Movie**	
The Minister's Cat	90	Thank You, Santa!	119
Good Times	96	◆ **Home Alone**	
Willy Wonka & The Chocolate Factory		Somewhere In My Memory	123
The Candy Man	100	Star Of Bethlehem	126

Dr. Dolittle © 1967 Twentieth Century Fox Film Corporation All Rights Reserved

Goodbye, Mr. Chips © 1969 Turner Entertainment Co. All Rights Reserved

Peter Pan © 1975 ITC Entertainment Group, Ltd. All Rights Reserved

■ MUSIC FROM TELEVISION

Reflections by Leslie Bricusse   129

◆ Peter Pan

Growing Up	130
I'm Better With You	138
Once Upon A Bedtime	142
Peter Pan	146
Pretending	156
Little Darlings	164
Never-Never Land	169
A Song Called Love	174
The House On Happiness Hill	180
You Can Fly	184

◆ Babes In Toyland

C-I-N-C-I-N-N-A-T-I	193
Through The Eyes Of A Child	198

Scrooge © MCMLXX Cinema Center Films, Inc. All Rights Reserved

Willy Wonka & The Chocolate Factory © 1971 Wolper Pictures Ltd. And The Quaker Oats Company All Rights Reserved

■ MUSIC FROM THE STAGE

Reflections by Leslie Bricusse	201

◆ Stop The World–I Want To Get Off

The ABC Song	202

◆ The Roar Of The Greasepaint– The Smell Of The Crowd

The Beautiful Land	203
Look At That Face	208
That's What It Is To Be Young	212
Things To Remember	216

◆ The Good Old Bad Old Days

It's A Musical World	224

◆ Noah's Ark

Faith In The Future	228

◆ Ondine

The World Is Beautiful	232

■ JUST FOR FUN

Reflections by Leslie Bricusse	236
Amy Rainbow	237
Tumbarumba	242

◆ COMPLETE LYRICS 245

Illustrated by Evie Bricusse

ALPHABETICAL LISTING

202	ABC Song, The	Stop The World—I Want To Get Off
237	Amy Rainbow	
74	Beautiful Day, The	Scrooge
203	Beautiful Land, The	The Roar Of The Greasepaint—The Smell Of The Crowd
14	Beautiful Things	Doctor Dolittle
100	Candy Man, The	Willy Wonka & The Chocolate Factory
108	Cheer Up, Charlie	Willy Wonka & The Chocolate Factory
71	Christmas Carol, A	Scrooge
76	Christmas Children	Scrooge
193	C-I-N-C-I-N-N-A-T-I	Babes In Toyland
52	Day Has A Hundred Pocket, A	Goodbye, Mr. Chips
12	Doctor Dolittle	Doctor Dolittle
22	Fabulous Places	Doctor Dolittle
228	Faith In The Future	Noah's Ark
84	Father Christmas	Scrooge
40	Fill The World With Love	Goodbye, Mr. Chips
96	Good Times	Scrooge
130	Growing Up	Peter Pan
180	House On Happiness Hill, The	Peter Pan
87	I Like Life	Scrooge
138	I'm Better With You	Peter Pan
112	I've Got A Golden Ticket	Willy Wonka & The Chocolate Factory
18	I've Never Seen Anything Like It	Doctor Dolittle
224	It's A Musical World	The Good Old Bad Old Days
164	Little Darlings	Peter Pan
208	Look At That Face	The Roar Of The Greasepaint—The Smell Of The Crowd
90	Minister's Cat, The	Scrooge
27	My Friend The Doctor	Doctor Dolittle
169	Never-Never Land	Peter Pan
142	Once Upon A Bedtime	Peter Pan
105	Oompa-Loompa Doompadee-Doo	Willy Wonka & The Chocolate Factory
146	Peter Pan	Peter Pan
156	Pretending	Peter Pan
116	Pure Imagination	Willy Wonka & The Chocolate Factory
34	Schooldays	Goodbye, Mr. Chips
123	Somewhere In My Memory	Home Alone
174	Song Called Love, A	Peter Pan
126	Star Of Bethlehem	Home Alone
5	Talk To The Animals	Doctor Dolittle
80	Thank You Very Much	Scrooge
119	Thank You, Santa!	Santa Claus: The Movie
56	That's A Boy!	Goodbye, Mr. Chips
212	That's What It Is To Be Young	The Roar Of The Greasepaint—The Smell Of The Crowd
216	Things To Remember	The Roar Of The Greasepaint—The Smell Of The Crowd
198	Through The Eyes Of A Child	Babes In Toyland
242	Tumbarumba	
44	When I Am Older	Goodbye, Mr. Chips
66	Where Did My Childhood Go?	Goodbye, Mr. Chips
232	World Is Beautiful, The	Ondine
184	You Can Fly	Peter Pan

Music From The Movies

Doctor Dolittle (1967)

Early in 1965, Arthur P. Jacobs (known as Apjac) called me in London to say that he was planning to make a major musical movie based on Hugh Lofting's "Doctor Dolittle" stories, and if invited, would I be interested to write it?

The plan had been for the film to re-unite the legendary Lerner and Loewe with Rex Harrison, but for various reasons of health and schedule, Lerner and Loewe had passed on the project, but Rex was still keen on it. Apjac had put forward my name to Darryl Zanuck, whose son Richard was the new young head of the Fox studios, as an alternative writer.

A couple of weeks later, Apjac called to say that Fox were interested and he would meet me in San Francisco the following week.

Believe this or not, *a couple of weeks after that* I was given the triple assignment as screenwriter, composer and lyricist—on the basis that I had already written a score *about animals*—viz. *Noah's Ark*.

I had no illusions about the fact that Rex was less than enchanted to be offered me as a replacement for both Lerner and Loewe. For the first several months, I think he condescendingly regarded me as a promising undergraduate who might eventually contribute a couple of good items to the college revue.

Wonderfully cantankerous and delighting in his wickedness, he was also very amusing. I think he went through life playing Rex Harrison without ever quite knowing who he really was. But during the following two years was born a friendship that continued until the end of his life.

I had to battle with Rex for many months, though, to keep the first song I'd written for him, "Talk to the Animals," in the score.

"*It's such a silly song*," he complained. I pointed out that Doctor Dolittle was a children's story and he would not be judged as Henry Higgins singing it. "I should bloody well hope not," he grumbled.

Only when the song was finally filmed did Rex grudgingly conceded that it was "all right." Even when "Talk to the Animals" won the Academy Award for Best Song the following year, he still retained lingering doubts about it.

"'Of courseros' does *not* rhyme with 'Rhinoceros,'" he sniffed. And he's probably right.

Goodbye, Mr. Chips (1969)

I knew about the musical version of *Goodbye, Mr. Chips* almost three years before I became involved in it, because it was already "in the works" at MGM when I arrived at Fox to write *Doctor Dolittle*.

Chips, at one time or another, was going to star, be directed, written, and composed by almost every major name in the industry. First this one was in and that one was out, then this one was out and the next one was in. This went on for *six years*!

Anyway, it eventually got made, starring Peter O'Toole and Petula Clark and directed by Herb Ross, who had been the choreographer on *Doctor Dolittle*.

Boy, Peter O'Toole can act!—and boy, oh boy, Peter *cannot* sing! But his wondrous acting art overcame even his non-singing, and he was nominated for an Academy Award as Best Actor. He also finally achieved a strangely touching performance in all his songs, so much so that before we knew it, he went straight on to his second musical, playing Don Quixote in The Man of La Mancha, no less!

I had immense trouble getting the last song—the score's big ballad. In all, I wrote *eighteen* songs for that one spot—more songs than there are in the whole film! The first seventeen somehow lacked the exact tenderness that defined the special romance of the relationship between Chips and his adored and adoring Katherine.

In the end, as so often before and since, I turned to my own adored and adoring Evie for the answer.

I wrote the song about *us*, and the weeks and weeks of frustration were solved in minutes. The song, called "You and I," has become, like most "Evie songs," one of my permanent favourites among my own songs.

Scrooge (1970)

Bob Solo gets the solo credit for causing this, one of my favourite projects, to happen. This young American film producer working in London wanted to create a definitive musical film version of Charles Dickens' first great Christmas story, A Christmas Carol, which The Great Author had dashed off in a matter of days as a means of paying off a bunch of bills owing in 1843. How lucky for all of us! And how *especially* lucky for me, a century and a quarter later!

The role of Scrooge was originally intended to be played by my old friend Richard Harris, which delighted me. He just had finished playing King Arthur in the film of Camelot, and I anticipated he would be brilliant in the role.

Then disaster struck—quiet unexpectedly, as disaster tends to do. The film Richard Harris was completing in Israel fell heavily behind schedule. He couldn't leave, and we couldn't wait for him because of our Christmas opening commitment a year hence. We had to re-cast, and fast!

I had some say in the matter, as in addition to being the film's screenwriter, composer and lyricist, I was also the executive producer. I promptly suggested Rex Harrison, with whom I had just worked for two years on Doctor Dolittle.

Rex was appearing at London's Lyric Theatre at the time. He was highly enthusiastic about Scrooge, and was readily available to discuss and rehearse musical material on non-matinee days. No question, he too was going to be fabulous in the role.

Then disaster suddenly decided to strike again! Rex suddenly became very sick and had to withdraw not only from the play, but the film, too! Now our backs were really to the wall. Cinema Centre Films gave us three actors to choose from and three days in which to get one of them to commit—Peter O'Toole, Richard Burton and Albert Finney.

My gut instinct was for Albert Finney, so I tried him first. By a happy chance, Albert was in London.

I called him and explained the project, the situation and the urgency. He invited me to his home for dinner that same evening. We sat and ate and talked in the kitchen until I had run out of killer persuasive chit-chat, and at dawn I left him with the script and score of Scrooge.

Less than 24 hours later, Albie was having his first wardrobe fittings, and Scrooge was finally on its way! We never heard from disaster again.

Willy Wonka & The Chocolate Factory (1971)

David Wolper, the pre-eminent Hollywood producer, brought this project to Tony Newley and me—a film musical based on the most successful of all Roald Dahl's wonderful children's books, *Charlie & the Chocolate Factory*. We met at David's house in Holmby Hills on a Saturday morning in early June, 1970. Newley and I said yes before he had even finished describing the project, and we went right to work.

In the film, Gene Wilder played Willy Wonka with charm and eccentricity—a touch of madness, almost—but I often wondered to myself why a 34-year-old actor was playing an old man retiring from the candy business and wanting to give his factory away.

Since there was nothing I could do about it—the die and Mr. Wilder were both cast—I let the matter rest, until one evening a couple of years later, when Fred Astaire was at our house in Beverly Hills for dinner. Late in the evening we played pool, and between games he suddenly turned to me and said in that famous shy, modest voice of his, "Leslie, I've been wanting to ask you this for years, but I didn't like to mention it! Why do you suppose it was they didn't want me to play Willy Wonka?"

I did not believe what I had just heard. Here was the greatest song-and-dance man in the history of the world telling me that he had actually asked to play the role of Willy Wonka, and they had *turned him down*! Ho Hum! Let's not discuss it!

Willy Wonka was kind to us all (Newley and I were nominated for a Best Original Song Score Oscar, and "The Candy Man" was a humongous, multi-million selling number one single for Sammy Davis, Jr.), and I'll always love and be grateful for it—but I'll also remain forever slightly testy at the mere thought of that miraculous might-have-been that was there for the taking—the never-to-be-repeated golden opportunity to work with my magical musical genius neighbor up the street in Beverly Hills—the one, the only, Fred Astaire!

Santa Claus: The Movie (1985)

In 1985, Alexander and Ilya Salkind, they of the "Superman" movies, launched their massive fifty-million dollar epic, *Santa Claus: The Movie*.

I was originally meant to write the songs with John Williams, with whom I worked on the original *Superman*, but I somehow ended up writing them with Hank Mancini, with whom I'd just done *Victor/Victoria*. Either way, a very nice collaboration for me!

The film was intended to breathe the very spirit of Christmas, and ended up being a less-than-hilarious contemporary comedy with a heavy-handed moral about the commercial greed of Christmas. It was neither Scrooge nor Santa Claus, because the canvas was large without being big, if you get my meaning.

What we did not know at the time was that the producers, in exchange for a large sum of money, had already made a deal beforehand with a major record company, which allowed virtually indiscriminate interpolation of their commercial material into the final soundtrack. Fragments of disjointed pop songs emerged from every toy store and hamburger joint that the camera passed and the film ended with an unrelated Christmas aria that had nothing whatsoever to do with the film, either musically, lyrically or stylistically. The end result was that ironically, the film was ruined by the application of the very same values it criticized in the story.

For me the abiding moral is "If you mess with Santa, your toys won't work!"

Home Alone (1990)

It is one of the classic ongoing inconsistencies of musicals and songwriting that you can work for weeks, months, or even years on a project that comes to nothing, and conversely, receive huge rewards and lasting acclaim for work that has taken only days, sometimes even hours, to achieve.

Happily for me, the songs for *Home Alone* fall into the latter category. One Friday evening in October, 1990, the telephone rang. It was John Williams, calling from California. John said, "I'm just finishing scoring this enchanting little film called *Home Alone*, and there's this theme I think would make a charming song."

By Monday morning we had the song "Somewhere in My Memory"...and indeed by Tuesday night we had *two* songs, as John had also composed a hauntingly beautiful Christmas carol, to which I added a lyric entitled "Star of Bethlehem."

In February of 1991, *Home Alone* was nominated for two Academy Awards, Best Score and Best Song—two for John, one for me—in my case, a wondrous reward for my long weekend's work.

Leslie Bricusse and Rex Harrison.

TALK TO THE ANIMALS
from the motion picture *Doctor Dolittle*

Words and Music by
Leslie Bricusse

Moderately

If I could Talk To The An-i-mals, just im-ag-ine it,
sult-ed with quad-ru-peds, think what fun we'd have,

Chat-ting to a chimp in chim-pan-zee, Im-ag-ine talk-ing to a
Ask-ing o-ver croc-o-diles for tea, Or may-be lunch with two or

ti-ger, chat-ting to a chee-tah, What a neat a-
three lions, wal-rus-es and sea lions, What a love-ly

Copyright © 1967 20th Century Music Corp.
All Rights Controlled by Hastings Music Corporation
1350 Ave. Of The Americas, New York, NY 10019
International Copyright Secured All Rights Reserved

chieve-ment it would be. If we could Talk To The An-i-mals,
place the world would be. If I spoke slang to o-rang-u-tangs,

learn their lan-gua-ges, May-be take an an-i-mal de-gree,
the ad-van-ta-ges, An-y fool on earth can plain-ly see.

I'd stud-y el-e-phant and ea-gle, buf-fa-lo and bea-gle,
Dis-cuss-ing east-ern art and dra-mas with in-tel-lec-tual lla-mas,

Al-li-ga-tor, guin-ea pig and flea. I would con-
That's a big step for-ward, you'll a-gree. I'd learn to

verse in polar bear and python, And I would
speak in antelope and turtle, My Pekin-

curse in fluent kangaroo. If people
ese would be extremely good. If I were

asked me, "Can you speak rhinoceros?" I'd say, "Of
asked to sing in hippopotamus, I'd say, "Why

course-er-os!"
not-a-mus?" Can't you?" If I con-
 And would! If I could

Cm Ab F Eb Abm F
ferred with our fur - ry friends, man to an - i - mal,
par - ley with pach - y - derms, it's a fair - y tale
Bb F+ Bb F7 Bb Cm7 Bb Gm Cm
Think of the a - maz - ing rep - ar - tee, If I could walk with the
Wor - thy of Hans An - der - sen or Grimm, A man who walks with the
F7 Dm Dm7-5 G7 Ebmaj9 Eb6 Am7 D7
an - i - mals, talk with the an - i - mals, Grunt and squeak and
an - i - mals, talks with the an - i - mals, Grunts and squeaks and
poco a poco cresc.
Gm7 C7 Cm Cm7 F11
squawk with the an - i - mals, And they could talk to
squawks with the an - i - mals, And they could talk to
f

1.
Bb Gm Cm G7 Cm7 Gb7 F7 Tacet
me. If I con -
mf
2.
Bb Bb7 G7 D7 (G Bass) G7 Tacet
him. I'd stud - y
mf
Gm Cdim Edim Bb Cdim C7 F Gb F D11 F#dim
ev - 'ry liv - ing crea - ture's lan - guage, So I could
Gm7 C7 F#dim Gm7 C7 F E F7 E7
speak to all of them on sight. If friends said,

"Can he talk in crab or pel-i-can?" You'd say, "Like hel-i-can!" And you'd be right! And if you just stop and think a bit, there's no doubt of it, I would win a place in his-to-ry, If I could

A tempo (as before)

walk with the an-i-mals, talk with the an-i-mals, Grunt and squeak and squawk with the an-i-mals, And they could squeak and squawk and speak and talk to me.

DOCTOR DOLITTLE
from the motion picture *Doctor Dolittle*

Words and Music by
Leslie Bricusse

Slow schottische

This is the world of Doctor Dolittle, The wonderful world of Doctor Dolittle, Where crocodiles talk and elephants sing and animals do most any old thing, Where polar bears wear top hats And leopards with spots wear spats. Well, that's

Say how d'you do to Doctor Dolittle, Life is a zoo to Doctor Dolittle, Where antelopes lope and ostriches fan and kangaroos do what kangaroos can to make the hyenas laugh As long as a long giraffe. Ev'ry

Copyright © 1967 20th Century Music Corp.
All Rights Controlled by Hastings Music Corporation
1350 Ave. Of The Americas, New York, NY 10019
International Copyright Secured All Rights Reserved

C
A7
life in the world of Doc-tor Do - lit-tle, Doves start to coo when they see
calf starts to moo when they see Do - lit-tle, E - ven the few who used to
F♯m7 B7 E13 E7+5 Em7 A7 F♯m D
Do - lit-tle. He has a pro-found phi - los-o-phy if an-i-mals can be
moo - lit-tle. For all of the birds and beasts a-gree he has a pro-found phi -
B7 A Dm B7 E11 E7 A7
1.
D Dm7 G7
friends says he, well then why can't we?
los - o - phy and so why can't
2.
D F♯ C7 B7+5 E11 E7 A11 A7-9 A7 D
we do lit-tle things to help them. Why can't we?

BEAUTIFUL THINGS
from the motion picture *Doctor Dolittle*

Words and Music by
Leslie Bricusse

Moderately, with warmth

1. The world is full of Beau-ti-ful Things, but-ter-fly wings, fai-ry-tale kings, And each new day un-doubt-ed-ly brings still more Beau-ti-ful Things.

2. (The) world is full of Beau-ti-ful Things, daf-fo-dil springs, chil-dren on swings, And each new day un-doubt-ed-ly brings still more Beau-ti-ful Things.

Copyright © 1967 20th Century Music Corp.
All Rights Controlled by Hastings Music Corporation
1350 Ave. Of The Americas, New York, NY 10019
International Copyright Secured All Rights Reserved

Lyrics:

The world abounds with many delights,
magical sights, fanciful flights, And those who dream on beautiful nights dream of Beautiful Things.
Beautiful days for

The world is dipped in delicate dreams,
sparkling streams, lullaby themes, Where ev'ry flight of fantasy seems filled with Beautiful Things.
Beautiful days of

15

G Eb7 G Am7 Cm7 Cm6 G Em7
sun - shine laz - in', beau - ti - ful skies and shores,
sun - kissed flow - ers, beau - ti - ful sea - kissed breeze,
Am7-5 D7 G G#m7-5 G#dim Dmaj7 D6
Beau - ti - ful days when I can gaze in beau - ti - ful eyes
Beau - ti - ful nights of moon - kissed hours, beau - ti - ful dreams
F7 A11 A7 D A7sus4 A7 Fmaj7 F7 A7sus4 A7 Dm Dm7
like yours. You won - der why the
like these. Our lives tick by like
poco rit.
a tempo
E7 E7-5 Gm(A bass) A7 Bb7 Gm7 Dm A7
night - in - gale sings, lov - ers have wings, peo - ple wear rings. The
pen - du - lum swings, poor lit - tle things, pup - pets on strings. But

Dm Dm7 G Gm
world is full of Beau - ti - ful Things,
life is full of Beau - ti - ful Things,
poco a poco cresc.
Bb(Abbass) D(A bass) G6 Gmaj7 Em7 Cmaj7 A7
Beau-ti-ful peo - ple too, Beau-ti-ful peo - ple like
Beau-ti-ful peo - ple too, Beau-ti-ful peo - ple like
poco rit.
1.
Dm Dm7 E(D bass) A7(D bass) Dm Dm7 E(D bass) A7(D bass)
you. 2. The
a tempo poco a poco decresc.
mp
2.
D D7 E7 Gm6 Gm D(add 9)
you.
a tempo poco a poco decresc.
ritard.
p

I'VE NEVER SEEN ANYTHING LIKE IT

from the motion picture *Doctor Dolittle*

Words and Music by
Leslie Bricusse

1. I've seen the world, I've been a-round, I could tell you sto-ries that would quite as-tound you.
2. I know the game, I've seen 'em all, I could tell you sto-ries that would quite en-thrall you.
3. I'm down to earth, I'll tell you straight, I could tell you sto-ries that would fas-ci-nate you.

I'm not a fool, I went to school, I've been from Liv-er-pool to Is-tan-bul,
I know me job, pleas-ing the mob, I give 'em what they want for just two bob,
I know the trade, I know the tricks, Once bought an e-le-phant for two pound six,

Is-tan-bul. I'm no fool. And an-y-one will tell you that I'm
just two bob. That's my job but this is so fan-tas-tic I can't
two pound six. Taught it tricks but for a push-mi-pull-yu I'd pay

Copyright © 1967 20th Century Music Corp.
All Rights Controlled by Hastings Music Corporation
1350 Ave. Of The Americas, New York, NY 10019
International Copyright Secured All Rights Reserved

sharp-er than a knife, But I've Nev-er Seen An-y-thing Like It in my
wait to tell the wife, 'Cause I've Nev-er Seen An-y-thing Like It in my
three pounds, four pounds, five, 'Cause I've Nev-er Seen An-y-thing Like It that's a-

life. No, I've Nev-er Seen An-y-thing Like It,
life. No, I've Nev-er Seen An-y-thing Like It,
live. No, I've Nev-er Seen An-y-thing Like It,

3rd time to Coda

Nev-er Seen An-y-thing Like It, I've Nev-er Seen An-y-thing Like It in my
Nev-er Seen An-y-thing Like It, I've Nev-er Seen An-y-thing Like It in my
Nev-er Seen An-y-thing Like It, I've Nev-er Seen An-y-thing Like It in my

life.
life.
I thought I'd seen ev-'ry
I thought I'd seen ev-'ry

Gm C7 Fmaj9 F6 Fmaj7 F#dim Gm7
won - der in the world, I've seen the Col - i - se - um in
mir - a - cle on earth, I've seen the lean - ing Tow - er of
C7 Bb Ebdim C7 F C7 F Gbdim Gm Gm7#
Rome and the A - crop - o - lis. I made the big - gest
Pi - sa and the Pyr - a - mids. They're not worth half what the
Gm C7 F Dm7 G7
blun - der in the world, Be - cause I've nev - er seen an - y - thing
push - mi - pull - yu's worth, Be - cause they real - ly don't have an ap -
C7
1.
2.
D. S. al Coda
G7 C7
quite like this. 2. I mean
peal for kids. 3. I mean
D. S. al Coda

Coda
F Fm G7 Gm7 C7 F D7 G7 C7
life. No I've Nev-er Seen An-y-thing Like It, There's
F7 C7 F7 Bb Bbm6 F7 Bbmaj7 A7
nev-er been an-y-thing like it, I've Nev-er Seen An-y-thing Like It,
Dm Dm7 Dm6 Bbm F D7 Gm Gm7
in all my
C7 F F7 Dm Db+ Bbm F Db7 Gm C7 F
life.

FABULOUS PLACES
from the motion picture *Doctor Dolittle*

Words and Music by
Leslie Bricusse

There's so many exciting and wonderful places, Mountains and jungles and desert oases, Pleasant as home is, it isn't what Rome is, So why stay there. When there are

G (add 9) G Gmaj7 G♯dim
so man - y fab - u - lous, far - a - way pla - ces to
so man - y sim - ply in - cred - i - ble pla - ces to
Am7 D9 D7-9 G (add 9)
see. Why should Spain and Ta -
see. When I think of the
G Dm7 G7 Cmaj7 C6
hi - ti and Ri - o just be on - ly names to you and
warm Car - ib - be - an, I see a new world for you and
Cmaj7 C6 F♯m7-5 B7 Em C Em6 Em7
me. I feel cer - tain they're peo - ple we'd be glad to
me. I'd give an - y - thing just to have one sin - gle

know there, So tell me why don't we get up and go there,
day there, And once we get there, I know that we'll stay there,

Go to those Fab - u - lous Pla - ces where we long to be, _____
Stay in those Fab - u - lous Pla - ces where we long to be, _____

Go to Bang - kok and Hong Kong and
Such as Si - am, Si - en - na, Vi -

Par - is and Ven - ice, To - kyo and Cai - ro and Lis - bon and
en - na, Ve - ro - na, Ja - va, Ja - mai - ca, Bom - bay, Bar - ce -

poco a poco cresc.

F7 F# G E7 G#dim (A Bass) Am7
Lon - don, Won - der - ful Fab - u - lous Pla - ces we're
lo - na, Show me those Fab - u - lous Pla - ces we're
1. D11 D7 G Em7 Am7 D9 (add 6) Tacet
long - ing to see. There are
rubato
mf a tempo
2. Bm A♭ B♭ Gmaj7 Gm7 C6/9
long - ing to see.
f a tempo
E♭maj9 Gadd9

MY FRIEND THE DOCTOR
from the motion picture *Doctor Dolittle*

Words and Music by
Leslie Bricusse

(Spoken:) "He understands the Irish!" And any man who understands the Irish can't be reckoned altogether bad, The same way that a lunatic whose patron saint is Patterick can't be reckoned altogether

Copyright © 1967 20th Century Music Corp.
All Rights Controlled by Hastings Music Corporation
1350 Ave. Of The Americas, New York, NY 10019
International Copyright Secured All Rights Reserved

mad._____ The doc-tor's ver-y smart, An I-rish man at heart, His fa-v'rite col-or, sure, it must be green._____ And al-so he's a man who'll blar-ney when he can,_____ Let me ex-plain the sort of thing I mean.

Chorus

1. My Friend The Doctor says the moon is made of apple pie and once a month it's eaten by the sun. And
2. My Friend The Doctor says the stars are made of lemon drops, the bigger ones are lollipops and ice. The

that is why up in the sky you'll find as ev'ry month goes by
clouds have shops up on the tops that sell you sweets and soda pops,

somebody in the sky's making another one.
What do they call the place? Isn't it paradise?

My Friend The Doctor says the sun is made of cheddar cheese, The
My Friend The Doctor says that ev-'ry time it starts to rain and

doctor even knows the reason why,
people run indoors again in swarms,
The
If

facts are these, Try, if you please, pretending you're a lonely cheese,
you remain out in the rain, you'll think you're drinking pink champagne,

Wouldn't you want to try finding an apple pie? *"Of course you would!"*
And you will spend your life praying for thunderstorms.

Maybe what the doctor tells me _____

isn't altogether true, _____ But

I _____ love ev'ry tale he tells me, _____

I don't know an-y bet-ter ones, Do you? My Friend The Doc-tor says the world is full of fan-ta-sy, And who are you and I to dis-a-gree? Let's hope and pray that is the way the life we love will al-ways stay for

Fm C Ab6 Fm7 Bb7
My Friend The Doc - tor and
poco a poco cresc.
1. Eb Abmaj7 Eb Fm7 Bb7
me.
f
poco a poco decresc.
2. Eb Eb7 Am7- 5 Abm6 Eb Cb7
me.
f
Fm7 Bbdim Bb7 Eb
My Friend The Doc - tor and me.
3
ff

SCHOOLDAYS
from the motion picture *Goodbye, Mr. Chips*

Words and Music by
Leslie Bricusse

Moderately with a lilt

School-days, so they tell us, are the most sub-lime of our lives. We'll have the time of our lives. It's the ab-so-lute prime of our lives. They tell us School-days are gold-en. In the old-en days it might have been true. But in the

Copyright © 1968, 1969 Metro-Goldwyn Mayer Inc., New York, N.Y.
Rights Throughout the World Controlled by Hastings Music Corporation, New York, N.Y.
International Copyright Secured All Rights Reserved

old-en days they liked tor-ture and slav-er-y too. What are you going to do?

School-days, so we gath-er are the sweet-est days that we'll know. And

if that real-ly is so, well, it comes as a bit of a blow. I mean if

School-days are the best of our lives, im-ag-ine the rest of our lives.

School-days, School-days, nev-er let me go.

School-days _____ are sub-lime.
We're in the thick of them. And we are sick of them.

School-days. _____ What a
You can take your pick of them. Work-ing for schol-ar-ships.

time! School - days,
Lov-a-ble Mis-ter Chips. Talk a-bout dic-ta-tor-ships. Stud-y-ing

How di-vine!
An-cient Greek all the week. Lat-in is all we speak.

School days. They're so
Class at nine, rain or shine,

fine. School days, they're the You can have all of mine. Oh, what a pain they are!

best. School - days, Think of the strain they are. Cruel and in-hu-mane they are. Slight-ly in-

that's the test. Have you guessed that sane they are. Is-n't it plain they are?

Eb6
D7
Gm7
I'll miss my School - days, my Tom Brown's tom -
Fun - ny days, sun - ny days, jol - ly days,
C7
Ebm6 (Gb Bass)
Bb (F Bass)
D7 (F# Bass)
Fm6 (Ab Bass)
G7
fool days? School - days, School - days,
hol - i - days. School - days, School - days,
Cm7
Cm7 (F Bass)
F9
Bb
Eb
Bb
nev - er let me go.
nev - er let me go.

FILL THE WORLD WITH LOVE

from the motion picture *Goodbye, Mr. Chips*

Words and Music by
Leslie Bricusse

Moderately with movement

In the morn-ing of my life I shall look to the sun-rise,
At a mo-ment in my life when the world is new.
And the bless-ing I shall ask is that God will grant me,

In the noon-time of my life I shall look to the sun-shine,
At a mo-ment in my life when the sky is blue.
And the bless-ing I shall ask will re-main un-chang-ing,

To be brave and strong and

Copyright © 1968, 1969 Metro-Goldwyn Mayer Inc., New York, N.Y.
Rights Throughout the World Controlled by Hastings Music Corporation, New York, N.Y.
International Copyright Secured   All Rights Reserved

G (B Bass) G Dm (F Bass) E7 Am Am (C Bass) D Am7 D
true, And to Fill The World With Love my whole life
C (G Bass) G G (B Bass) C G (B Bass) D (A Bass) G (B Bass) G7
through. And to Fill The World With Love, And to
C A7 (C♯ Bass) D F♯m7-5 (C Bass) B B7 (D♯ Bass)
Fill The World With Love, And to Fill The World With
Em A (sus 4) A D Am7 D
Love my whole life through. In the

evening of my life I shall look to the sunset, ___ At a moment in my life when the night is due. ___ And the question I shall ask only { I / you } can answer. ___ Was I brave and strong and true? ___ Did I

Fill The World With Love my whole life through? _____ Did I
Fill The World With Love, Did I Fill The World With
Love, Did I Fill The World With Love my
whole life through? _____

WHEN I AM OLDER
from the motion picture *Goodbye, Mr. Chips*

Words and Music by
Leslie Bricusse

Slowly

Sev-en weeks of home sweet home are o-ver. They're o-ver Sev-en weeks of moth-er's cook-ing, moth-er's love and moth-er's look-ing aft-er and laugh-ter and liv-ing in clo-ver are

Copyright © 1968, 1969 Metro-Goldwyn Mayer Inc., New York, N.Y.
Rights Throughout the World Controlled by Hastings Music Corporation, New York, N.Y.
International Copyright Secured   All Rights Reserved

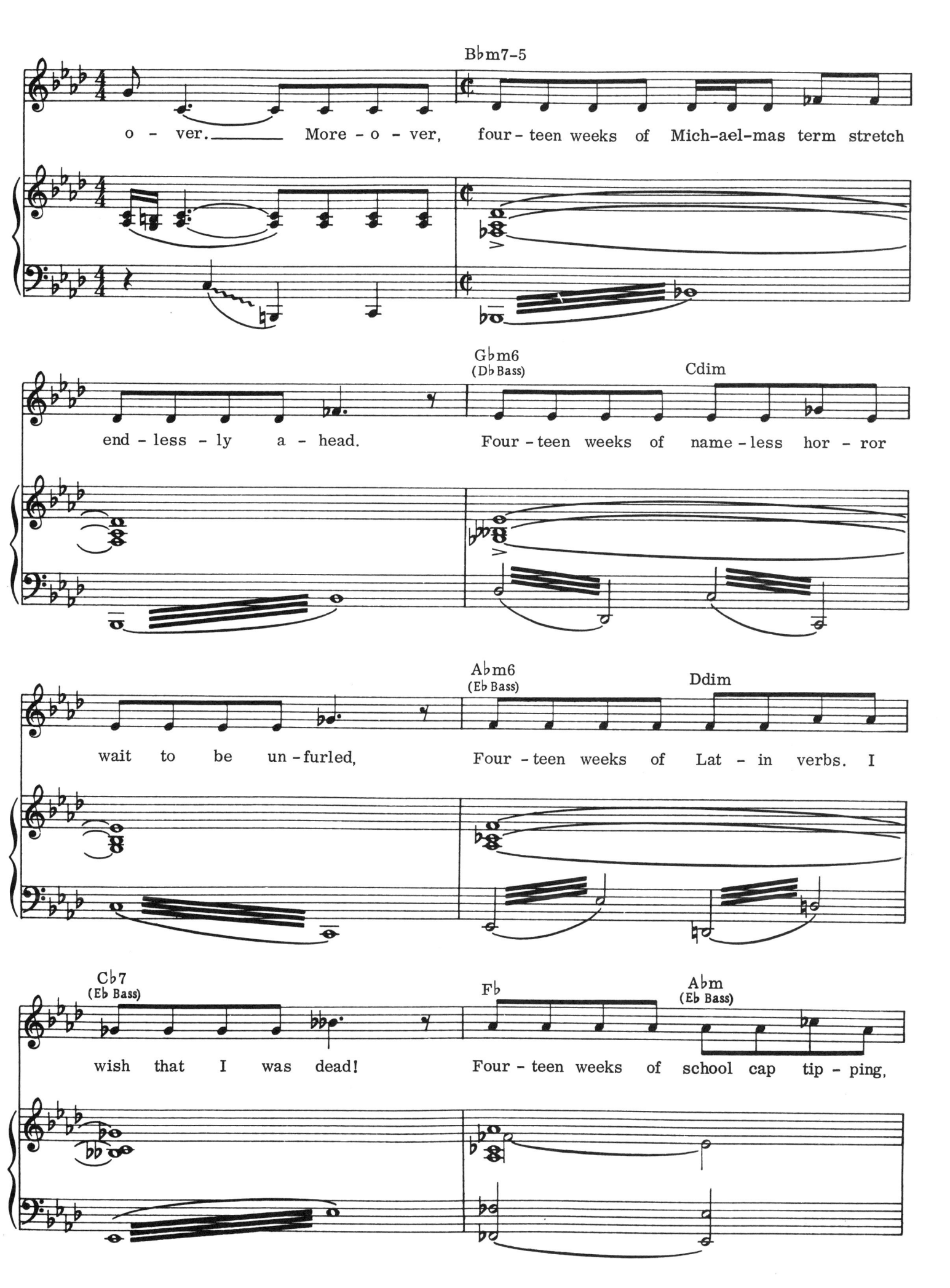

o - ver._____ More-o-ver, four-teen weeks of Mich-ael-mas term stretch end-less-ly a-head. Four-teen weeks of name-less hor-ror wait to be un-furled, Four-teen weeks of Lat-in verbs. I wish that I was dead! Four-teen weeks of school cap tip-ping, filth-y food and Mis-ter Chip-ping.

Four-teen weeks in the dun-geon of a school-boy's world.

But one day, one day:

Chorus: Brightly

When I Am Old-er, I'll be the pres-i-dent of Pe - ru, I'll own an
When I Am Old-er, I'll be the nov-el-ist of the year, I'll be an

em-er-ald mine or two. I'll swim for Eng-land in the next O-lym-pic games.
em-i-nent en-gi-neer. I'll be the ac-tor that the au-di-ence ap-plauds.

I'm gon-na be a play-boy farm-er. I'm gon-na be a la-dy charm-er.
I'm gon-na be a fine mu-si-cian. I'm gon-na be a rich phy-si-cian.

I'm gon-na be a knight in ar-mor. Find a dam-sel and dis-arm her.
I'm gon-na be a pol-i-ti-cian. I shall be an ob-ste-tri-cian.

When I Am Old-er, I'll be the mul-ti-est mil-lion-aire. I'll be the fel-low be-yond com-pare. I'll be the he-ro that the pop-u-lace ac-claims. I'm gon-na carve the world in piec-es. I'm gon-na be as rich as Croe-sus. Think of the might-y em-pire I shall rule. When I Am Old-er, wis-er and

bold-er, on the day that I get out of school.

D. S. al Coda

Coda

I'll a-chieve my great am-bi-tion. When I Am Old-er I'll be the fel-low who makes the rules. I will a-bol-ish our pub-lic schools. I'll be the chair-man of at least a hun-dred boards.

Gm
Gm7
C7
I'll run a fleet of o - cean tank - ers.
mp
Db
D7
I'll buy a street of mer - chant bank - ers.
Gb7 (Db Bass)
C13
C7
Gm7 (Bb Bass)
C7 (Bb Bass)
I'll be the great - est man you've ev - er
poco cresc.
Am7
D7
Am7
D7
seen.
mf

Lyrics:

When I Am Old-er, wis-er and bold-er, Just as soon as I am sev-en-teen!

A DAY HAS A HUNDRED POCKETS

from the stage production of *Goodbye, Mr. Chips*

Words and Music by
Leslie Bricusse

Moderately fast swing

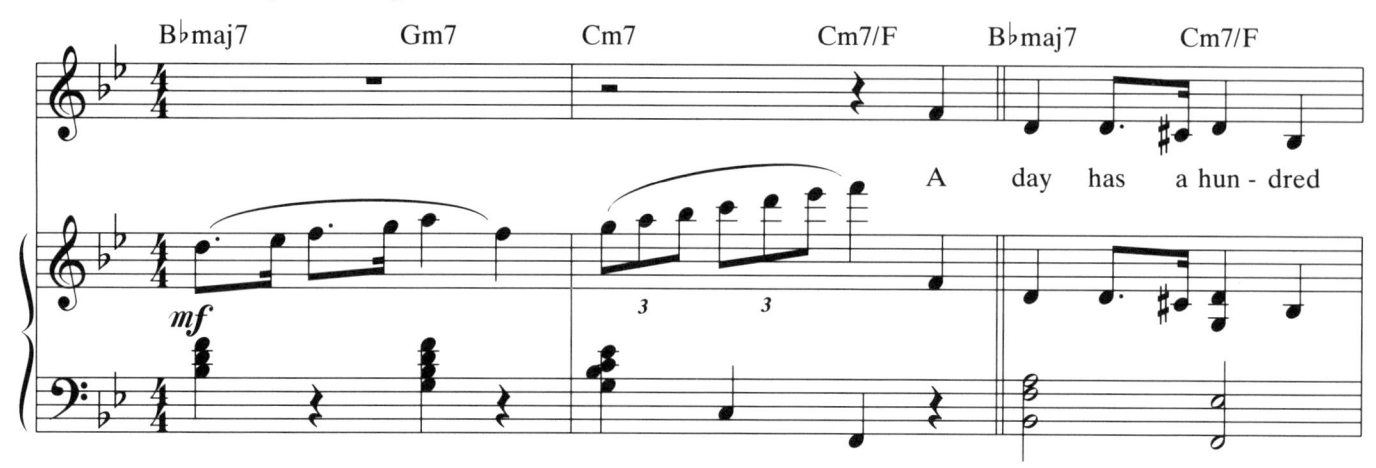

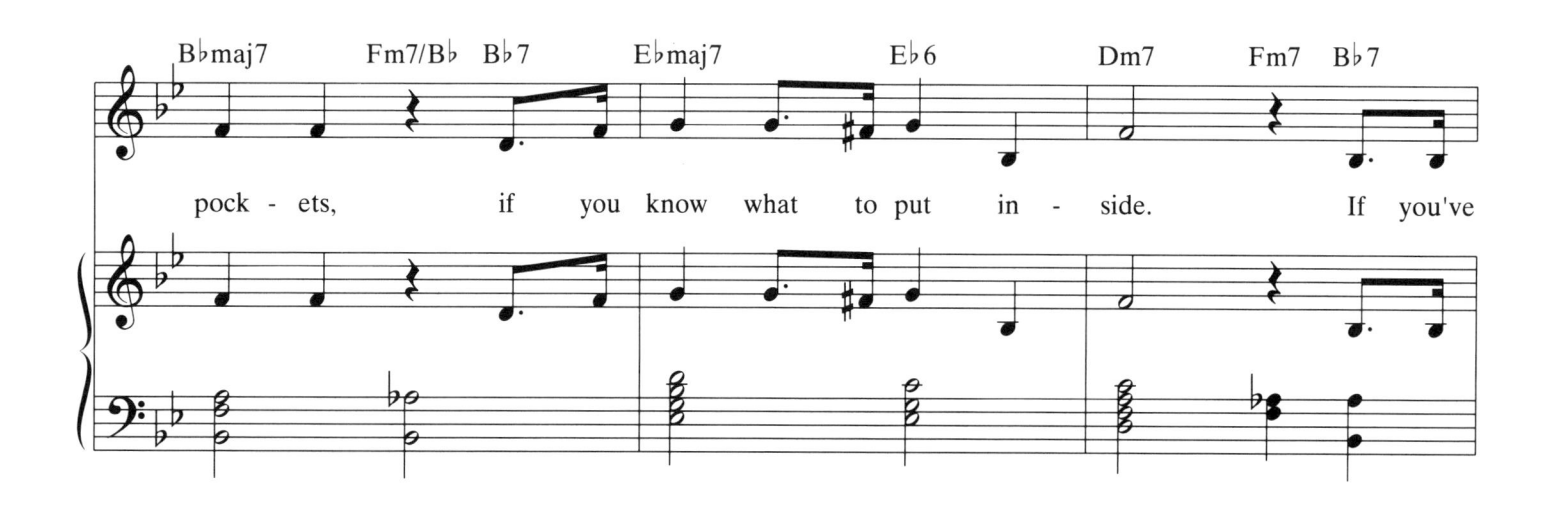

A day has a hun-dred pock-ets, if you know what to put in-side. If you've got e-nough schemes and you've got e-nough dreams, you can fill 'em un-til they

Copyright © 1981 Stage And Screen Music, Inc.
Worldwide Rights Administered by Cherry River Music (BMI)
International Copyright Secured All Rights Reserved

Cm7 G7/D E♭6 F7 C7/G F7/A A+/B
burst their seams. I know, I've tried. Each
B♭maj7 Cm7/F B♭maj7 Fm7/B♭ B♭7 E♭maj7 E♭6
one of the hun - dred pock - ets can be squeezed in - to ev - 'ry
day has a hun - dred pock - ets, if you know what to put in -
Dm7 Fm7 B♭7 E♭maj7 E♭7 Dm7 E♭maj7 E♭7 Dm7
day. You can fill the day up like a bot - tom - less cup; if you're
side. If you've got e - nough schemes and you've got e - nough dreams, you can
F/C Gm7/C C7 Cm7 G7/D E♭maj7 F7 Cm7/F F7
clev - er you'll nev - er spill a drop. Or so they say...
fill 'em un - til they burst their seams. I know I've tried...

B♭ B♭7 E♭maj7 B♭sus2/D B♭ Cm7 F13
There's a pock - et for hope and a pock - et for rope, and a
There's a pock - et for fears and a pock - et for tears, and a
B♭sus4 B♭ Fm7/B♭ B♭7 E♭maj7 B♭sus2/D
pock - et for odds and ends. There's a pock - et for plans and a
pock - et for stor - ing sun. There's a pock - et for glad and a
E♭maj7 Am7/D D7♭9 Gm7 C7 Cm7/F Dm7/F Cm7/F
cou - ple for hands, and a beau - ti - ful pock - et full of friends. It
pock - et for sad, and a won - der-ful pock - et just for fun. My
F7 Cm7/F F7 B♭maj7 Cm7/F
all de - pends...
fa - v'rite one...
We all have a hun - dred

pock-ets, on-ly we know what they should hold. When you're plan-ning your day, you should plan in a way that the day be-comes big and bold. A hun-dred pock-ets im-prove a day a hun-dred-fold. A fold.

THAT'S A BOY!
from the stage production of *Goodbye, Mr. Chips*

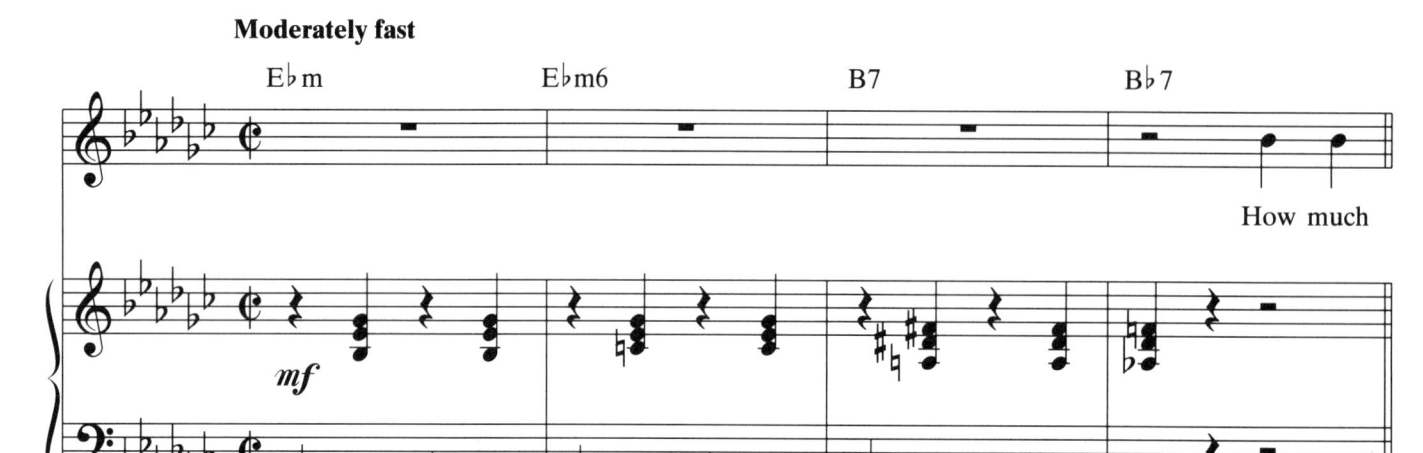

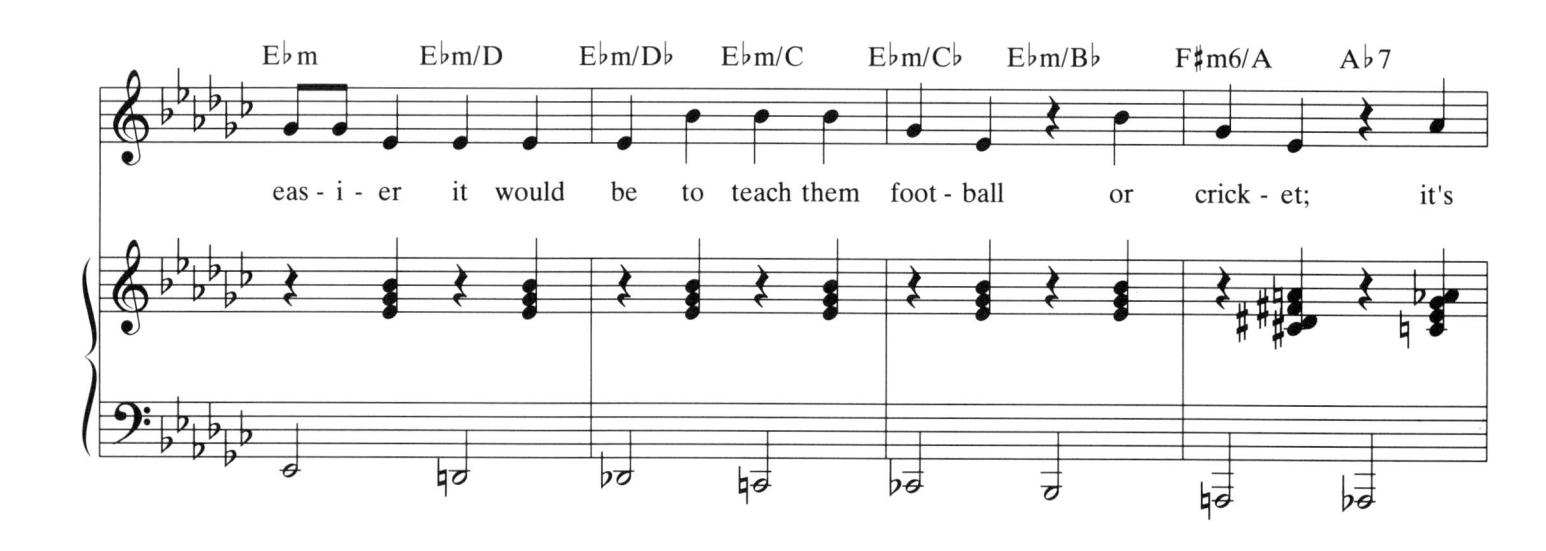

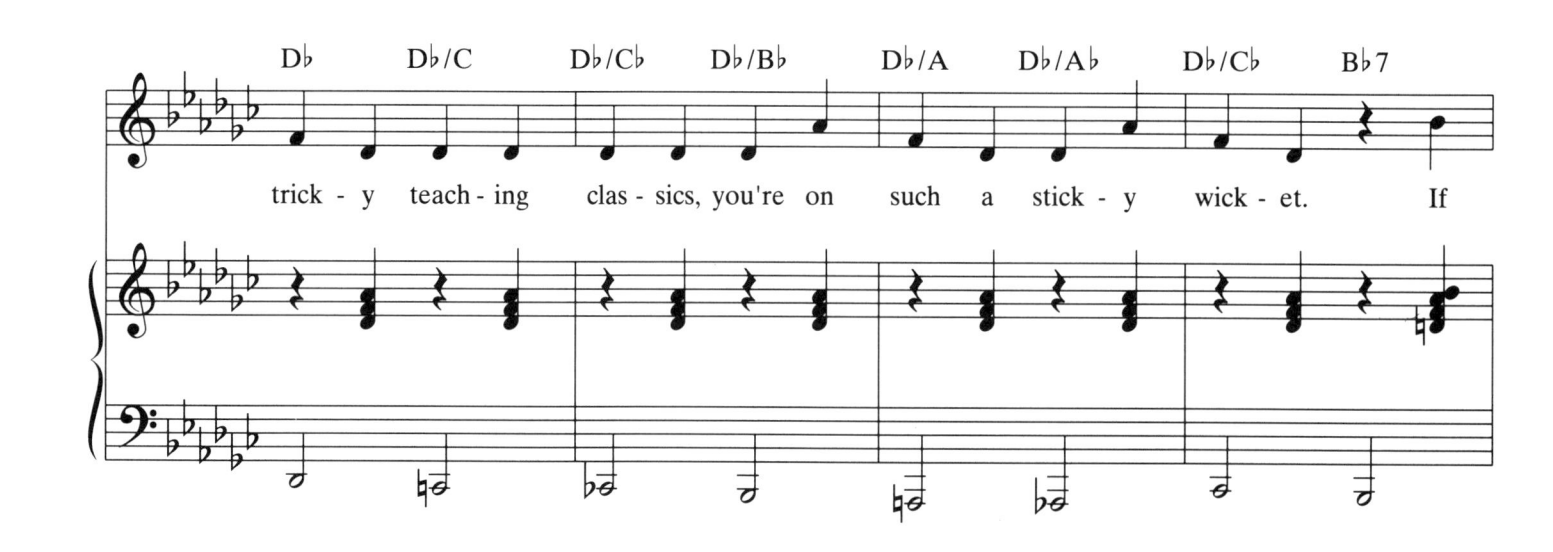

Words and Music by
Leslie Bricusse

Moderately fast

How much easier it would be to teach them football or cricket; it's tricky teaching classics, you're on such a sticky wicket. If

all we taught was games I know they'd all be thrilled to see us, but
heaven help the classics teacher off'ring them Aeneas.
Boys are venemous with Virgil,
horrified by Homer, Cicero in Verrem throws them

all in-to a co-ma. And Pindar's ver-y name is like some ter-ri-ble a-ro-ma. The ex-pres-sions on their fac-es you should see._____ But no, I can't blame Pindar, I blame me. *(Spoken) It must be my fault...*

G7
Gm7/C
...a lack of communication...
I mean,
F
What is a boy? A
Why does a boy ram -
boy is a thing with string in his pock - et and a
page like a fool through school and through col - lege with a
F♯° C7/G C7 F♯° C7/G C7
grin on its face, rac - ing 'round like a rock - et. Spread - ing
great deal of noise, and a vast lack of knowl - edge and a

dirt a - round the place, an ab - so - lute dis -
to - tal lack of poise? P'raps that's what he en -

grace. That's a boy!
joys. That's a boy!

Re -

gard - less of cli - mate or sea - son, boys are
told boys are del - i - cate crea - tures, to be

born to de - file and de - stroy. Yet for
han - dled with lim - it - less care. I've ob -

some in - ex - pli - ca - ble rea - son, to their
served all their del - i - cate fea - tures; they're as

moth - ers they're a foun - tain of in - fi - nite joy. It's
del - i - cate as some kind of small griz - zly bear. They're

sick - en - ing, the de - vas - tat - ing tricks they em - ploy.
el - e - phants, rhi - noc - er - os - es look o - ver there!

I mean, why should it be? To me they're a curse. Their nurse-maid-cum-father, that's the job that I've got. There are times when I'd rather like to drown the bloody lot. No, now I'm talking rot... no, I'm

Ah well, all I can say is, maybe a boy is more than we reckon. He is not just a lout, he's aware fate will beckon, and he knows what he's about. But now that I greatly doubt. Max, look

not! — I'm an ex-pert on Troy, I can
out! — Youth's a thing to en-joy, for like

speak flu-ent Greek, but there's one thing that mys-ti-fies me
faith, it's a gift. They say faith can move moun-tains, but there's

sev-en days a week: that's a
one thing it can't shift: that's a

Slowly

boy! And I'm bound to ad-mit that the
boy! And I re-fuse to be-lieve that can

future is his, but I still don't know what a boy
grow up to be a ma-ture hu-man be-ing like

is.

How can a boy re-tain an-y hope to cope as a schol-ar, when there's mud in his brain and there's blood on his col-lar? It can drive a man in-sane, the an-swer's ver-y plain: That's a boy! We're me!

WHERE DID MY CHILDHOOD GO?

from the motion picture *Goodbye, Mr. Chips*

Words and Music by
Leslie Bricusse

They think I do not understand them. They think I do not hear or see. I only wish they knew that I do understand them. I only wish they understood me. Yesterday I was their age. Tomorrow they'll be my age.

Copyright © 1968, 1969 Metro-Goldwyn Mayer Inc., New York, N.Y.
Rights Throughout the World Controlled by Hastings Music Corporation, New York, N.Y.
International Copyright Secured   All Rights Reserved

Em
F
Dm6
Soon-er, much soon-er than they know. And sud-den-ly they will ask what
Poco mosso
Eb
E (B Bass)
Bm7-5
F (B Bass)
E
Bm7-5 (E Bass)
E
Bm7-5 (E Bass)
ev-'ry child must ask, "Where Did My Child-hood Go?"
In a slow reflective manner
E
Bm7-5 (E Bass)
E
Bm7-5 (E Bass)
E
G#m7-5
G#m7-5 (C# Bass)
C#7-9
Where Did My Child-hood Go? When did my youth, so sweet and free,
mf
F#m7
Cmaj7
C6
E (B Bass)
G#m7-5
G#m7 (C# Bass)
C#7
sud-den-ly slip a-way from me? Was it so long a-go?

F#m7 Cmaj7 C6 E Bm7-5 (E Bass) E Bm7-5 (E Bass) E Bm7-5 (E Bass)
Where Did My Child-hood Go? When did the mag - ic
E Bm7-5 (E Bass) E G#m7-5 G#m7-5 (C# Bass) C#7-9 F#m7
end? When did the fu - ture meet the past, end - ing a dream too
Cmaj7 C6 E (B Bass) G#m7-5 G#m7 (C# Bass) C#7 F#m7 Cmaj7 C6
good to last, tak - ing a-way a friend? When did my child - hood
Poco più mosso
E Bm7-5 (E Bass) E F#m7 C#7 F#m7 B7 (A Bass) G#m7 E (G# Bass)
end? Was it that day in ear - ly Spring that lin - gers

F#m7-5 B13 G#m7 E (G#Bass) Cmaj7 Am7 D9 Gmaj7 C
on, when some-how I knew this pre-cious time would soon be
F#m7 B7 E Bm7-5 (E Bass) E Bm7-5 (E Bass) E G#m7-5
gone? What does the fu-ture show? Spring will re-turn a-
G#m7-5 (C#Bass) C#7-9 F#m7 Cmaj7 C6 E (B Bass) G#m7-5
gain next year, and when she does, she'll find me here, Won-der-ing still, I
G#m7 (C#Bass) C#7 F#m7 Cmaj7 C6 E Bm7-5 (E Bass) E Bm7-5 (E Bass)
know, Where Did My Child-hood Go?

Yes-ter-day I was their age. To-mor-row they'll be my age. Soon-er, much soon-er than they know. And sud-den-ly they will ask what ev-'ry child must ask, "Where Did My Child-hood Go?"

A CHRISTMAS CAROL
from the motion picture *Scrooge*

Words and Music by
Leslie Bricusse

Gm Fm7 B♭7 E♭maj7 B♭/D C9sus C7 C9
see What a world of won - der this
A♭6/C (Add B♭) Cm7 F Tacet
world can be Sing a Christ - mas
mp p
B♭/D E♭ C7/E F
Car - ol Sing a Christ - mas Car - ol,
cresc. poco a poco
D7/F♯ Gm Cm/E♭
Sing a Christ - mas Car - ol like the chil - dren
mf

Dsus D F7 Bb Bb/D Eb
do And en-joy the beau-ty
mp cresc. poco a poco
C7/E F D7/F#
All the joy and beau-ty That a mer-ry
Bb/Ab Eb/G Ebm6/Gb Fsus F
Christ-mas can bring to
f
1. Bb Ebmaj7 Eb6 F7
you.
mf mp
2. Bb Bb/D Eb (Add F) F7sus Bb
you.
mf rall. f

THE BEAUTIFUL DAY
from the motion picture *Scrooge*

Words and Music by
Leslie Bricusse

Slowly and Tenderly

Expressively rubato

On a beau-ti-ful day that I dream a-bout in a world I would love to see____ Is a beau-ti-ful place where the sun comes out, and it

Copyright © 1970 by Stage & Screen Music, Inc.
Worldwide Rights Administered by Cherry River Music (BMI)
International Copyright Secured All Rights Reserved

Bb/F Cm/Eb Dsus D D7/F# D7-9/F# D7/F# Gm
shines in the sky for me. On this beau-ti-ful win-ter's morn-ing, eve-ning, If my
Eb Eb/D Cm7 F (Add G) F Bbmaj7 Bb7 Ebmaj7 D7
wish could come true some-how, Then the beau-ti-ful day that I
cresc. poco a
Gm Cm D G7 Cm F9sus 1. Bb Bbmaj7 Cm/Bb
dream a-bout would be here and now. On a
poco
f mp p mp
2. Bb Ab6 Gm Ebm/Gb Bb/F E°/F F9sus F7 Bb
now.
p
rall.

CHRISTMAS CHILDREN
from the motion picture *Scrooge*

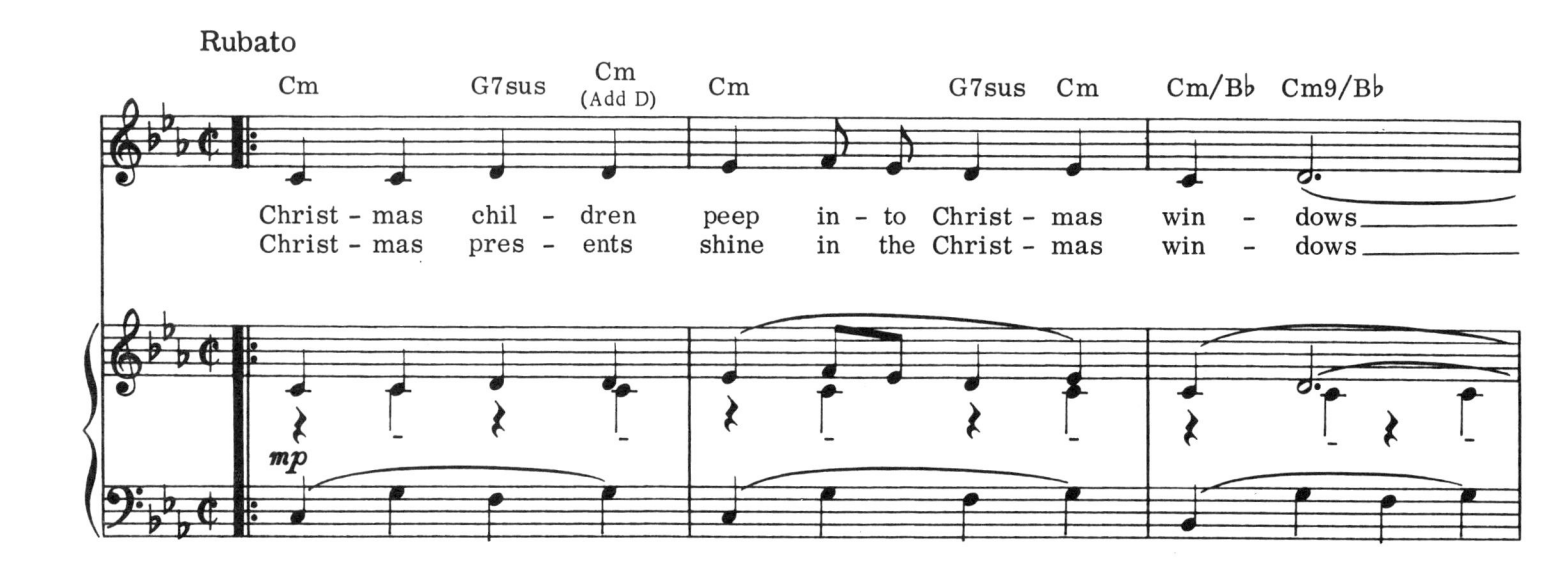

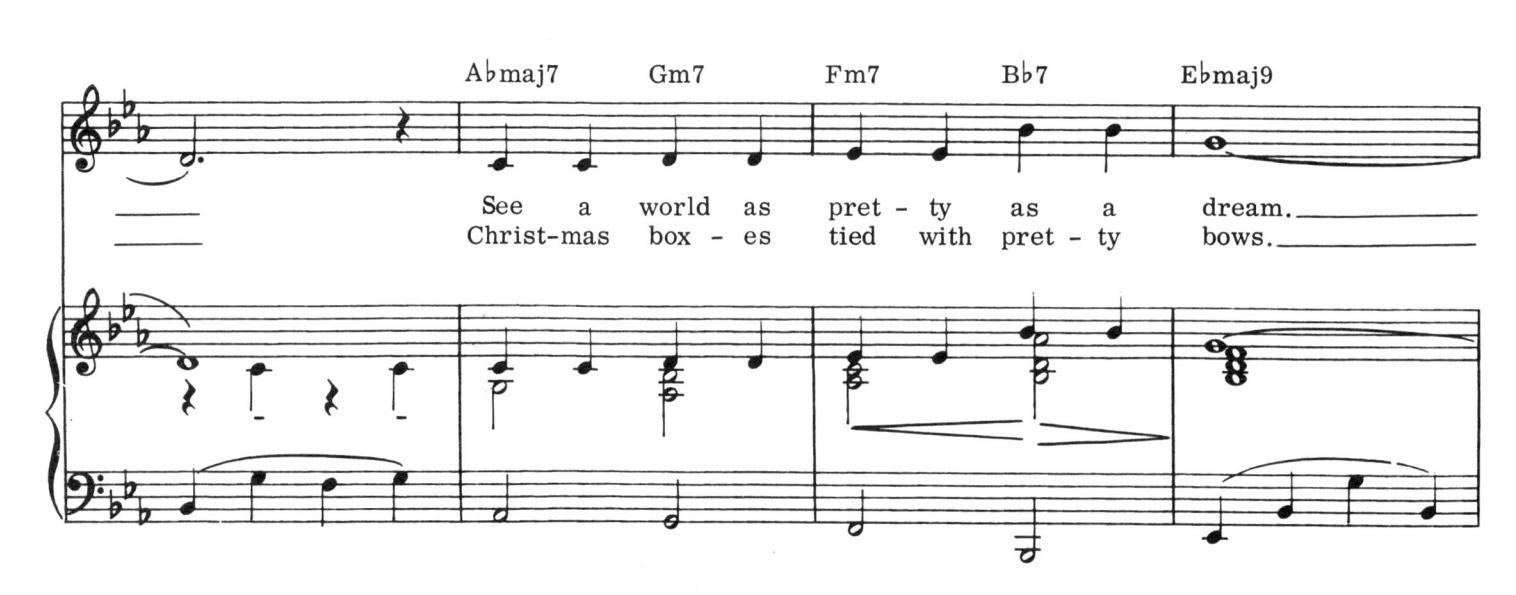

Words and Music by
Leslie Bricusse

Moderato, not too fast

Rubato

Christ-mas chil-dren peep in-to Christ-mas win-dows
Christ-mas pres-ents shine in the Christ-mas win-dows

See a world as pret-ty as a dream.
Christ-mas box-es tied with pret-ty bows.

Copyright © 1970 by Stage & Screen Music, Inc.
Worldwide Rights Administered by Cherry River Music (BMI)
International Copyright Secured All Rights Reserved

Christ-mas trees and toys Christ-mas hopes
Won-der what's in-side What de-lights

and joys Christ-mas pud-dings rich with Christ-mas
they hide But till Christ-mas morn-ing no - one

cream.
knows

Won't it be ex-cit-ing if it snows?

G9sus G7 Cmaj7
I sup - pose that chil - dren ev - ery - where
mp
C6 D7/A Am7 D7/A
will say a Christ - mas prayer till San - ta
Fm/A♭ C/G D7sus D7 G9sus G7
brings their Christ - mas things.
p
Cm G7sus Cm (Add D) Cm G7sus Cm Cm/B♭ Cm9/B♭
Christ - mas chil - dren hun - ger for Christ - mas morn - ing
mp

Christ-mas Day's a won-der to be-hold___

Young one's dreams come true, Not-so-young one's too,

I be-lieve that sto-ry we've been told___

Christ-mas is for chil-dren young and old.___

THANK YOU VERY MUCH
from the motion picture *Scrooge*

Words and Music by
Leslie Bricusse

Em7-5 Gm7/A A7 Dm Bbm/Db (Add A) Bbm/Db F/C F#o/C
done for us to - day And there - fore I would
Gm7/C C7 F7 Cm/G Ab7 F7/A Ab7 Cm/G Ab/Gb F7 Cm7 F7
sim - ply like to say:
Refrain
Bb F9sus Bb Bb D7
1. Thank you ver - y much, Thank you ver - y much, That's the nic - est thing that
2. Thank you ver - y much, Thank you ver - y much, That's the nic - est thing that
3. Thank you ver - y much, Thank you ver - y much, That's the nic - est thing that
4. Thank you ver - y much, Thank you ver - y much, That's the nic - est thing that
mp
Gm C7 F7 Eb/G (Add F) Abm6 F7/A Cm Cm-5 Cm (Add D) Fm7/C F7
an - y - one's ev - er done for me I may sound dou - ble Dutch But
an - y - one's ev - er done for me It sounds a bit bi - zarre But
an - y - one's ev - er done for me It is - n't ev - 'ry day Good
an - y - one's ev - er done for me The fu - ture looks al - right In

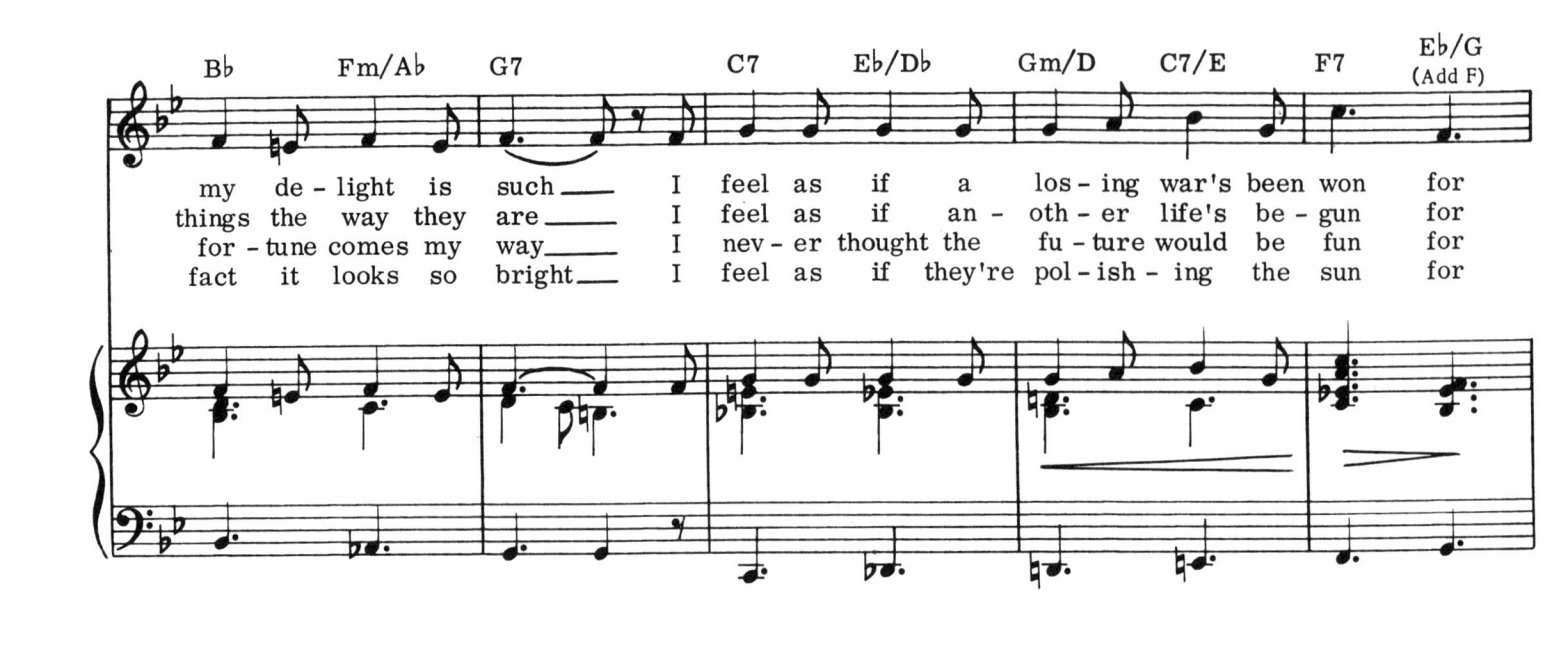

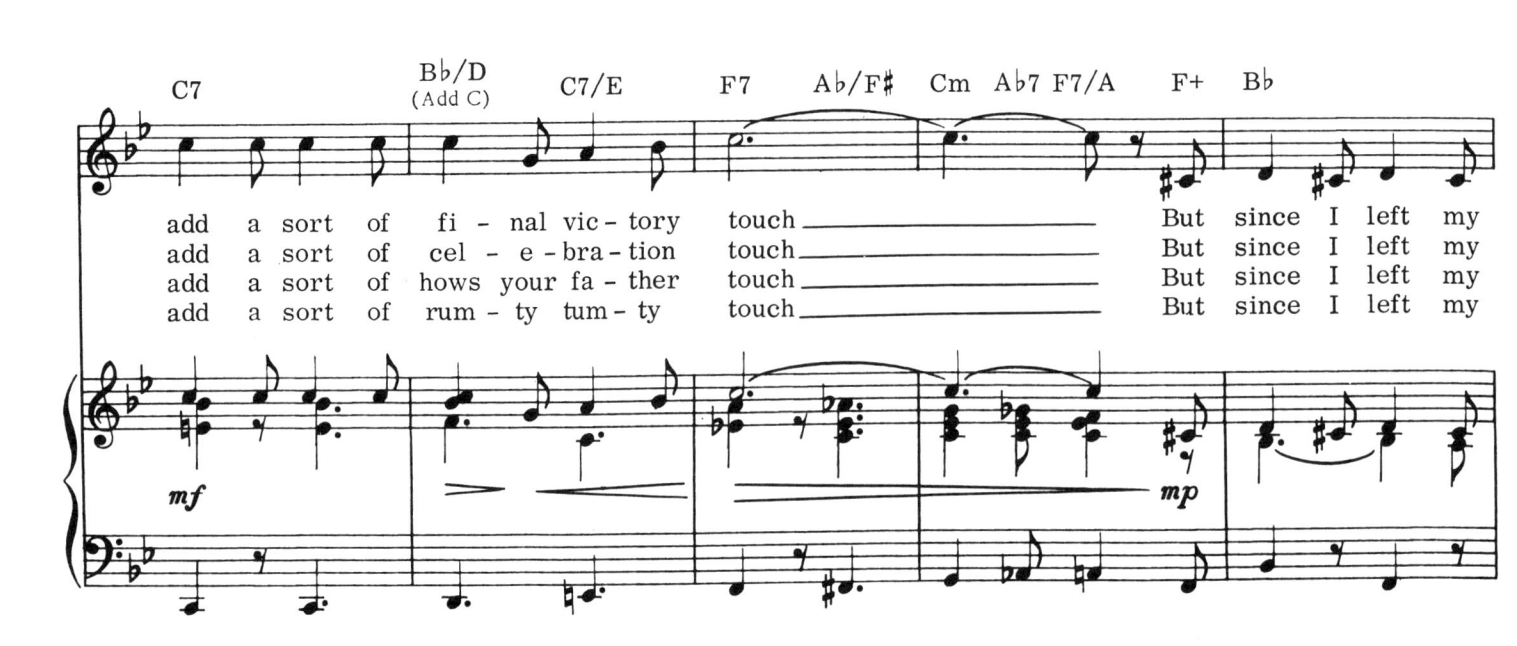

my de - light is such___ I feel as if a los - ing war's been won for
things the way they are___ I feel as if an - oth - er life's be - gun for
for - tune comes my way___ I nev - er thought the fu - ture would be fun for
fact it looks so bright___ I feel as if they're pol - ish - ing the sun for

me___ And if I had a flag I'd hang my flag out___ To
me___ And if I had a can - non I would fire it___ To
me___ And if I had a bu - gle I would blow it___ To
me___ And if I had a drum I'd have to bang it___ To

add a sort of fi - nal vic - tory touch___ But since I left my
add a sort of cel - e - bra - tion touch___ But since I left my
add a sort of hows your fa - ther touch___ But since I left my
add a sort of rum - ty tum - ty touch___ But since I left my

flag at home I'll sim - ply have to say: Thank you ver - y, ver - y, ver - y much.
can - non at home I'll sim - ply have to say: Thank you ver - y, ver - y, ver - y much.
bu - gle at home I'll sim - ply have to say: Thank you ver - y, ver - y, ver - y much.
drum - mer at home I'll sim - ply have to say: Thank you ver - y, ver - y, ver - y much.

Thank you ver - y ver - y ver - y much!

FATHER CHRISTMAS
from the motion picture *Scrooge*

Words and Music by
Leslie Bricusse

Moderato, not too slowly

Father Christmas_____ Father Christmas_____ He's the great-est man in the whole wide world, In the whole wide world, and he knows it, Ev-'ry
Christmas_____ Father Christmas_____ He's a dear old gent, He was heav-en sent It would not be Christmas with-out him. He's a

Copyright © 1970 by Stage & Screen Music, Inc.
Worldwide Rights Administered by Cherry River Music (BMI)
International Copyright Secured All Rights Reserved

Christ-mas___ Fa-ther Christ-mas___ Puts a great big sack on his
sweet-heart___ He's a dar-ling___ He's an "as-to-crat" He's a
dear old back 'Cause he loves us all and he shows it, And he goes___ for a
pus-sy cat We'd be fool-ish ev-er to doubt him, He's got style,___ such a
sleigh ride___ If it snows___ then he may ride all night But
man-ner___ and his smile___ is a ban-ner of joy you
that's all right___ In the morn-ing___ Christ-mas
can't de-stroy___ Mer-ry Christ-mas___ Fa-ther

Am A7 Dm7 G9 Em7 A9
morn - ing If you lift your eyes there's a big sur - prise on your
Christ - mas For it's thanks to you and the things you do that the
cresc. poco a poco
Dm7 Dm7/F A7/E Dm Dm9/C Bm7-5 E7 Am7 Am7 (Add D) D7sus D7 Dm7 C6/E
bed you'll see there's a gift from Fa - ther Christ - mas. That's how
likes of me think the world of Fa - ther Christ - mas Who makes
f
mf
Fmaj7 Dm7/G G7 1. C Am7 Dm7 Dm9 G7 G7 (Add E)
Christ - mas ought to be. Fa - ther
all our dreams come
mp
2. C C9sus C
true.
f
sfz

I LIKE LIFE
from the motion picture *Scrooge*

Words and Music by
Leslie Bricusse

I Like Life. Life likes me. Life and I fair-ly ful-ly a-gree Life is fine. Life is good.
I Like Life. Life likes me. I make life a per-pet-u-al spree, Eat-ing food, Drink-ing wine,

Copyright © 1970 by Stage & Screen Music, Inc.
Worldwide Rights Administered by Cherry River Music (BMI)
International Copyright Secured All Rights Reserved

D A9sus Dmaj7 A7/D D7 Gm7
'Spe - cially mine, which is just as it should be. I like
Think - ing who'd like the priv - i - lege to dine me. I like
C9sus C7 F F6 A (Add G) F Bb D7
pour-ing the wine and why not?
liv - ing the life of pleas - ure,
Life's a
Paus - ing
mf
Gm Gm/F E7sus E7 A9sus A7 D A9sus
pleas-ure that I de - ny not.
on - ly to take my lei - sure.
I Like Life,
I like songs.
mp
D A9sus D A9sus Dmaj7 A9sus
Here and now. Life and I made a mu - tu - al vow.
I like dance. I hear mu - sic and I'm in a trance.

Till I die, Life and I, We'll both try to be better somehow. And if life were a woman She would be my wife Why? Because I Like Life.

Tra-la-la, Oom-pah-pah, Chances are I shall get up and prance. Where there's music and laughter Happiness is rife Why? Because I Like Life.

THE MINISTER'S CAT
from the stage production of *Scrooge*

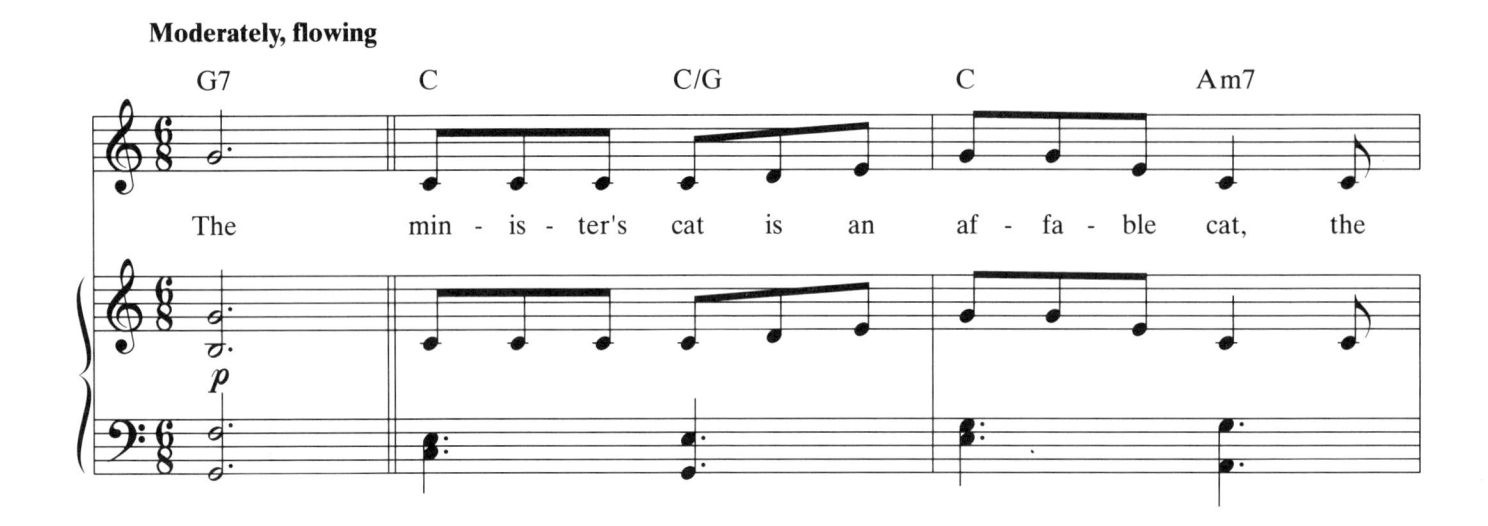

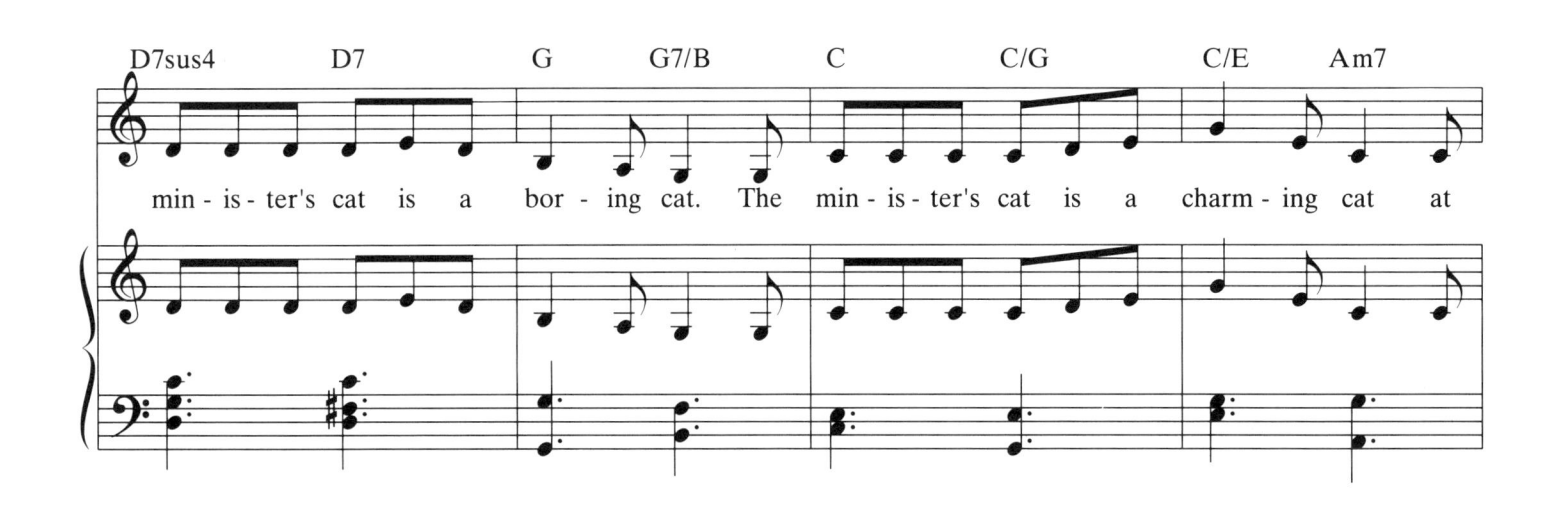

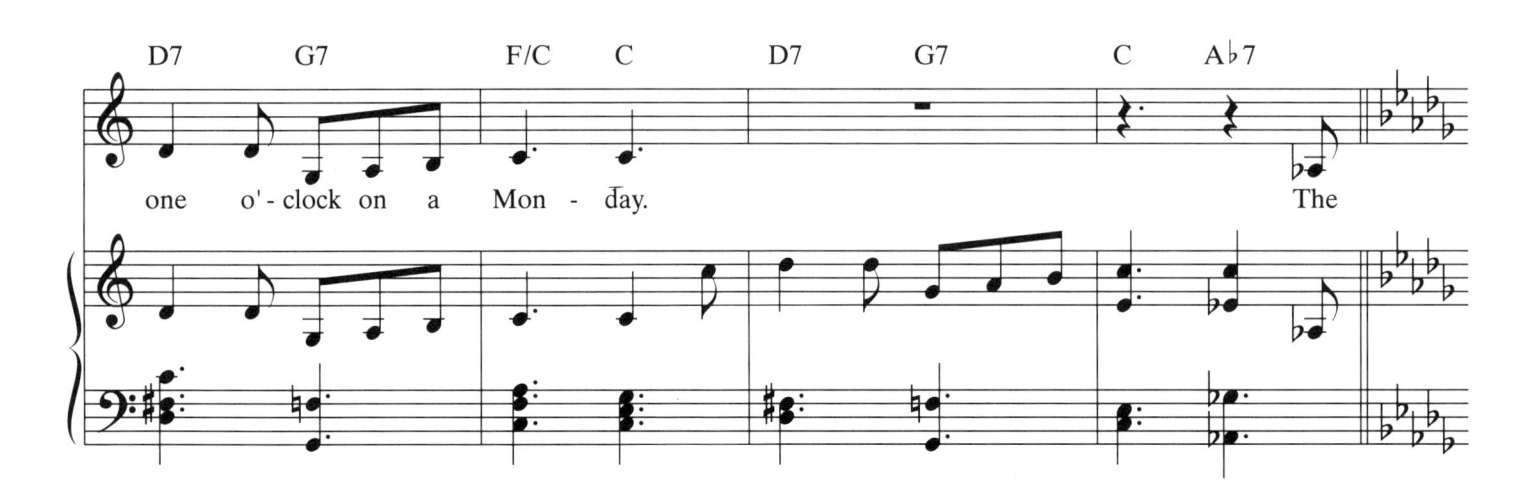

Words and Music by
Leslie Bricusse

Moderately, flowing

The min-is-ter's cat is an af-fa-ble cat, the min-is-ter's cat is a bor-ing cat. The min-is-ter's cat is a charm-ing cat at one o'-clock on a Mon-day. The

Copyright © 1982 by Stage & Screen Music, Inc.
Worldwide Rights Administered by Cherry River Music (BMI)
International Copyright Secured   All Rights Reserved

minister's cat is a darling cat, the minister's cat is an evil cat. The minister's cat is a frightful cat at two o'-clock on a Tuesday. The minister's cat is a grumpy cat, the minister's cat is a hungry cat. The minister's cat is an idiot cat at three o'-clock on a Wednes-day. The min-is-ter's cat is a jeal-ous cat, the min-is-ter's cat is a kind-ly cat. The min-is-ter's cat is a lone-ly cat at four o'-clock on a Thurs-day. The min-is-ter's cat is a mon-ster cat, the min-is-ter's cat is a

B B7/D♯ E E/D♯ C♯m7 E/B F♯7/A♯ B7
naugh - ty cat. The min - is - ter's cat is an o - val cat at five o'-clock on a
A/E E C7 F Dm Am Dm
Fri - day. The min - is - ter's cat is a per - fect cat, the
mp
E♭ G C G7/B C7/E F F/E♭ Dm7 B♭m6/D♭
min - is - ter's cat is a quirk - y cat. The min - is - ter's cat is a rev - er - ent cat at
C7sus4 C7 D♭/F F D♭7
six o' - clock on a Sat - ur - day. The

minister's cat is a silky cat, the minister's cat is a tiresome cat. The minister's cat is a useless cat at seven o'clock on a Sunday. The minister's cat is a vicious cat, the minister's cat is a wise old cat. The minister's cat's an extraord-'n'ry cat, a yel-low-dyed cat, a zip-py za-ny Zan-zi-bar cat. And what do you make of all of that? I'll tell you what we make of that: The min-is-ter tru-ly, tru-ly has an ab-so-lute-ly most re-mark-a-ble cat!

GOOD TIMES
from the stage production of *Scrooge*

Words and Music by
Leslie Bricusse

Moderately, freely

Some days are up days, some days are down days, some days are gold-en, some dark brown days. I nev-er mind when we have blue days;

Copyright © 1977 by Stage & Screen Music, Inc.
Worldwide Rights Administered by Cherry River Music (BMI)
International Copyright Secured All Rights Reserved

Cm7/F F7 Fm7 B♭7 A13 B♭13
they're al - ways fol - lowed by "we've come through" days. We've had
Medium fast cut time
E♭maj7 E♭6 B9 B6 B♭7
good times be - fore, and we'll have good times a - gain. What -
mf
E♭maj7 E♭6 B♭m7♭5 B♭m7 E9 E♭7
ev - er we've done, we've made life fun. And
A♭maj7 A♭m9 G7♯5 C7♭9♯5 C7
when things were bad, and bad times we've had, we've

Lyrics:

fought and we've won___ one for all, all for one. So if today things get rough,___ then we've just got-ta get tough.___ We're
made of the stuff___ that makes men men.___ We're
gon-na come through,___ and kids when we do,___ we'll

Chords by line:
- Cm7/F | F9♭5 | F7 | B♭7 Fm7/C C♯m7 B♭7/D | B♭13 A13
- E♭maj7 | E♭6 | B9 | B6 | B♭7
- E♭maj7 | E♭6 | B♭m7♭5 B♭m7 | E9 | E♭7
- A♭maj7 | A♭m9 | G7♯5 | C7♭9♯5 | C7 *To Coda*

F9 B♭7 E♭ B7
on - ly know good___ times a - gain.___
Cm7/F
D.S. al Coda
We've had
Coda
F9 B♭7
nev - er know bad___ times, good -
G13 G7♯5 C7 Cm7/F B♭7
bye to the sad___ times. We'll on - ly know good___
E♭ B7 B♭ E♭
times a - gain.___

THE CANDY MAN

from the motion picture *Willy Wonka & The Chocolate Factory*

Words and Music by
Leslie Bricusse and Anthony Newley

can - dy, Wil - ly's the con - quer - or.

Refrain—Moderato, joyfully

Who can take a sun - rise sprin - kle it with dew,
Who can take a rain - bow wrap it in a sigh,

cov - er it in choc - 'late and a mir - a - cle or two?
soak it in the sun and make a straw-b'ry lem - on pie?

The can - dy man, (The can - dy man, the can - dy man can. the

C Am7 D7sus D7 Dm7/G
can - dy man can.) The can - dy man can 'cause he mix - es it with love and makes the
mp
1. Cmaj7 F/G Cmaj7 Dm7/G
world_ taste good.
R.H.
2. Cmaj7 F/G C C7sus C7
world_ taste good. The
Fmaj7 F♯o C/G GnoD Cmaj7 C6
can-dy man makes ev-'ry-thing he bakes sat - is fy - ing and de - li - cious.
mf
mp
F♯m7-5 B7+ B7+(-9) Em Em7 Em7/A A7-9 Dm7 Tacet B♭7 A7 A♭7-5 G7 Tacet
Talk a-bout your child-hood wish-es! You can e-ven eat the dish - es!
mf
mp
mf

Who can take to-mor-row, dip it in a dream, sep-a-rate the sor-row and col-lect up all the cream? The can-dy man, (The can-dy man, the can-dy man can. the can-dy man can.) The can-dy man can 'cause he mix-es it with love and makes the

1.
Cmaj7 F/G C C7sus C7
world_ taste good.___ The
2.
Cmaj7 C C6
world_ taste good.___
rall.
Very slowly, ad lib.
Am9 Am7 D7sus D7 Dm7/G Dm9/G Dm7/G
And the world tastes good 'cause the can - dy man thinks_ it
mp
p
rall.
Moderato
B♭ (Add C)
C (Add D)
should.___
f
mp
B♭ (Add C)
C (Add D)
Repeat and fade out
dim. poco a poco

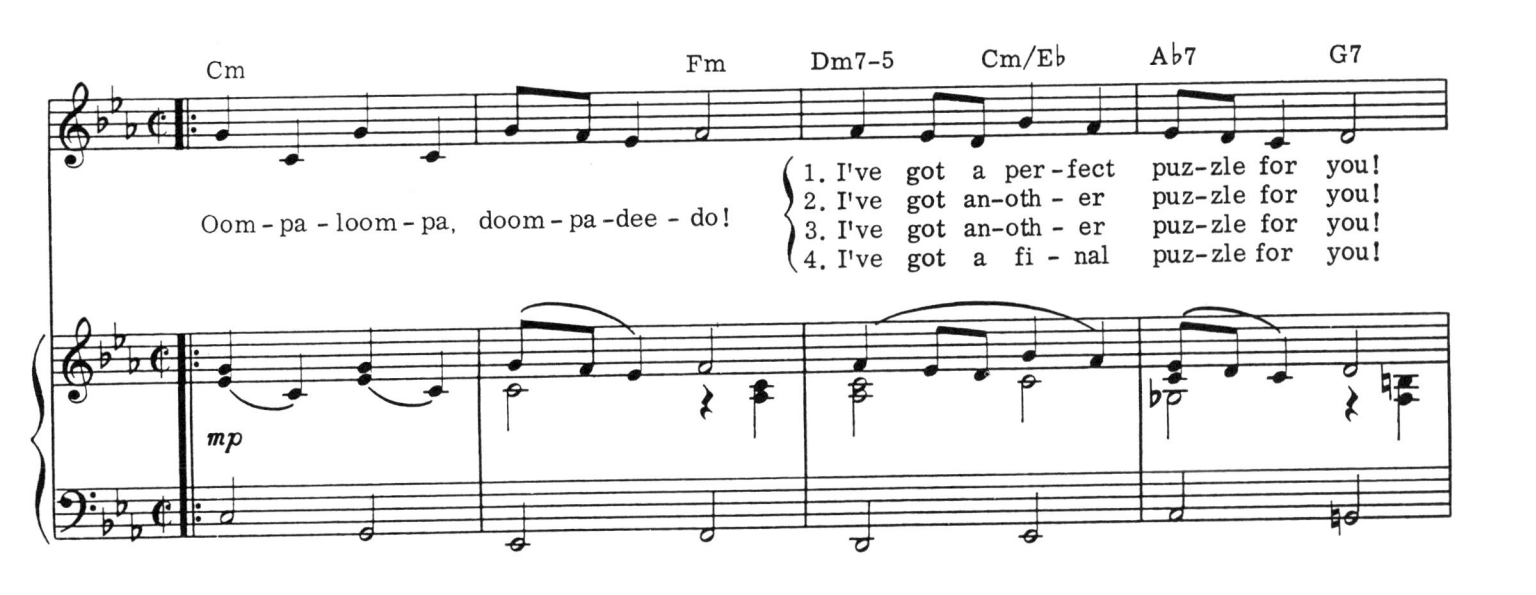

OOMPA-LOOMPA DOOMPADEE-DOO
from the motion picture *Willy Wonka & The Chocolate Factory*

Words and Music by
Leslie Bricusse and Anthony Newley

Oom-pa-loom-pa, doom-pa-dee-do!

1. I've got a per-fect puz-zle for you!
2. I've got an-oth-er puz-zle for you!
3. I've got an-oth-er puz-zle for you!
4. I've got a fi-nal puz-zle for you!

Oom-pa-loom-pa, doom-pa-dee-dee! If you are wise you-'ll lis-ten to me!

Copyright © 1970, 1971 Taradam Music
International Copyright Secured All Rights Reserved

What do you get when you guzzle down sweets, eating as much as an el-e-phant eats? What are you at getting ter-ri-bly fat? What do you think will come of that?

What do you get when your man-ners are bad? Why are you rude to your moth-er and dad? What do you gain driv-ing peo-ple in-sane? I should have thought the an-swers plain!

Who do you blame when a kid is a brat, pam-pered and spoiled like a Si-a-mese cat? What can you say when a kid is a curse? par-ents are us-u-ally ten times worse!

What do you get from a glut of T. V.? A pain in the neck and an I. Q. of three! Why don't you try sim-ply read-ing a book? Or could you just not bear to look? Or

I don't like the look of it!
You don't gain any-thing!
have-n't you no-ticed?
You'll get no com-mer-cials!

Oom - pa - loom - pa, doom - pa - dee - da!

If you're not greed-y you will go far!
Giv-en good man-ners you will go far!
If you're not spoiled then you will go far!
Do as I say and you will go far!

You will live in hap-pi-ness too!

Like the oom - pa - loom - pa, doom - pa - dee - doo!

4. Keep repeating and fade out

doo! Doom - pa - dee -

dim. poco a poco

CHEER UP, CHARLIE
from the motion picture *Willy Wonka & The Chocolate Factory*

Words and Music by
Leslie Bricusse and Anthony Newley

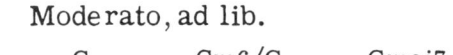

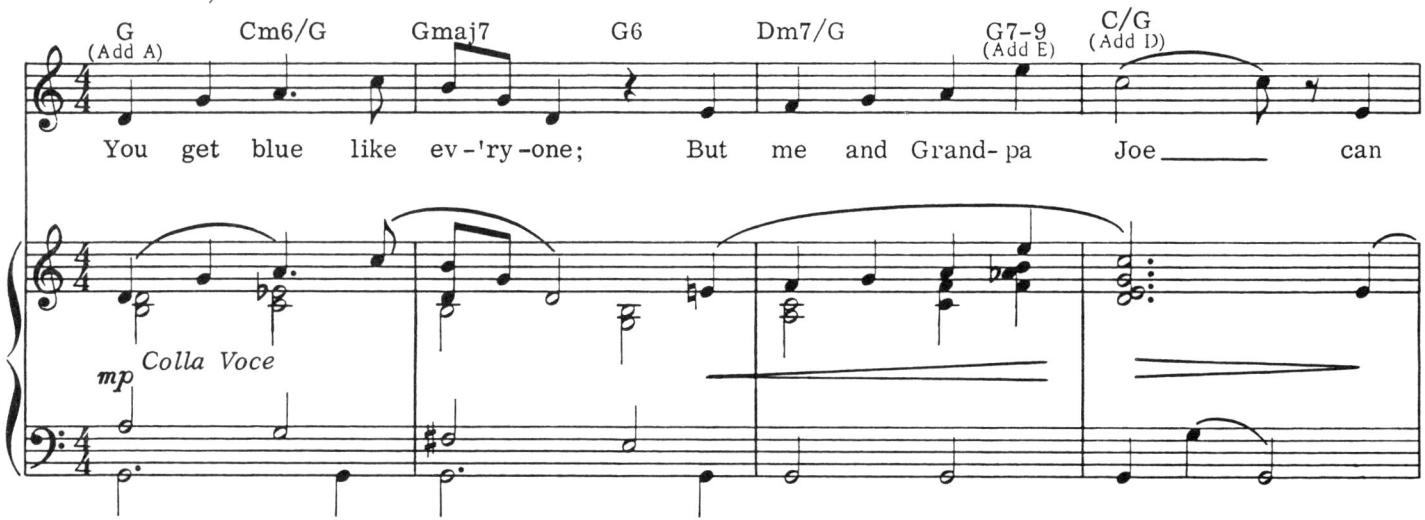

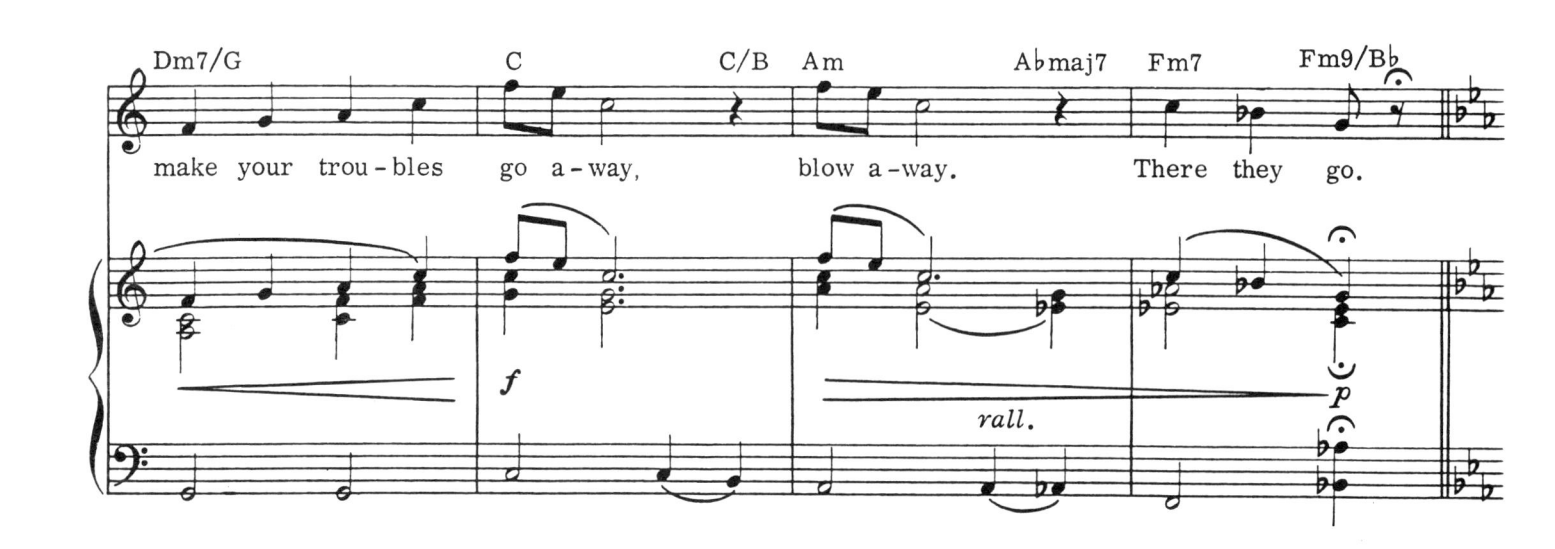

Refrain

Moderately slow, Rubato and Tenderly

Cheer up, Charlie, give me a smile. What happened to the smile I used to know? Don't you know your grin has always been my sunshine? Let that sunshine show! Come on, Charlie, no need to frown. Deep down you know tomorrow is your toy.

Fm7 Db9 Gm7 Cm9 ♮B Cm7 Fm9 Fm7/Bb
When the days get heav-y, nev-er pit - a-pat 'em! Up and at 'em,
mf
Eb Bbm7 Eb7 Ab Dbm/Ab Ab
boy! Some day, sweet as a song,
mp
Abmaj7 Ab6 Gm Gm7-5 C7-9
Char-lie's luck-y day will come a - long. 'Til that day you've got-ta stay in
mf
Fm Fm (Add E) Cm7/F F7 Bm7 E7 Fm7 (Add Bb) Bb7-9 (Add G)
strong, Char-lie. Up on top is right where you be - long. Look up,
mp
p
mp

Ebmaj Eb Abm/Eb Ebmaj7 Eb6 Gm7 Gm7-5/C C7
Char-lie, you'll see a star. Just fol-low it and keep your dreams in
Fm Am7-5 Abm6 Gm7 Bo/C Cm7
view. Pret-ty soon the skies are gon-na clear up, Char-lie.
Abmaj7 G7sus G7-9 Cm7 F7-5 -9 Tacet (Optional) Ebmaj7/Bb Eb/Bb Cm
Cheer up, Char-lie, do Cheer up, Char-lie,
mf rall. f a tempo mf
Fm7 Gm7 Ab (Add Bb) Fm7/Bb Am7-5 Abm6 Eb/G Ao/Gb F7 (Add Bb) Fbmaj7-5 Ebmaj7 Eb
just be glad you're you.
rall. a tempo rall. p

I'VE GOT A GOLDEN TICKET

from the motion picture *Willy Wonka & The Chocolate Factory*

Words and Music by
Leslie Bricusse and Anthony Newley

Moderately Fast

With abandon

I nev-er thought my life could be an-y-thing but ca-tas-tro-phe! But
I nev-er had a chance to shine. Nev-er a hap-py song to sing. But

sud-den-ly I be-gin to see a bit of good luck for me!____ 'Cos
sud-den-ly half the world is mine! What an a-maz-ing thing!____ 'Cos

I've got a gold-en tick-et!____
I've got a gold-en tick-et!____

Copyright © 1970, 1971 Taradam Music
International Copyright Secured All Rights Reserved

(Sheet music)

Lyrics:
I've got a gold-en twin-kle in my eye!
I've got a gold-en sun up in my sky!

I nev-er thought I'd see the day when I would face the world and say, "Good-morning. Look at the sun!"

I never thought that I would be slap in the lap of luxury! 'Cause I'd have said it couldn't be done! But it *can* be done! I never dreamed that I would climb over the moon in ecstasy; But nevertheless it's there that I'm

Dm7 G7 Cm7 F9 F7 Bb B° F/C F7
shortly about to be! 'Cos I've got a golden ticket!
Bb Bbm F/A Bb Bbmaj7 Am7-5 D7sus D7
I've got a golden chance to make my
G7 G7-5 Gm Gm (Add F#) Gm7 Tacet Gm7/C
way! And with a golden ticket it's a gold-
Tacet Gm7/C Tacet F Ab C7/G sus Gb7-5 F
en day!
f
ff
sfz

PURE IMAGINATION
from the motion picture *Willy Wonka & The Chocolate Factory*

Words and Music by
Leslie Bricusse and Anthony Newley

Ebmaj7/G Cm7 Fm9 Fm7 Fm11 Fm9/Bb Fm7/Bb G (Add A)
a - tion! What we'll see will de - fy ex - pla - na - tion!
mp
mf
Abmaj7 Gm7 Gm7/C C7-9 Fm9 Fm9/Bb
If you want to view par - a - dise, sim-ply look a-round and
f
mf
Ebmaj9 Am7-5 D7 Gm11 Gm7
view it! An - y - thing you want to, do it!
C7 (Add A) F9 Bb7 Ab/Bb E7/Bb Fm7/Bb Ab Eb/G
Want to change the world? There's noth - ing to it! There is
p
mp

Fm11 Fm7 Fm11/Bb Fm7/Bb Ebmaj7 Fm7 F#o
no life I know to com - pare with pure im - ag - i -
mp
mp
Gm7 Cm7 Fm9 Fm7 Fm11 Fm9/Bb Fm7/Bb G (Add A)
na - tion! Liv - ing there, you'll be free if you tru - ly
mp
1. Bbm7 Bb7 Eb Fm9/Bb Ab Eb/G
wish to be! Come with
p
mf
mp
2. Bbm7 Bb7 Eb Abmaj7 Ebmaj7
wish to be!
mf
rall.
p

THANK YOU, SANTA!
from the motion picture *Santa Claus: The Movie*

Words by Leslie Bricusse
Music by Henry Mancini

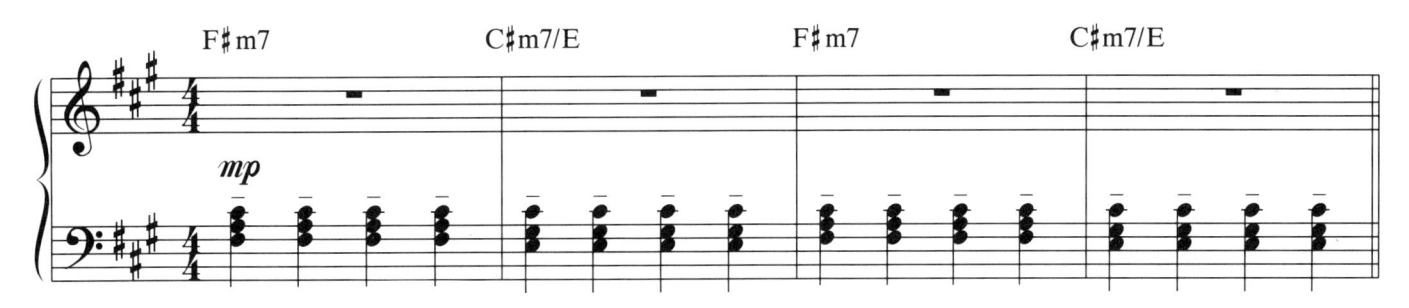

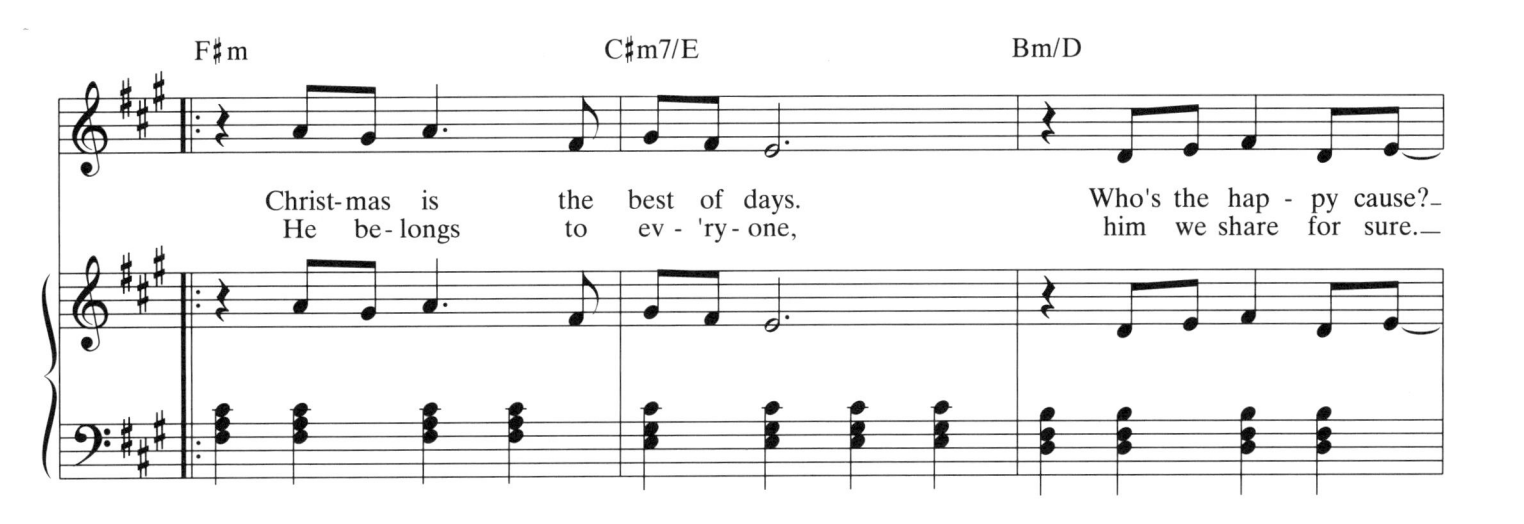

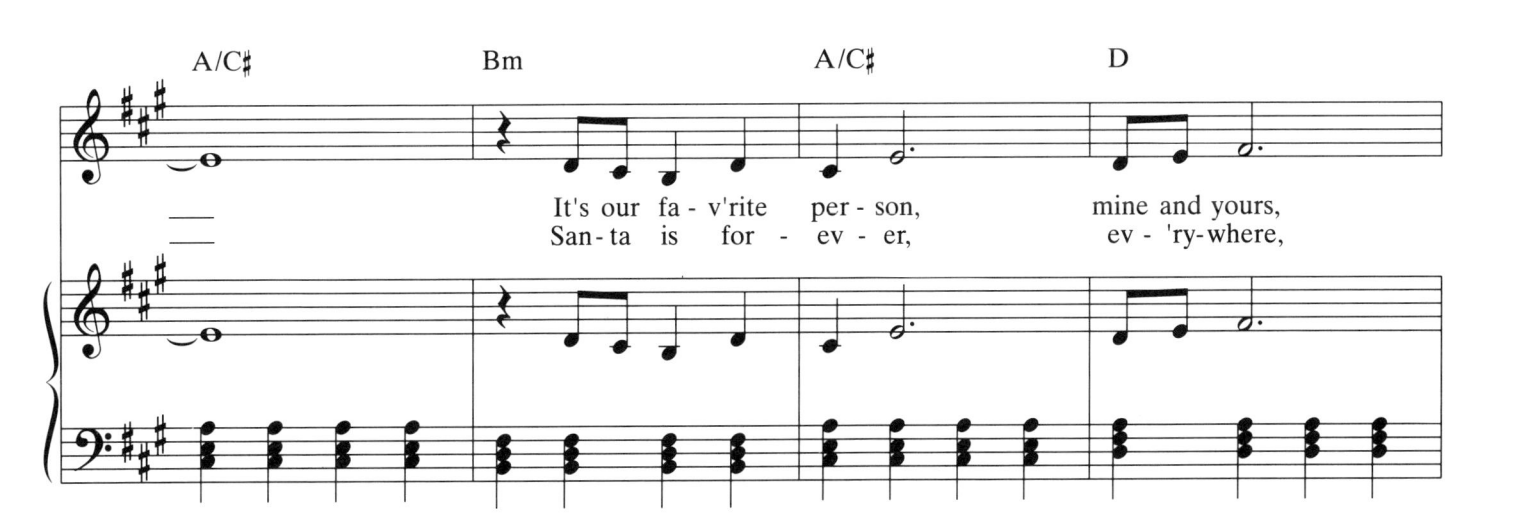

Christ-mas is the best of days. Who's the hap-py cause? him we share for sure.
He be-longs to ev-'ry-one,

It's our fa-v'rite per-son, mine and yours,
San-ta is for-ev-er, ev-'ry-where,

Copyright © 1985 The Calash Corporation N.V.
International Copyright Secured All Rights Reserved

119

E F♯m C♯m7/E Bm/D
San-ta Claus. San-ta gives to all of us, all he has to give.
ev-er-more. San-ta Claus is ours be-cause he's a friend in need.
A/C♯ D E Asus4 A
San-ta real-ly knows the way to live.
San-ta is our friend in word and deed.
Dsus4 D G C D
Thank you, San-ta! Thank you,
Thank you, San-ta! Thank you,
f
C G Em Am F
San-ta! When it snows we know you're near.
San-ta! You bring all the world good cheer.

D D7 C/E D7/F♯ G C D
We wan - ta thank you, San - ta! Thank you,
We're here ta thank you, San - ta! Frank - ly,
C G Em Am D G
San - ta! 'S nice to know you're com - ing back next
San - ta, we'd like Christ - mas twen - ty
1.
year.
2.
D G E♭7 D♭/F E♭/G
times a year. We wan - na
A♭ D♭ E♭ D♭ A♭
thank you, San - ta! Thank you, San - ta!

Fm
D♭
G♭
E♭ E♭7/G D♭/F E♭7/G
You bring all the world good cheer. We're here ta
A♭
D♭
E♭
D♭ A♭
thank you, San - ta! Thank you, San - ta!
Fm
B♭m7
E♭
A♭
'S nice to know you're com - ing back next
D♭
A♭
D♭
A♭
D♭
A♭ E♭7 A♭
year.

SOMEWHERE IN MY MEMORY
from the motion picture *Home Alone*

Words by Leslie Bricusse
Music by John Williams

Gently and with simplicity

smoothly
mp

Candles in the win - dow, shad - ows paint - ing the ceil - ing,

Copyright © 1990 Fox Film Music Corp.
International Copyright Secured   All Rights Reserved

gazing at the fire glow, feeling that "gingerbread" feeling. Precious moments, special people, happy faces I can see. Somewhere in my memory, Christmas joys all around me, living in my mem - 'ry, all of the mu - sic, all of the mag - ic, all of the fam - 'ly home here with me.

STAR OF BETHLEHEM
from the motion picture *Home Alone*

Words by Leslie Bricusse
Music by John Williams

Moderato

Star of Beth-le-hem shin-ing bright, bath-ing the world in
Star of Beth-le-hem, star on high, mir-a-cle of the

heav'n-ly light. Let the glow of your dis-tant glo-ry
mid-night sky. Let your lu-mi-nous light from heav-en

Copyright © 1990 Fox Film Music Corp.
International Copyright Secured All Rights Reserved

fill us with hope this Christmas night. Star of innocence,
enter our hearts and make us fly. Star of happiness,

star of goodness. Gazing down since time began.
star of wonder. You see ev'rything from afar.

You who've lived through endless ages, view with love the
Cast your eye upon the future, make us wiser

age of man. Star of beauty hear our plea,
than we are. Star of gentleness hear our plea,

whis-per your wis-dom ten-der-ly. Star of Beth-le-hem set us free, make us a world we long to see. make us a world we long to see.

Music From Television

Peter Pan (1975)

As a teenager, I was privileged to see Danny Kaye's first legendary, mould-breaking performances in music hall (all right, vaudeville) at the renowned London Palladium in 1949. He was a complete phenomenon.

I knew every lyric of every song that Danny ever sang—and most of the really good ones were written by his wonderful and dazzlingly clever wife, Sylvia Fine.

So when Newley and I were asked to write a brand-new song score for a musical version of Sir James Barrie's *Peter Pan*, to star Mia Farrow as Peter and Danny Kaye as Captain Hook, my cup ranneth (if that is the word) over. For Mia, too, was and is a very special person in my life. In our early days at Fox in the 60's, we would lunch together in the commissary every single day, daydreaming about all the wonderful fantasy projects we would like to make together—prime among them being *Peter Pan*! And now suddenly, a decade later, it was as though Somebody had known about it all along and decided to grant our wish!

So for me *Peter Pan* was pure serendipity. It brought the immense and rare satisfaction of working on a story I had loved all my life, starring two people I knew, admired and loved so well. And if that isn't serendipity, I don't know what is!

Babes In Toyland (1986)

Thanks to the good offices of my dear friend, the British film director and author Bryan Forbes, I was invited in the spring of 1986 to write a new song score for the classic 1903 Victor Herbert operetta, *Babes in Toyland*.

An eleven-year-old Drew Barrymore, still warm from the global glow of *E.T.*, played the little girl from Cincinnati whose dreams become dramas in Toyland, and became my new best friend for the three months we were in Germany.

My two favourite songs from the score are "Through the Eyes of a Child" and "C-I-N-C-I-N-N-A-T-I." I like the philosophy of the first and the tongue-twisting fun of the second.

If anyone from Cincinnati reads this, please tell the mayor that this song is the perfect theme song for your fair city—especially the ball teams! Reds and Bengals, please note!

GROWING UP

from the television production of *Peter Pan*

Words and Music by
Leslie Bricusse and Anthony Newley

Gmaj7
Asus4
To Coda
Asus4
A
be, liv - ing the life a child should.
tine. They would - n't know how
Dmaj7
E/D
I don't see why I've got to say good-bye
mf
C♯m7
F♯m7
Dmaj7
to my child - hood.
Let them take their closed-

up world___ and leave me an o - pen sky.

Here in my child - hood.___

I've got no time for grow - ing up.___ When you've got time,_

___ don't__ waste it. Taste it each__ and any way you choose. Use each love-ly mo-ment, youth is too good to lose. Raise your voice and make your choice. If you've got youth, re-joice.

Bm9 Bm E9♭5 E/D C♯m7
Grow - ing up is go - ing up a hill you ought to be go -
F♯m7 Dmaj7 E/D
ing down. I think grow - ing up is slow - ing up a dream
C♯m7 F♯m7 Dmaj7
that does - n't need slow - ing down. Grow - ing up is
E/D C♯m7 E/F♯ F♯m7
throw-ing up a chal-lenge you should be throw-ing down. And I've

got no time for grow-ing up,_____ ev - er.

Tempo primo

They

D.S. al Coda

Coda

not to.

Grow-ing up is go - ing up a hill you ought to be going down. I think grow-ing up is slow-ing up a dream that does-n't need slow-ing down. Grow-ing up is throw-ing up a chal-lenge you should be throw-ing down. And that's why I'm not grow-ing up, nev-er,

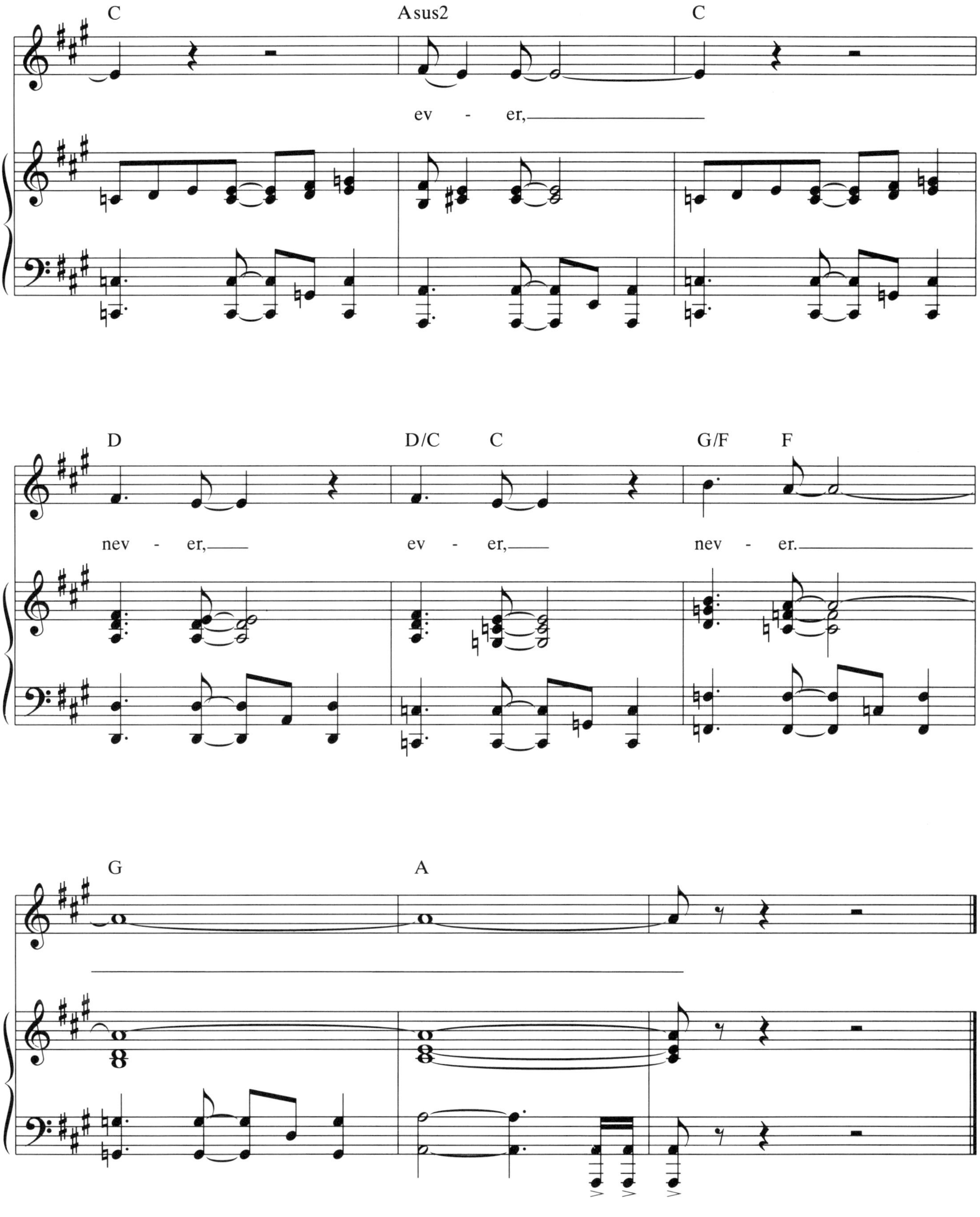
C
Asus2
C
ev - er,
D
D/C
C
G/F
F
nev - er,
ev - er,
nev - er.
G
A

I'M BETTER WITH YOU
from the television production of *Peter Pan*

Words and Music by
Leslie Bricusse and Anthony Newley

Moderately fast, with a swing

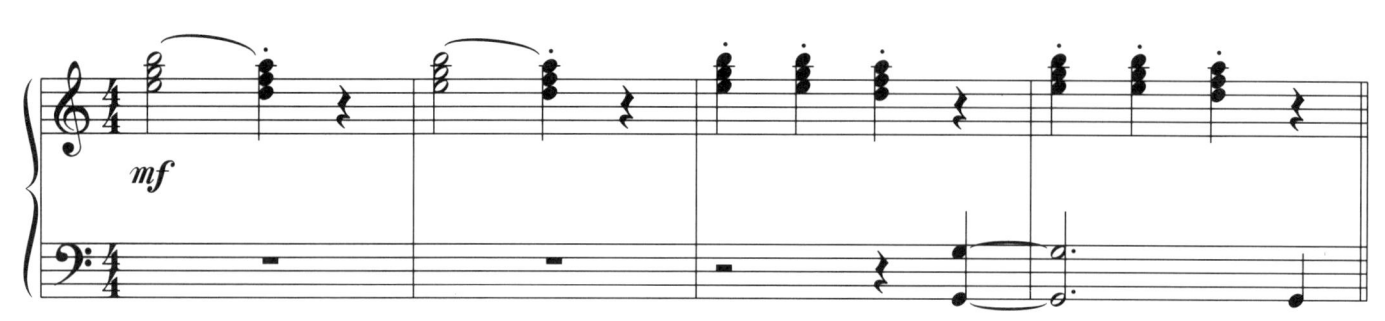

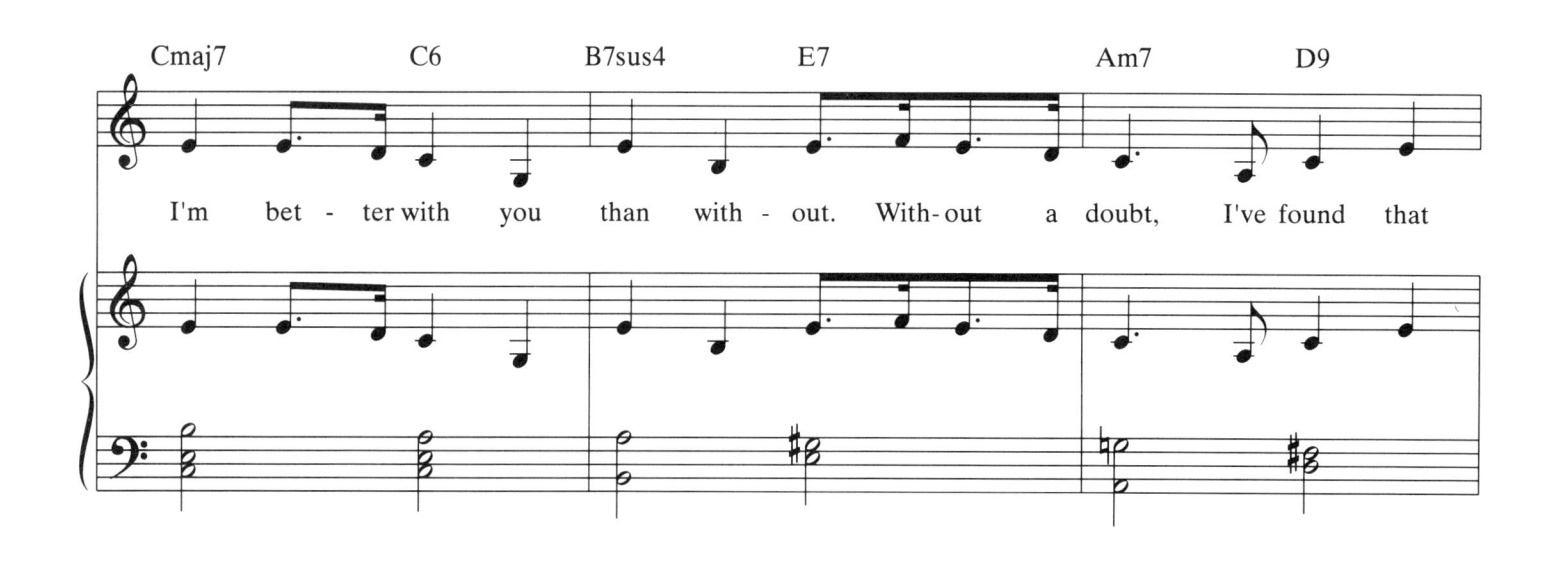

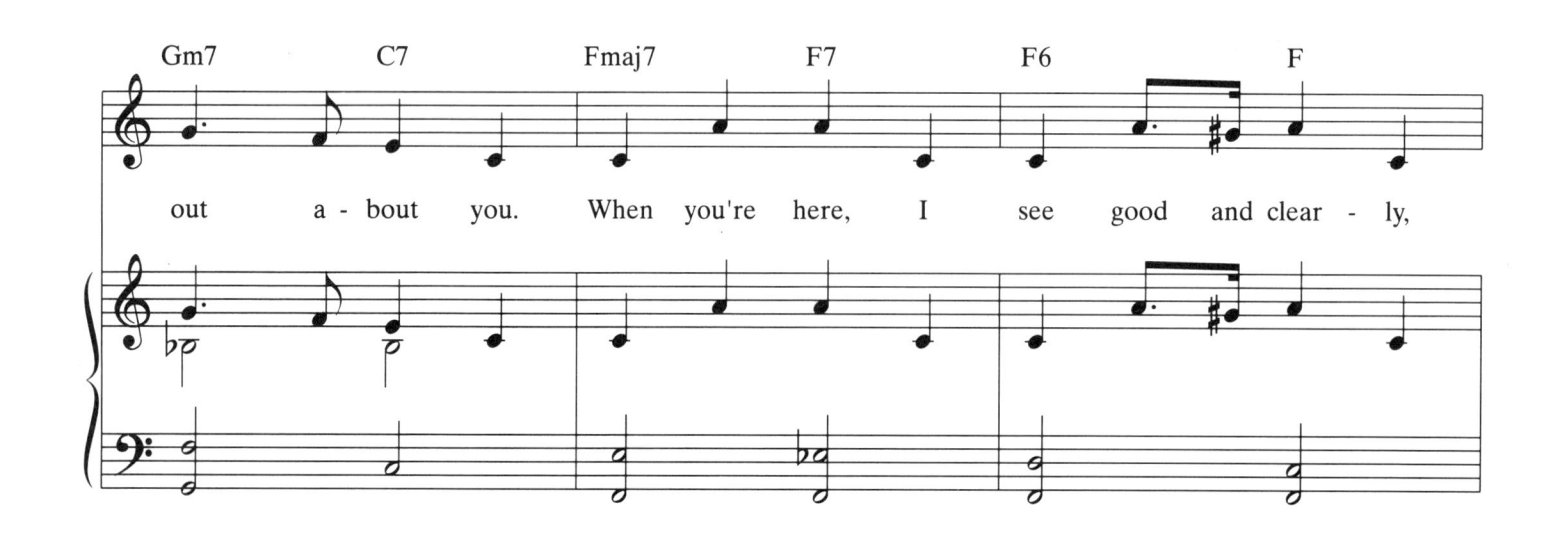

mf

I'm better with you than without. Without a doubt, I've found that out about you. When you're here, I see good and clearly,

Copyright © 1975 Taradam Music, Inc.
International Copyright Secured All Rights Reserved

| Bm7♭5 | E7 | Am7 | Gm7 C7 | Fmaj7 F7 |

get to do a lot - ta things I've got to do. When you're not,

| Dm7 | | G7 F/A G7/C C#° |

dun - no what to do, fret - ting and get - ting up - set and for - get - ting the

| Dm Dm7 | G9♭5 G7 | Gm7/C C7 |

sort - a things I ought - a not to.

| F F+ F6 F+ | F G7/F |

When you're gone, it's as though the sun had nev - er

Em11 A7 Am9/D D13 Am9/D
shone. Life's bou - quet goes and the
D13 Dm7 Em7 Fmaj7 Em7 D7sus4 D7
day goes on and on and on.
Dm7 G7 Cmaj7 C6 B7sus4 E7
And so you see, it's clear to me that we should
Am7 D9 Gm7 C7 Fmaj7 F7
be to - geth - er now and al - ways. Big and small ways,

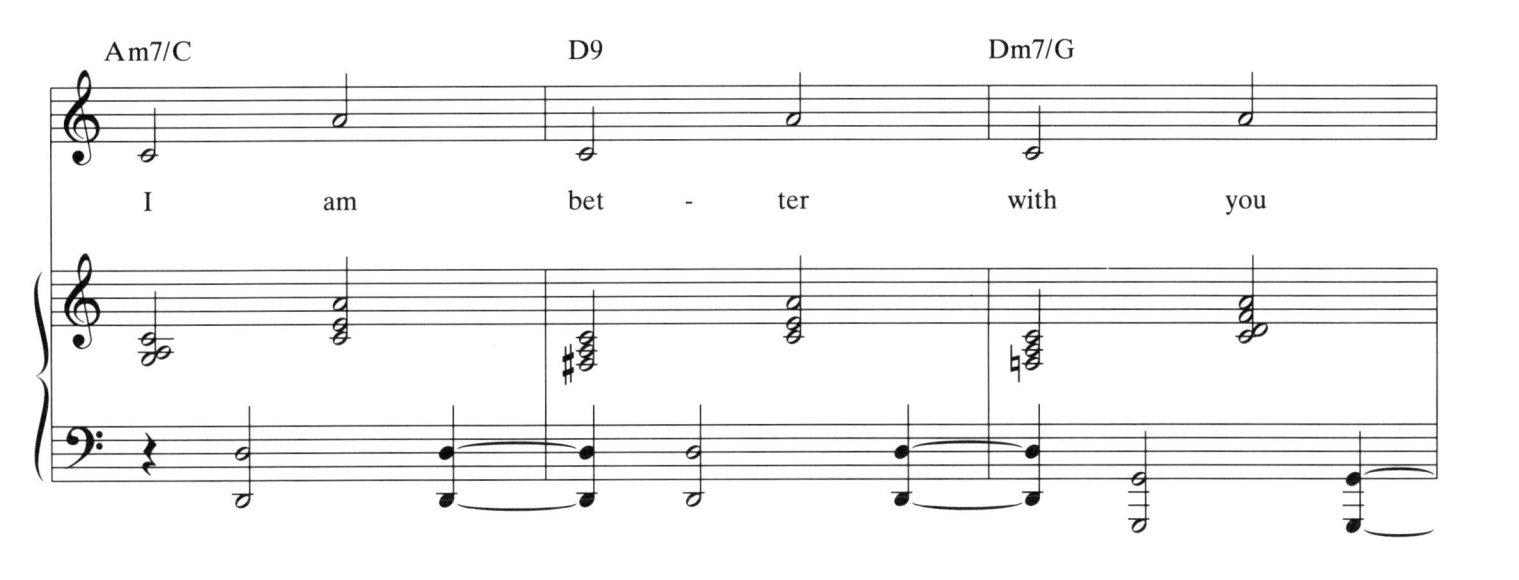

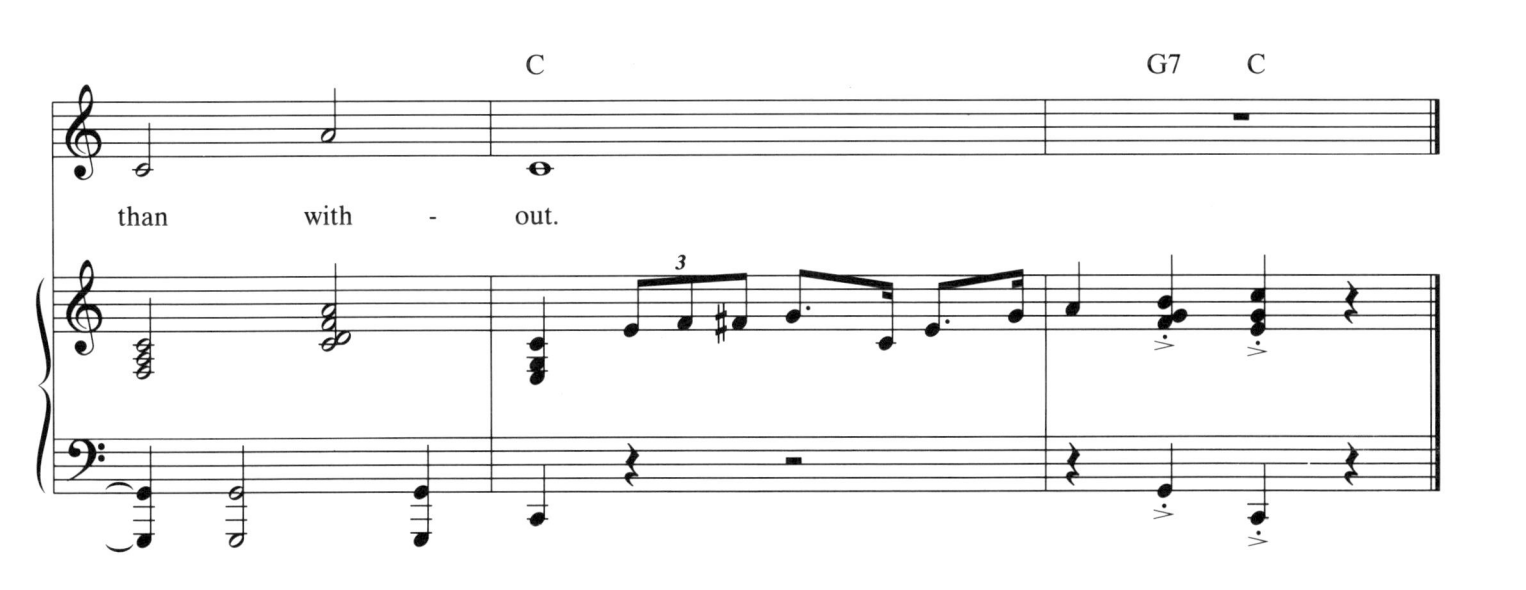

ball - rooms or hall - ways, you're what my life's a - bout.

I am bet - ter with you

than with - out.

ONCE UPON A BEDTIME
from the television production of *Peter Pan*

Words and Music by
Leslie Bricusse and Anthony Newley

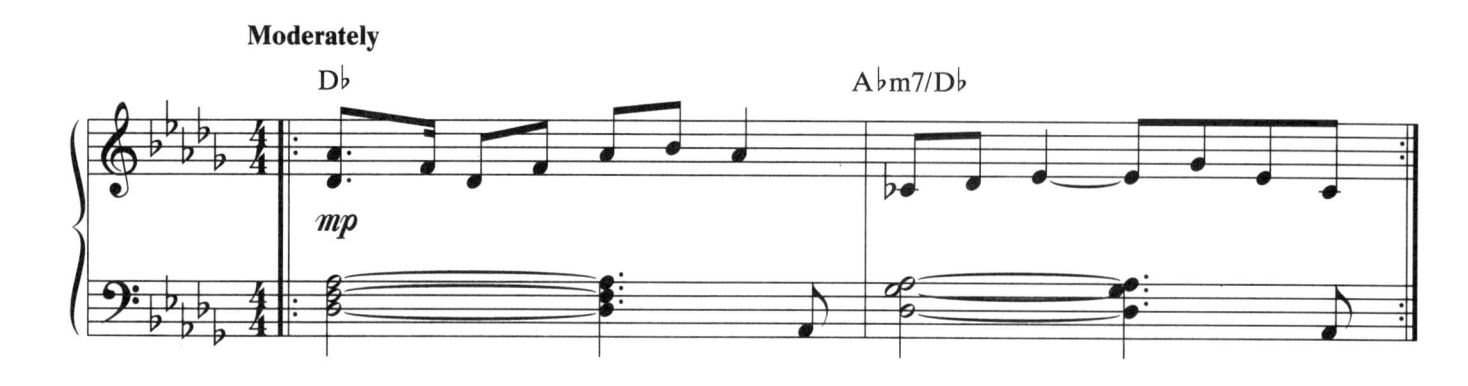

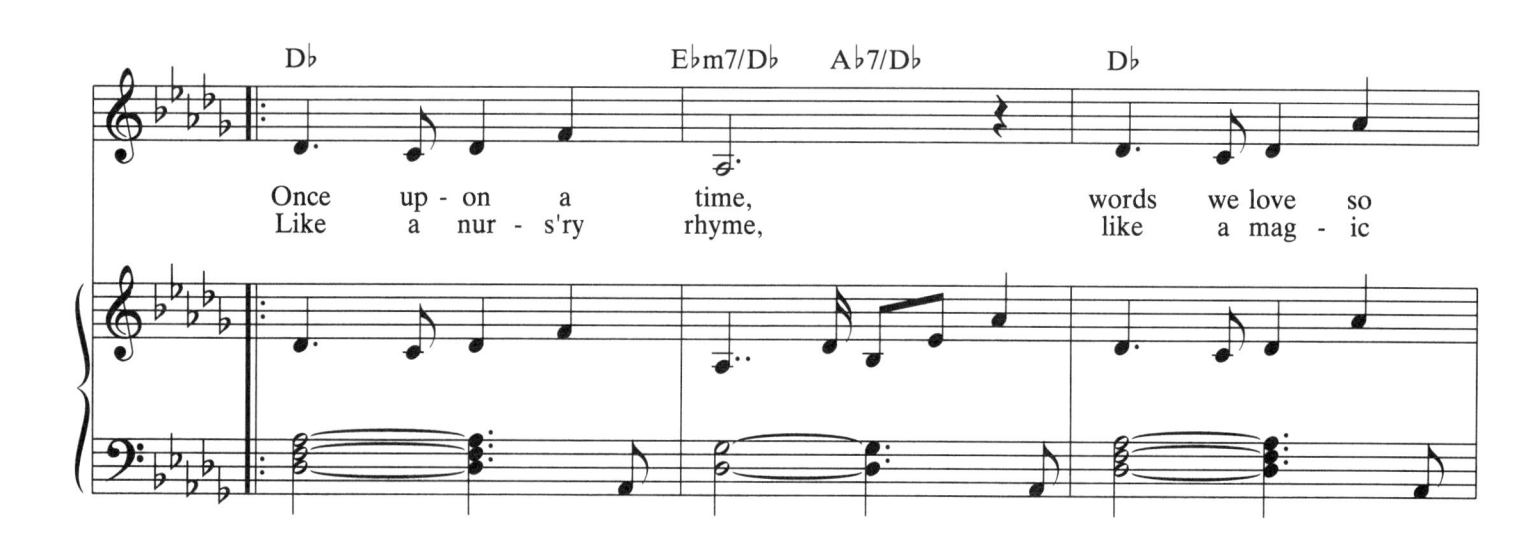

Moderately

Once up-on a time, words we love so well.
Like a nur-s'ry rhyme, like a mag-ic spell,
Sto-ry-tell-ers tell in
ev-'ry dream we weave is

Copyright © 1975 Taradam Music, Inc.
International Copyright Secured All Rights Reserved

Cm7♭5 F7♭9♭5 F7♭9 B♭m7
words with wings of knaves and
make - be - lieve that tugs the
E♭9♭5 E♭9 E♭m7 A♭sus4 A♭7 A♭9
1. 2.
kings and won - drous things. time.
sleeve of
A♭m7/D♭ D♭9 G♭maj7 Gm7♭5 C7♭9 Fm7
Tales were told, bold and
B♭sus4 B♭7 E♭m7 A♭sus4 A♭7 D♭maj9 D♭6
true; though we all grow up,

sto- ries nev- er do. I know why sto- ries nev- er die: they just wait for chil- dren passing by. Time to go to sleep, count your pretty

A♭m7/D♭ G♭ G♭♯5 E♭m/G♭ Fsus4 F7
sheep. Dream a dream to keep to-mor-row
B♭m7 G♭m6/A D♭maj9/A♭ G♭maj9♯11 G♭maj9
new. Hap-py end-ings too,
Fm7 B♭7♭9♭5 B♭7♭9 E♭m9 Fm7
hope your dreams come true. Once up-on a bed-time
G♭maj9 Gm7♭5 E♭m7/A♭ A♭sus4 D♭
sto-ry, they do.

PETER PAN
from the television production of *Peter Pan*

Words and Music by
Leslie Bricusse and Anthony Newley

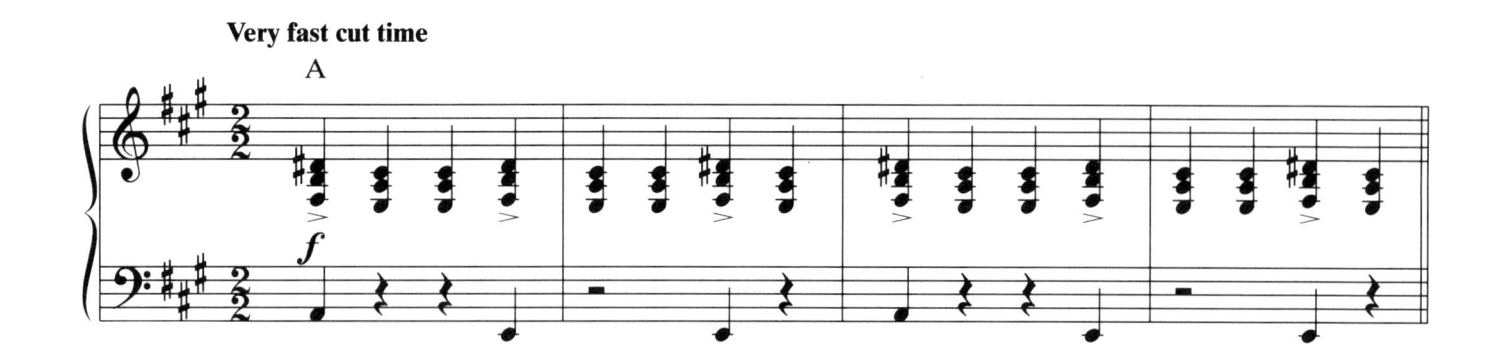

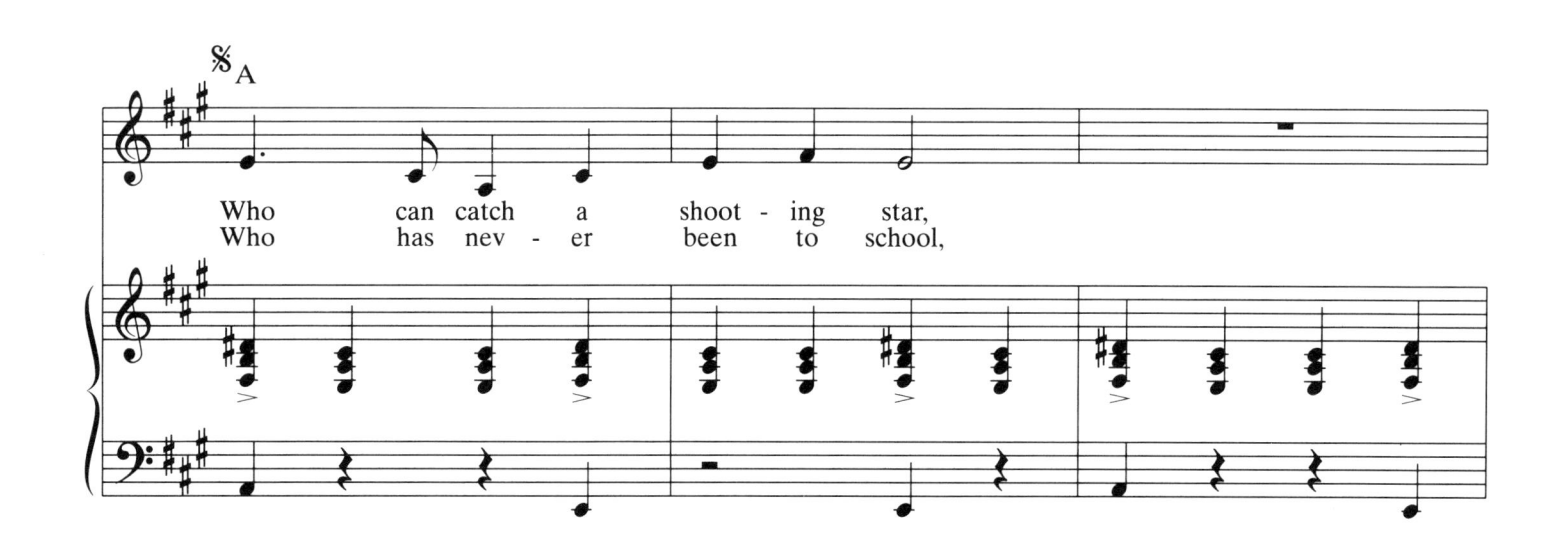

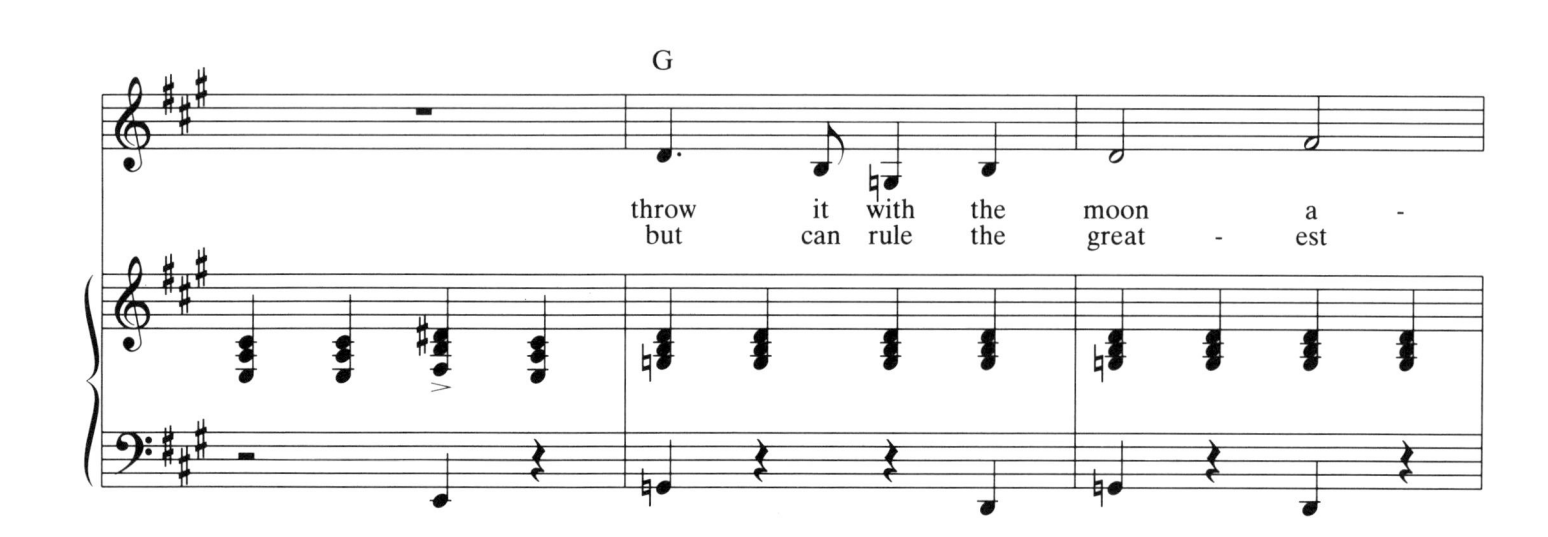

Very fast cut time

Who can catch a shoot-ing star,
Who has nev-er been to school,

throw it with the moon a-
but can rule the great-est

A
mong his toys?
land there is?
Keep a sun - beam in a jar?
Make the wis - est man a fool?
G
Pe - ter Pan,
Pe - ter Pan.
Em7
To Coda
the King of
The world is
A
Boys.

Dmaj7
Who can fling a rain - bow 'round the
C♯m7
F♯7sus4
sun and make life fun?
F♯7
Dmaj9
B♭m7
E♭
Sweet Pe - ter can!

Who can tie a tin can to the wind and grin with joy? Only one boy can, Pe - ter Pan! Who has nev - er read a book,

but could rook the Em - p'ror of Ja - pan?

Who's a match for Cap - tain Hook or an - y man?

Sweet Pe - ter

152

Who is as quick as a light-ning flash? Whizz, bang, crash! It's me, Pe-ter Pan.

Catch me if you can, but no man can.

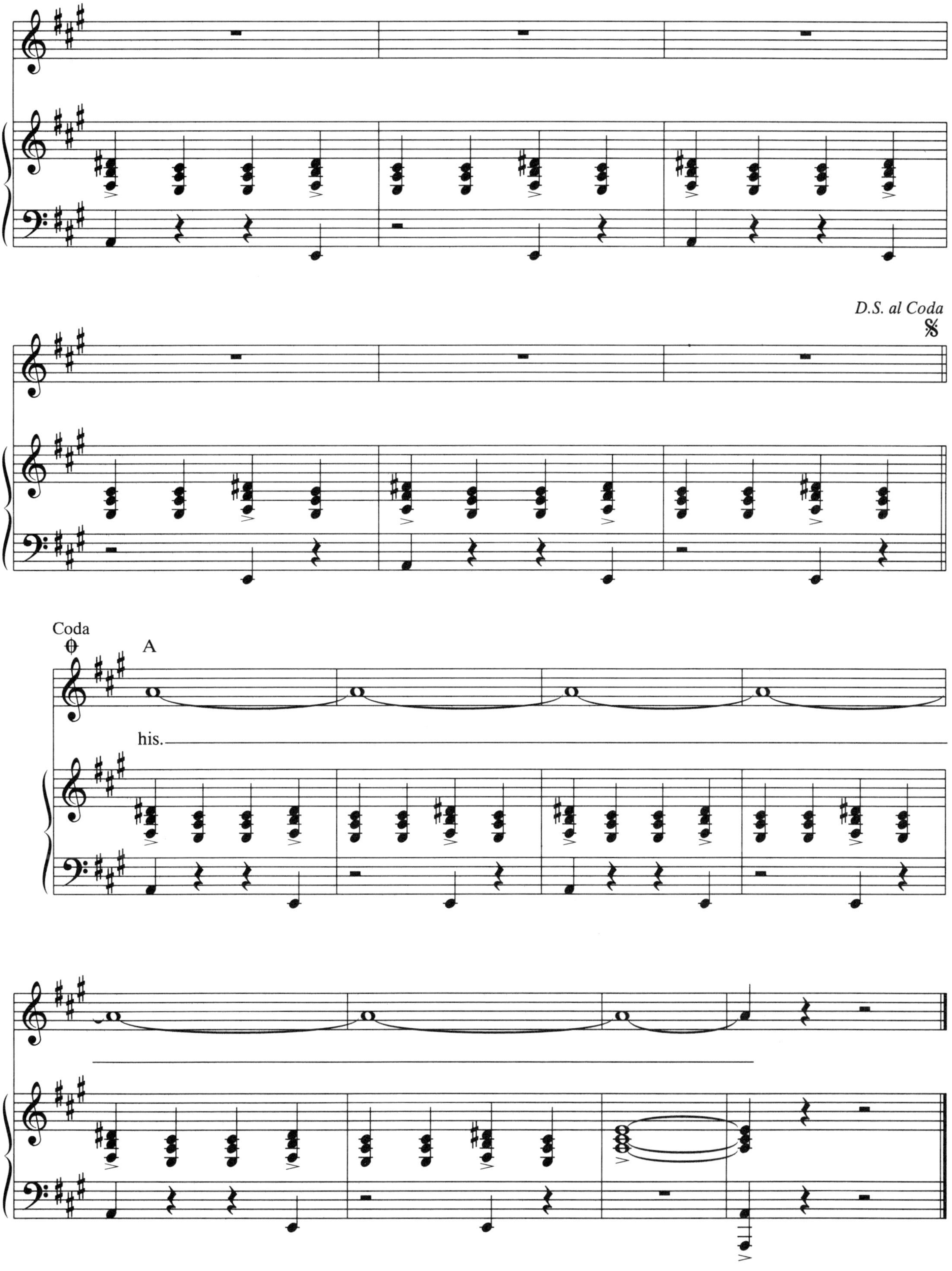
D.S. al Coda
Coda
A
his.

PRETENDING
from the television production of *Peter Pan*

Words and Music by
Leslie Bricusse and Anthony Newley

Bright waltz, in one

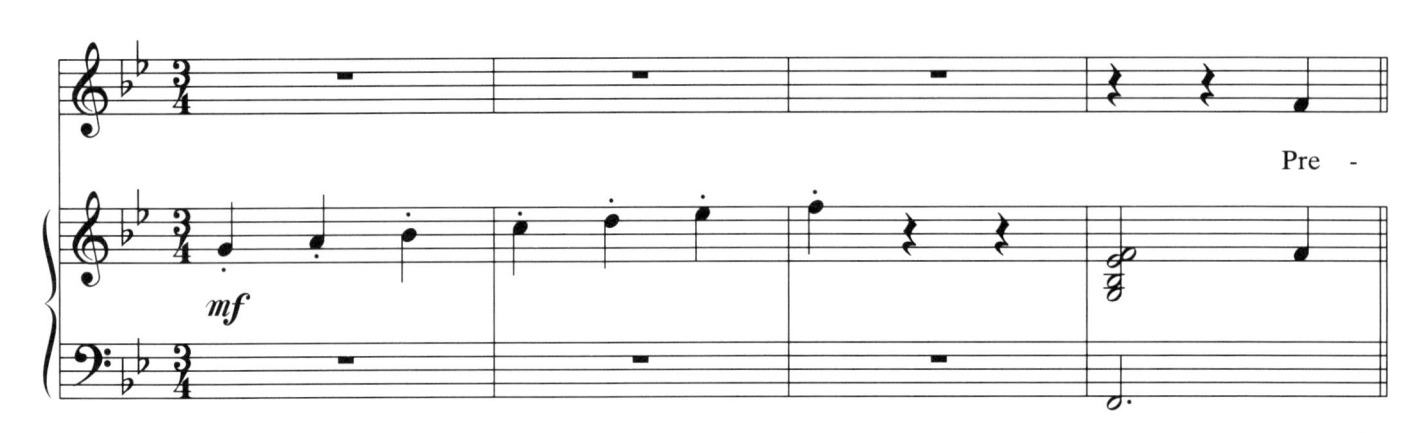

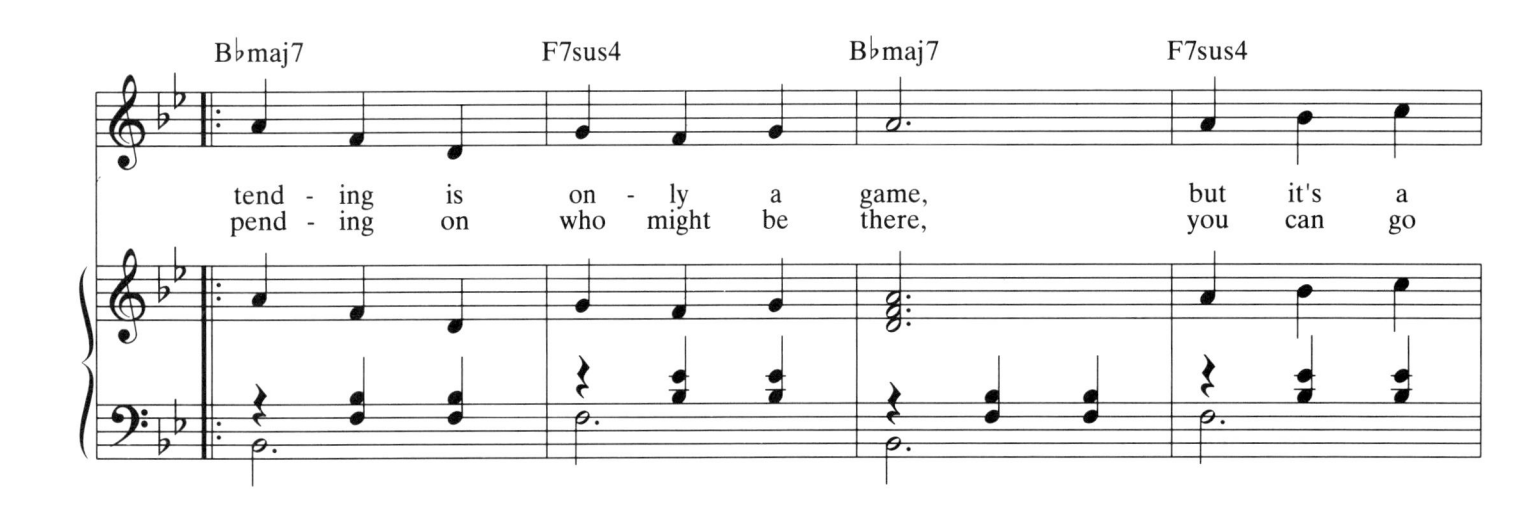

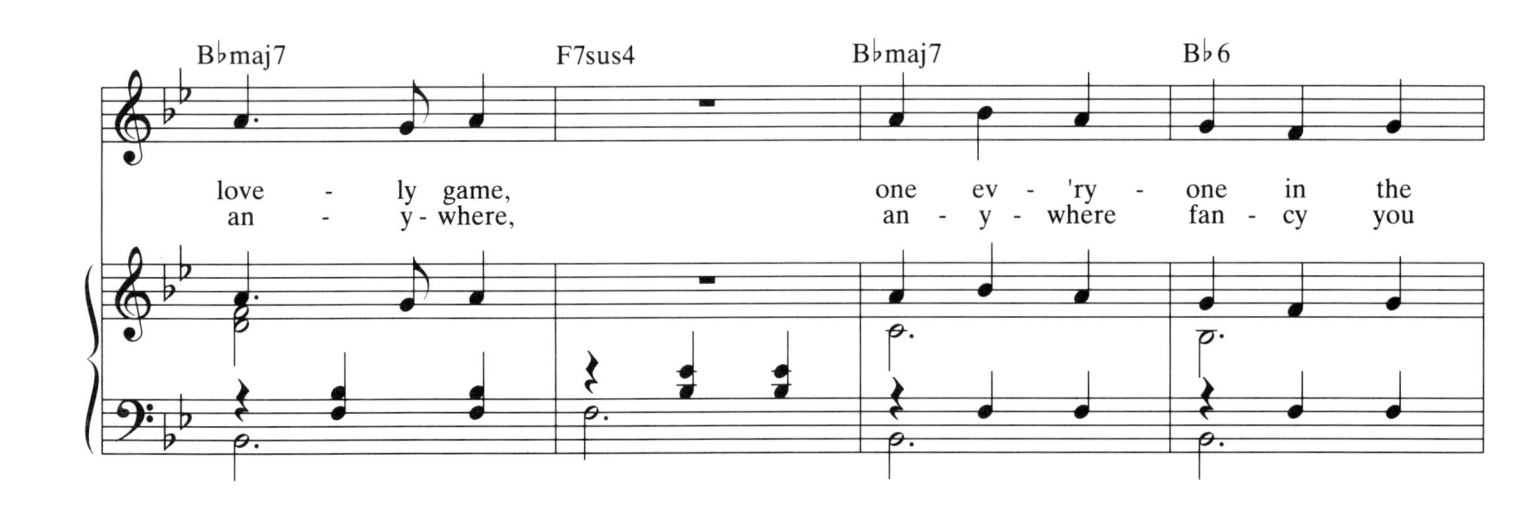

Pre-tending is only a game, but it's a lovely game, one ev'ry-one in the
Pre-pending on who might be there, you can go anywhere, anywhere fancy you

Dm7
G7
F/A
world can play.
care to find.
B♭m6
G7/B
E♭maj7
All that you do is to
And since it's all in your
1.
Dm7
G7♭5
G7
C7♭5
C7
make a wish and
mind, you'll

Cm7/F
B♭maj7
B♭6
Gm7
you're a fish.
Or you can
Gm7/C
C7
F7
be a king or a flea by pre - tend - ing.
Cm7/F
2.
Cm7
De - find
Cm7/F
B♭maj7
Em7
E°7
fan - ta - sies that are nev - er -

Fm7
B♭13
E♭
end - ing. Close your
B♭/D
E♭
eyes, the sky's the
B♭/D
E♭maj7
lim - it. Now you've found the
Dm7
B♭/D
G7
F/A
B♭m6
G7/B
mag - ic po - tion.

Lyrics:
If the ocean's wide just swim it.
Nothing you can't do, just pretend it's true. Pre-

B♭maj7
F7sus4
B♭maj7
F7sus4
tend - ing you're mend - ing the moon, put - ting the
a tempo
B♭maj7
F7sus4
B♭maj7
B♭6
world in tune. Make ev - 'ry day an un -
Dm7
G7
F/A
end - ing spree.
B♭m6
G7/B
E♭maj7
An - y - thing splen - did you

long to be, pre- tend to be. Mimic or mime, just do it like I'm re-com-mend-ing. Then your world will grow, when pre-tending makes it so.

LITTLE DARLINGS
from the television production of *Peter Pan*

Words and Music by
Leslie Bricusse and Anthony Newley

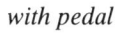

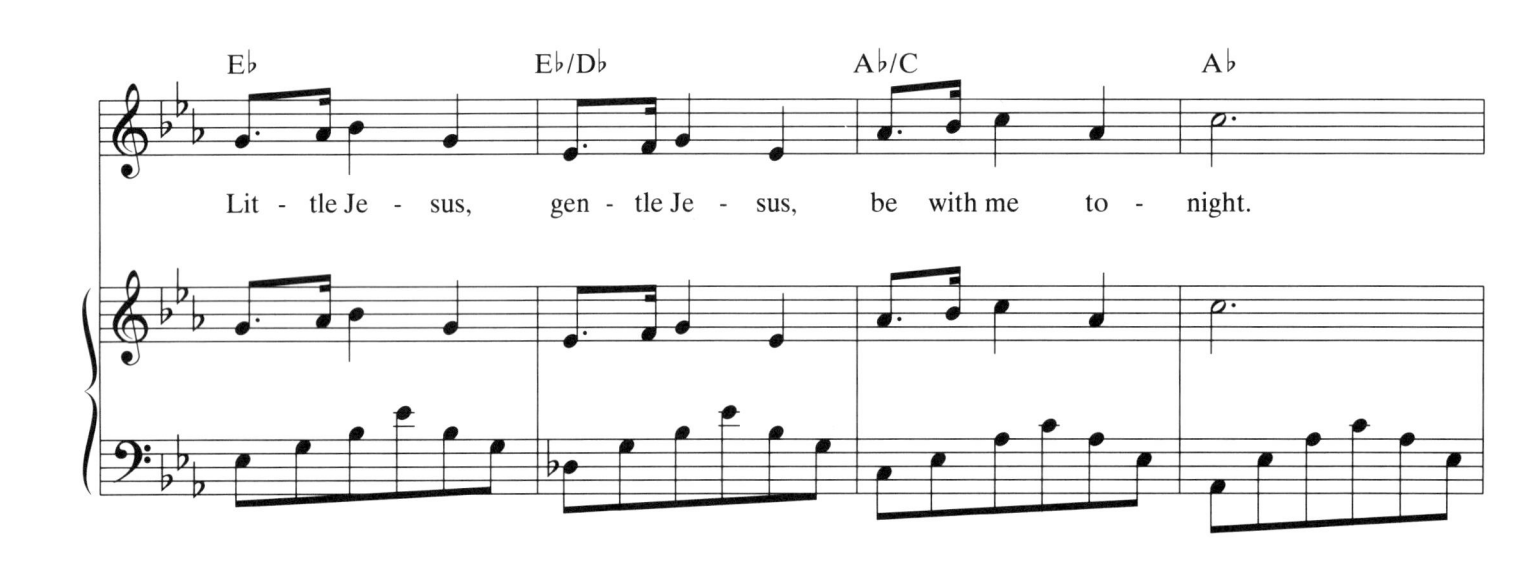

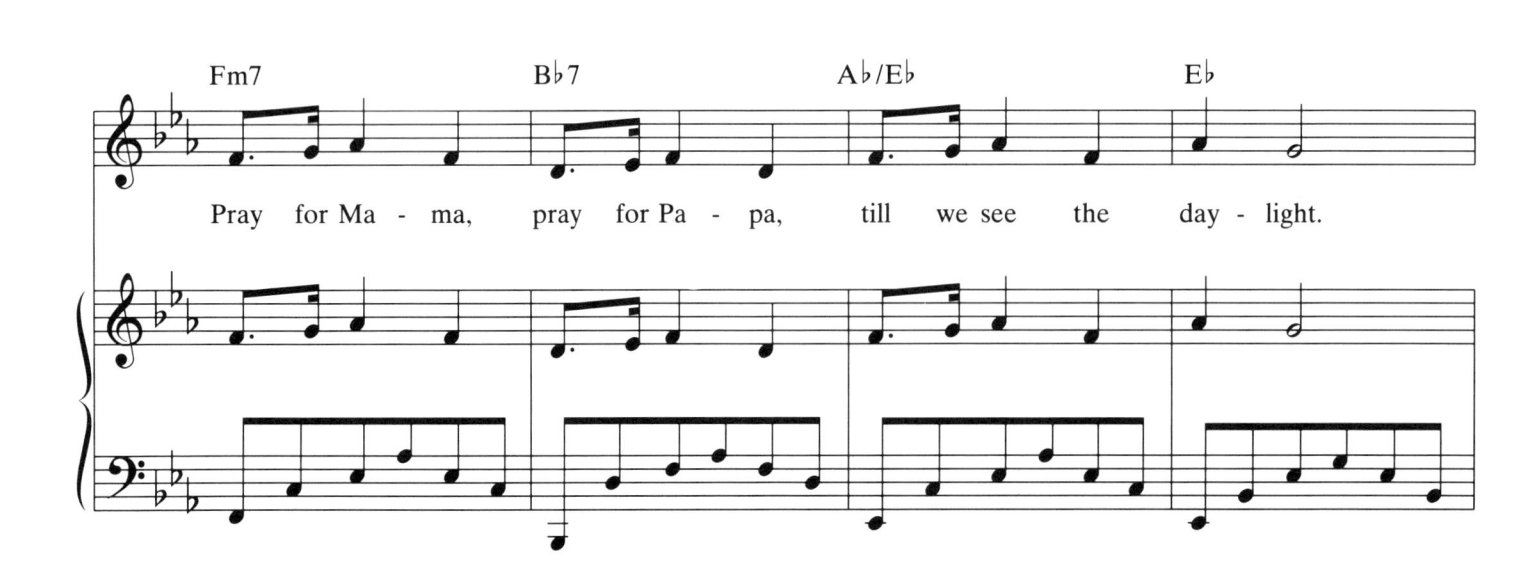

Lit - tle Je - sus, gen - tle Je - sus, be with me to - night.

Pray for Ma - ma, pray for Pa - pa, till we see the day - light.

Copyright © 1975 Taradam Music, Inc.
International Copyright Secured All Rights Reserved

Pray for John and pray for Wendy, pray for Michael too.

Little Jesus, gentle Jesus, keep me safe with you.

Little light, burning bright, bid the night wel-

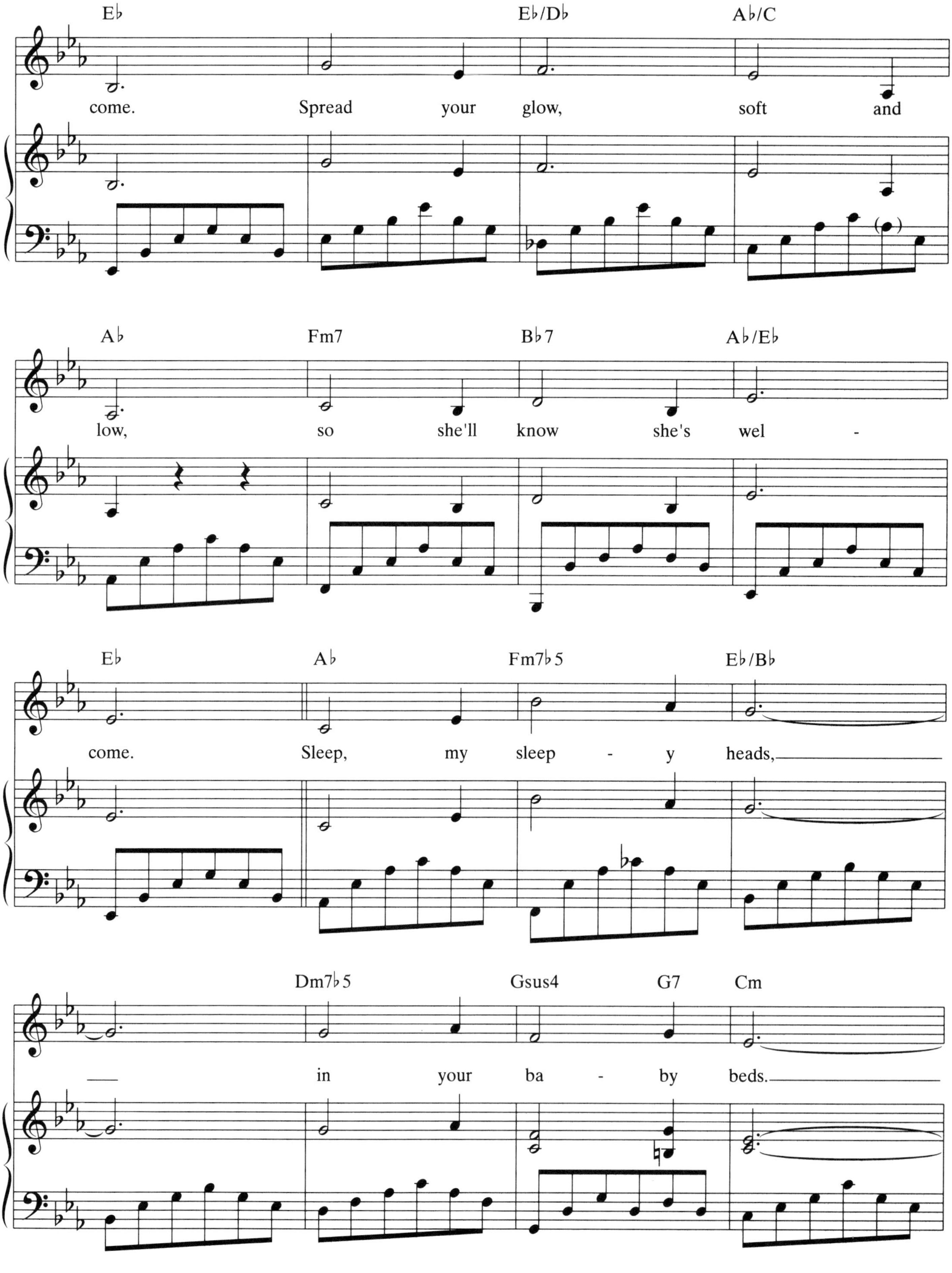
E♭ E♭/D♭ A♭/C
come. Spread your glow, soft and
A♭ Fm7 B♭7 A♭/E♭
low, so she'll know she's wel -
E♭ A♭ Fm7♭5 E♭/B♭
come. Sleep, my sleep - y heads,
Dm7♭5 Gsus4 G7 Cm
in your ba - by beds.

B♭m11 E♭7 A♭maj7 Fm7♭5 E♭/B♭
Send the world a - way,
Cm7 F13 F7 B♭9
till there's a brand - new day.
(duet)
E♭ E♭/D♭ A♭/C
Lit - tle Je - sus, gen - tle Je - sus, be with me to -
Friend - ly light, burn - ing
A♭ Fm7 B♭7 A♭/E♭
night. Pray for Ma - ma, pray for Pa - pa, till we see the
bright, be the night's eye -

E♭ E♭/D♭ A♭/C
day - light. Pray for John and pray for Wen - dy, pray for Mi - chael
sight. Guard my chil - dren's dreams un -
Fm7♭5/C♭ E♭/B♭ B♭13/A♭ B♭7/A♭ Gm7♭5
too. Lit - tle Je - sus, gen - tle Je - sus,
til bye and bye, day draws
C7♭9 Fm9 B♭sus4 B♭ A♭/E♭ E♭
keep me safe with you. A - men.
night. Hush - a - bye, lit - tle dar - lings.

NEVER-NEVER LAND

from the television production of *Peter Pan*

Words and Music by
Leslie Bricusse and Anthony Newley

E♭maj9
shores. Ev - 'ry child - hood dream I ev - er
go in that part of chil - dren's minds they
hand ev - 'ry pre - cious se - cret chil - dren
B♭m7/E♭
had was yours. The most
nev - er show. Ev - 'ry
un - der - stand. In what
A♭maj7
Fm9
love - ly land that was ev - er planned,
fan - ta - sy chil - dren plan to see,
ev - er land we may ev - er land,

where my mind still ex - plores
it is here, it will grow,
on - ly here can we live

still ex - plores.
it will
what we

For to grow.

Tigers and blue-eyed el-e-phants, bits of a fall-ing star. If ev-er you eyed el-e-phants, here's where they are. Mon-keys and gray-nosed por-cu-pines, flunk-ies in pur-ple coats.

B♭m7 B♭m7/E♭ A♭maj7 A♭m7 A♭m7/D♭
(𝅗𝅥=♩)
Chil - dren have seen those por - cu - pines, sail - ing in boats,
Tempo primo
D.S. al Coda
Cm7♭5 B7 Fm7/E♭
beau - ti - ful boats. Nev - er
Coda
Bsus2 B F♯m7/B Esus4 E
dream. And we dream that we
F♯sus2 F♯ D♭sus4 B♭sus4
live here in Nev - er - land.

A SONG CALLED LOVE
from the television production of *Peter Pan*

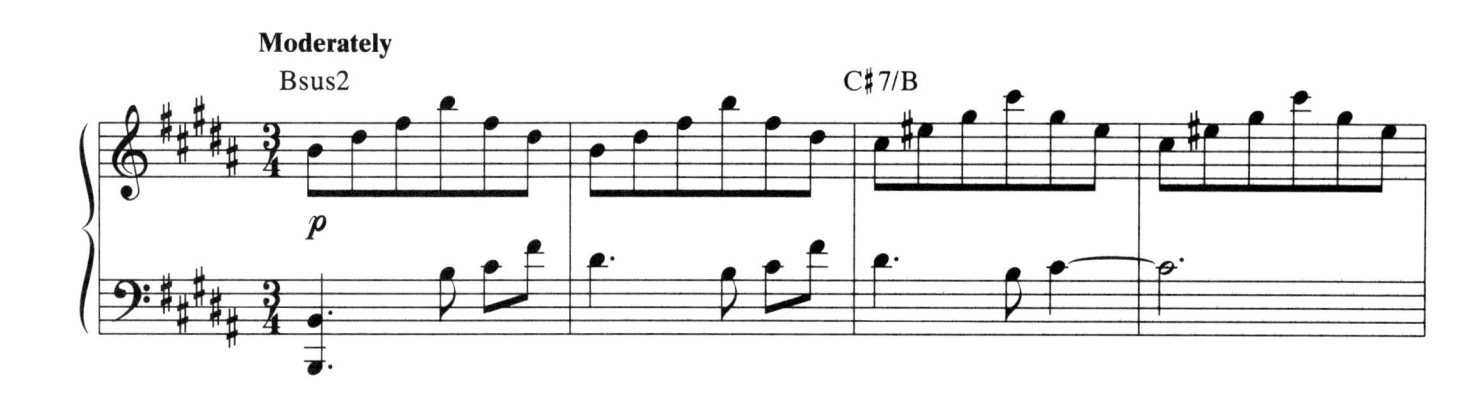

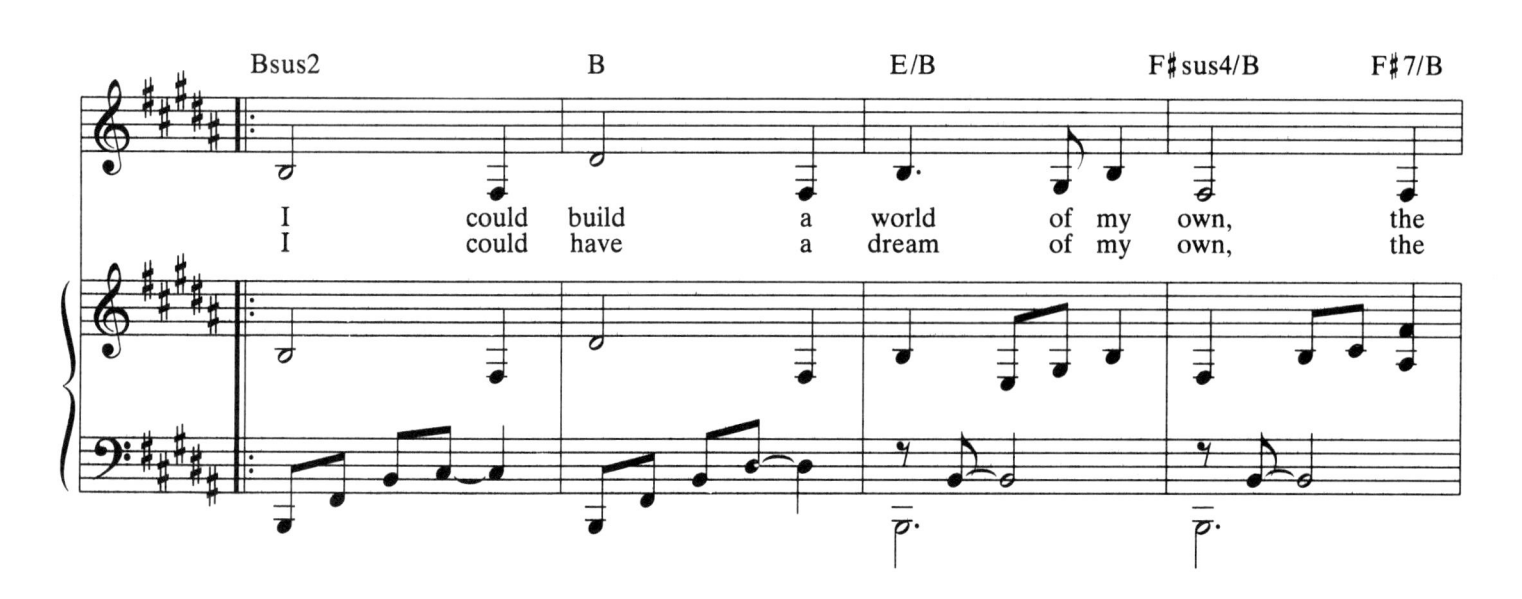

Words and Music by
Leslie Bricusse and Anthony Newley

Copyright © 1975 Taradam Music, Inc.
International Copyright Secured   All Rights Reserved

B Bmaj7 F♯m7/B B7
world would nev - er be lone - ly. On a
night would nev - er be lone - ly. I would
Emaj7 F♯9/E D♯m7 G♯m B/F♯
gold - en day that would nev - er end,
dream of mo - ments I'd nev - er known,
Emaj7 F♯9/E D♯m7 G♯m7/C♯ C♯7 F♯sus4
ev - 'ry - bod - y would be my friend. And the
warm and co - zy but not a - lone. And the

world | I would build | would be called _____
dream | I would dream | would be called _____

love. _____

If

For of

all the peo-ple that I re-call,

B/F♯ G♯m Em/G C♯m7
no one knows who I am at all.
(duet) Love is a
D♯m7 Emaj7 D♯m7 C♯m7 F♯7 B
If I could
house, high up on Hap - pi-ness Hill.
B/D♯ E F♯7sus4 F♯7 B
sing a song of my own, my heart would
Hap - pi-ness Hill.

Bmaj7 F♯m7/B B7 Emaj7
nev - er be lone - ly. I would sing of
Peace is the key to the door.
F♯9/E D♯m7 G♯m B/F♯ E♯m7♭5
days that I hope to see, days I
Live there in love,
A♯7sus4 A♯7 G♯7sus4 G♯7 G♯m7/C♯ C♯7 C♯m7/F♯
hope you will spend with me. And the
live there. Love is high up on Hap - pi - ness

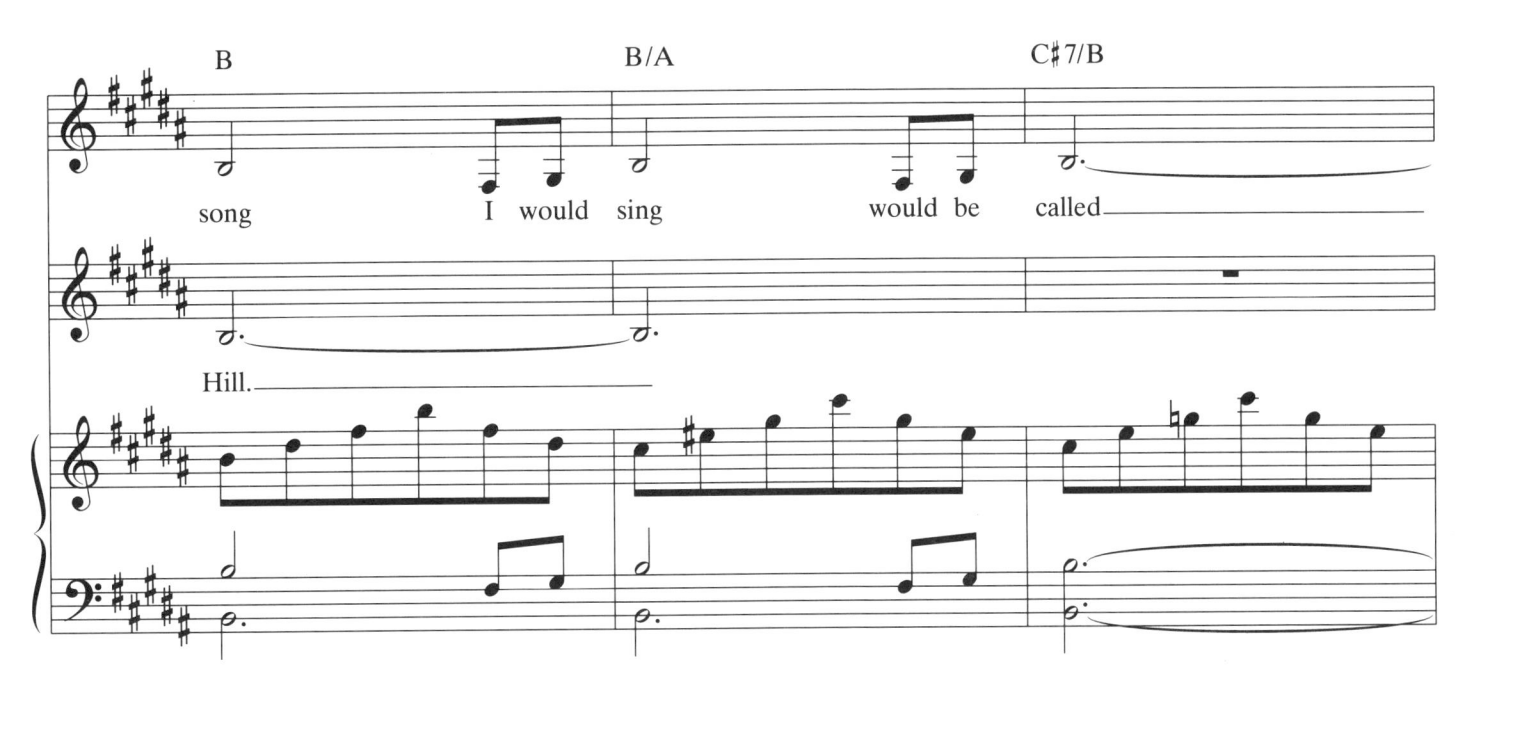

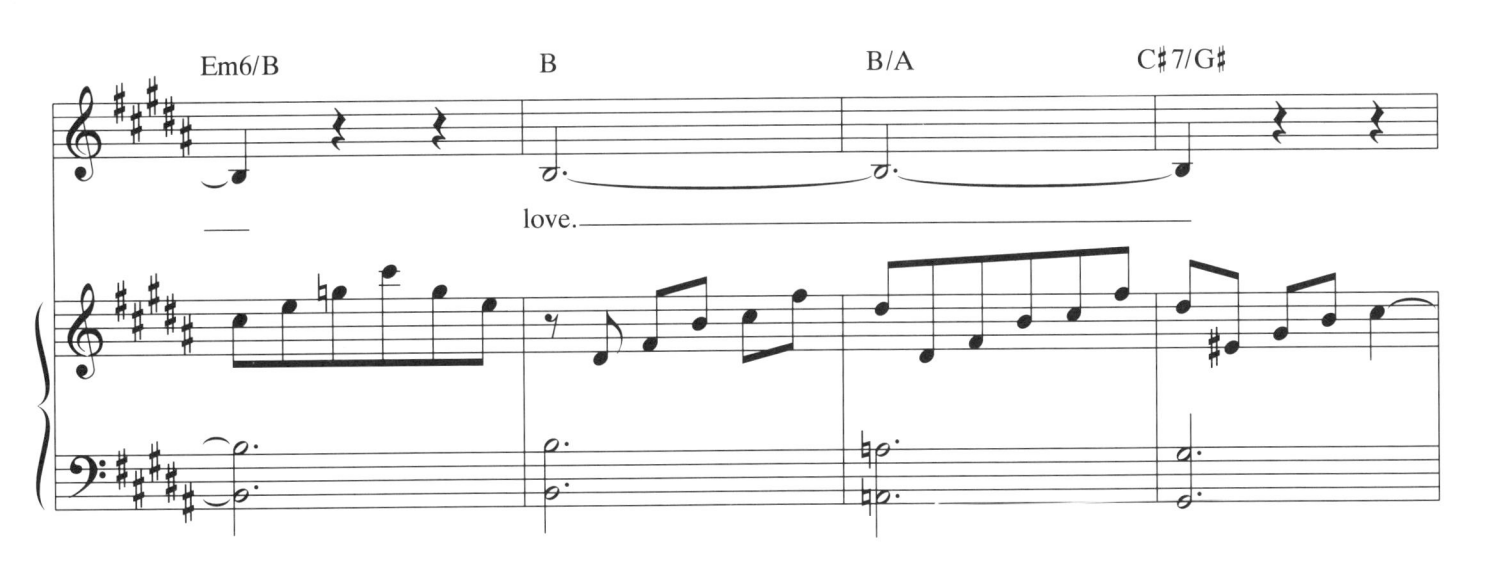

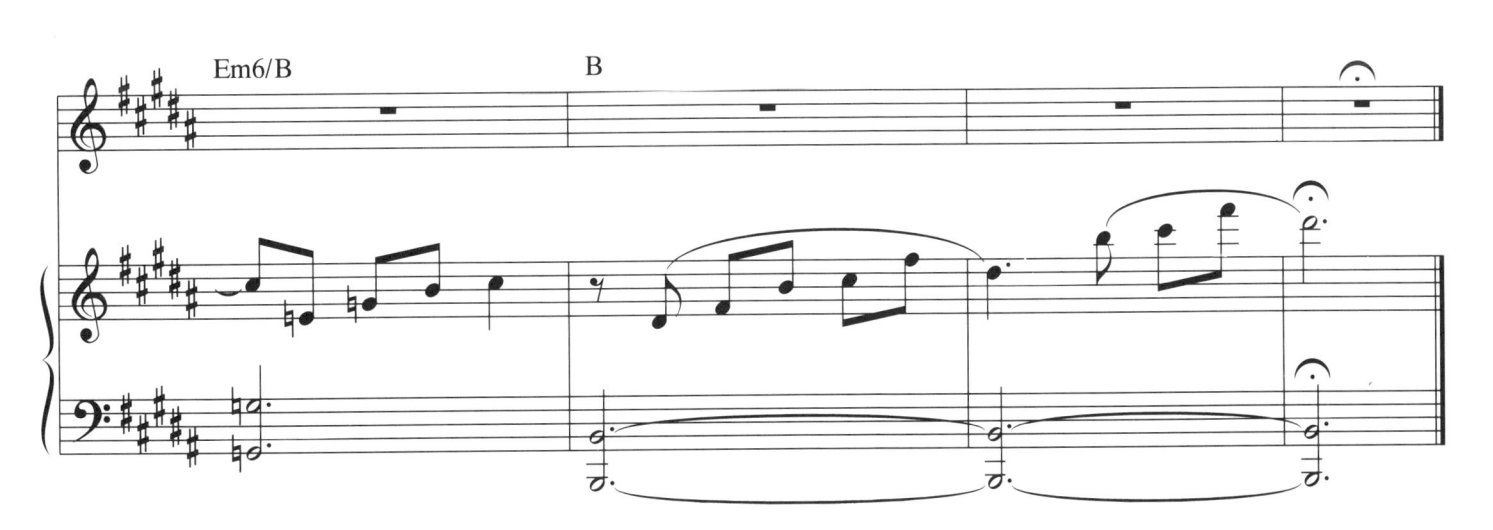

Lyrics: song I would sing would be called Hill. love.

THE HOUSE ON HAPPINESS HILL
from the television production of *Peter Pan*

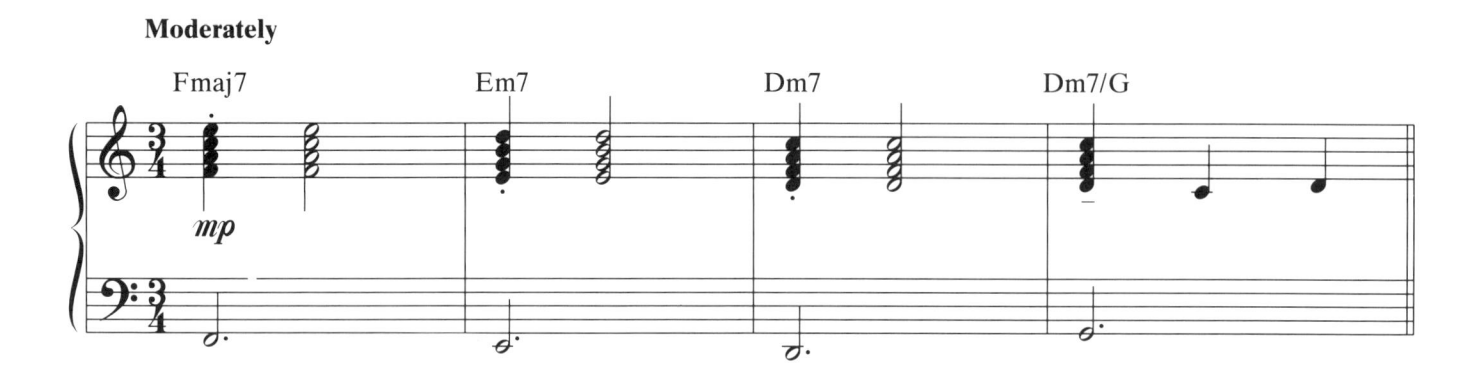

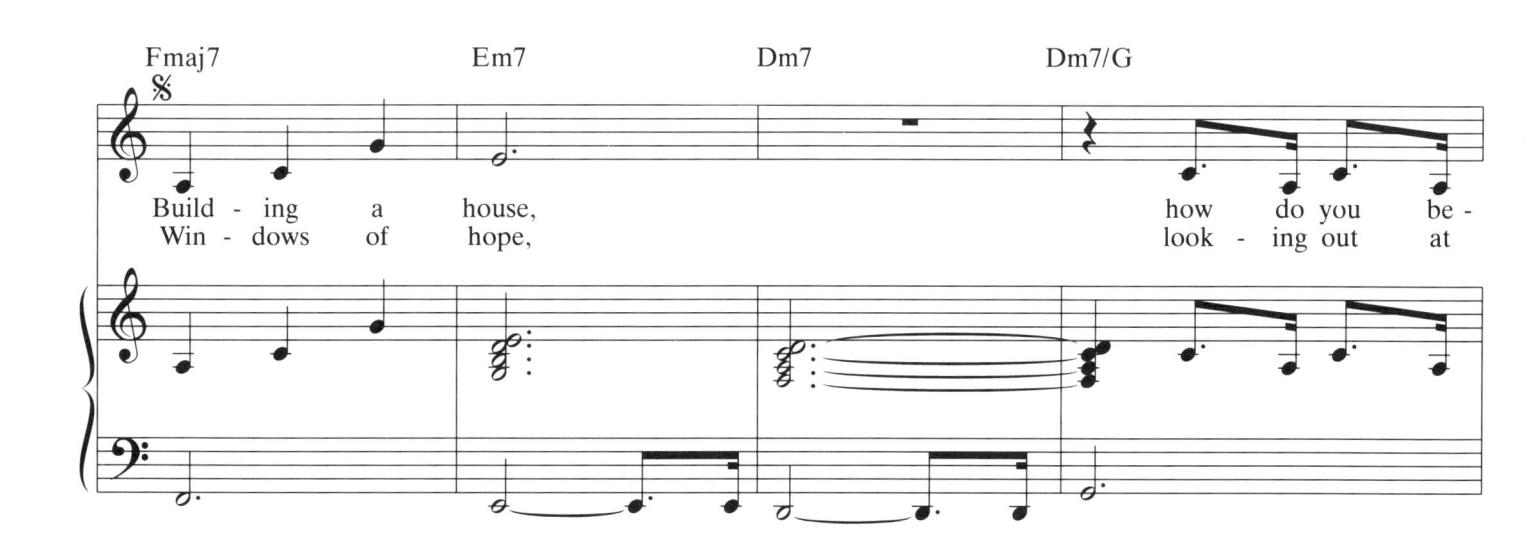

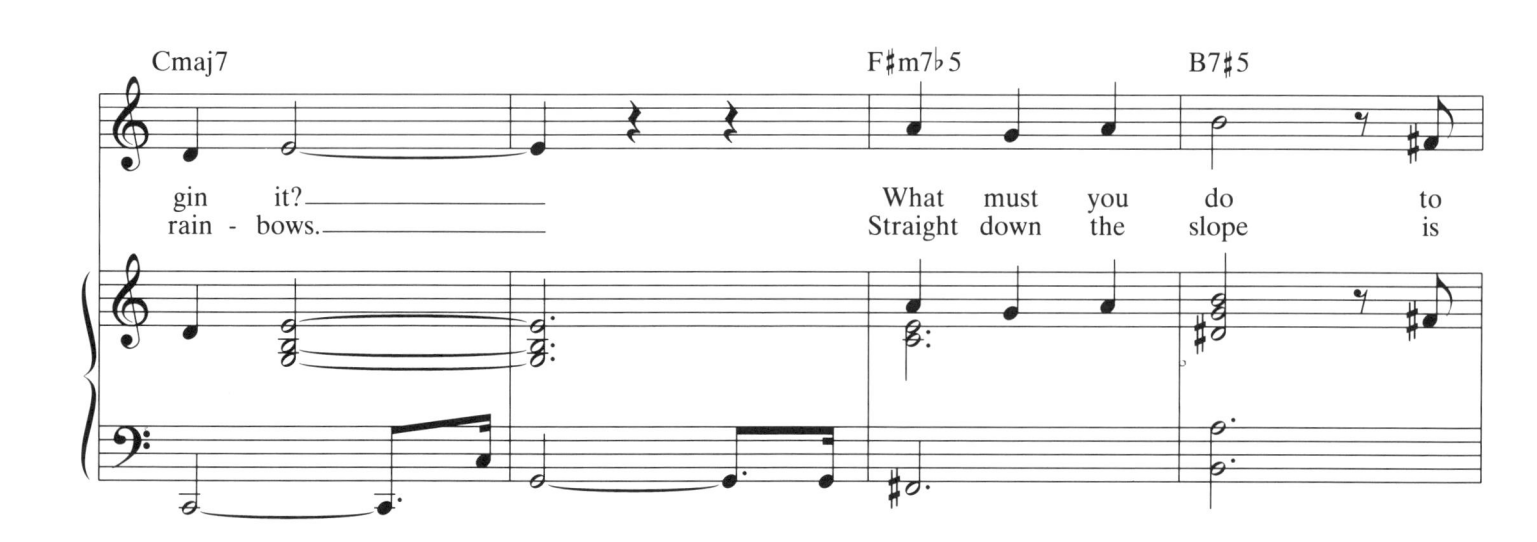

Words and Music by
Leslie Bricusse and Anthony Newley

Moderately

Build - ing a house, how do you be -
Win - dows of hope, look - ing out at

gin it?
rain - bows.
What must you do to
Straight down the slope is

Copyright © 1975 Taradam Music, Inc.
International Copyright Secured All Rights Reserved

| Em7♭5 | A7sus4 | A7 | Dm7 |

be hap - py in it?
where all the rain goes.
I know a
Friend - ship's the

| Em7 | Fmaj7 | Dm7/G | Cmaj7 |

hill, one with the sun on its face.
roof, peace is the key to the door.

| | F#m7♭5 | | B7♭9♭5 |

Hap - pi - ness Hill, it's a good place.
If you need proof, what it's there for.

| B7♭9 | Cmaj7 | C6 | F#m7 |

This house needs love and care.
Live there in all good will,

B7
Em
Em (maj7)
There's some - one spe - cial liv - ing there.
as in my heart I know you will.
Em7
To Coda
A7♭9
Dm7
We'll use con - tent - ment for the
B♭9
E7♭9♯5
A7♭9
floor of it, and wel - come for the door of it. There's
Am7/D
D9♭5
Dm7
G13
D.S. al Coda
F♯13
more of it.

Coda

Love is a house, high up on Happiness Hill.

Live there in love, high up on Happiness Hill.

YOU CAN FLY

from the television production of *Peter Pan*

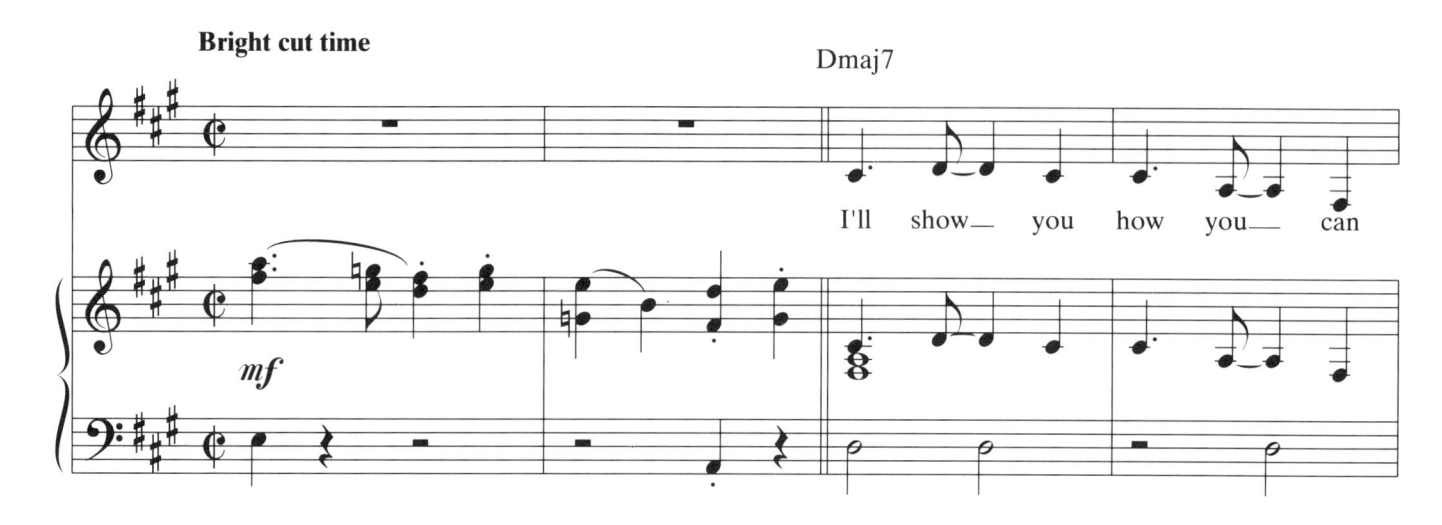

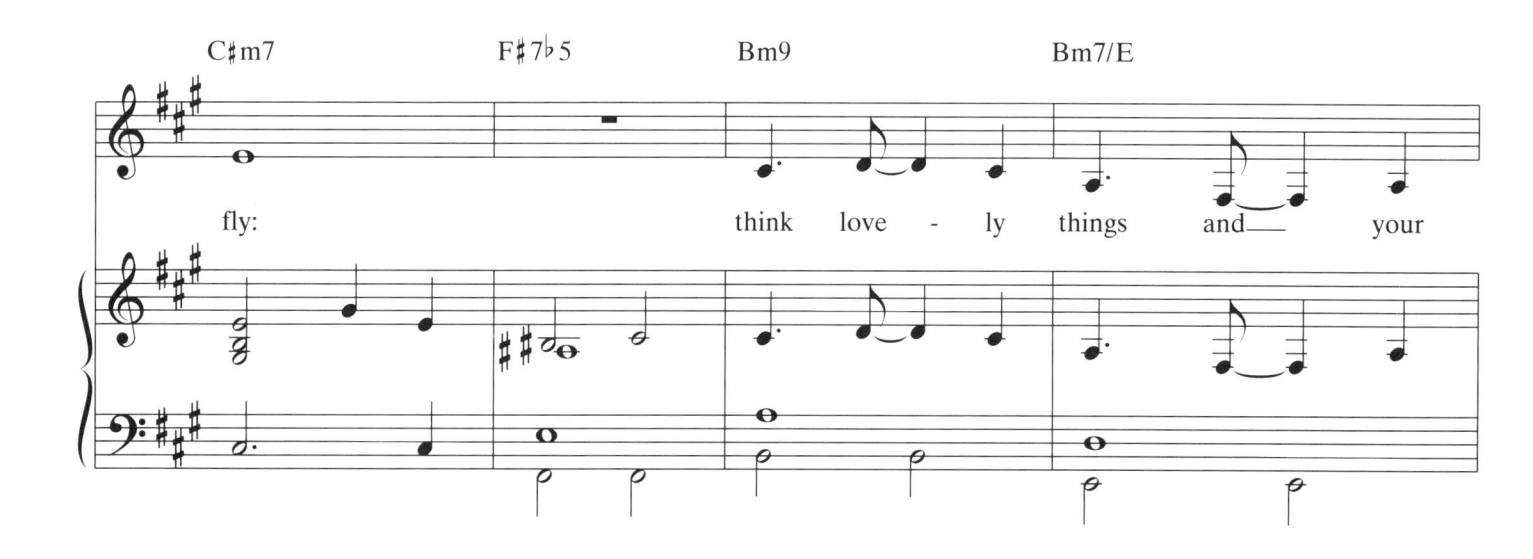

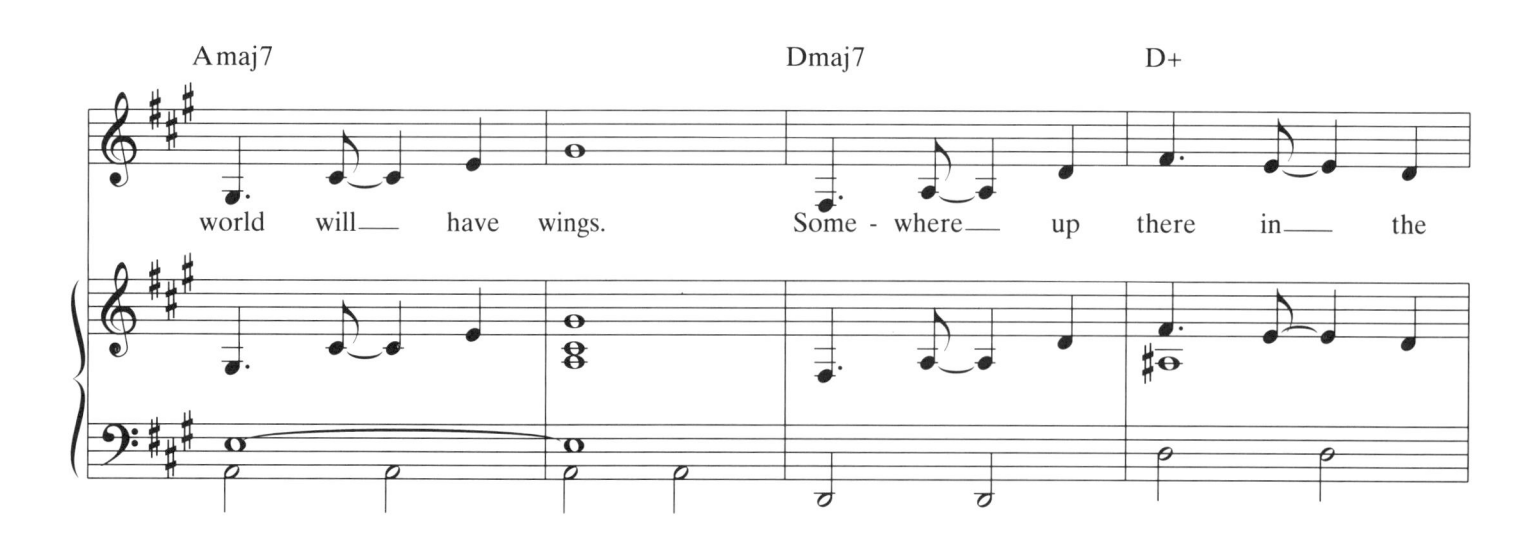

Words and Music by
Leslie Bricusse and Anthony Newley

Bright cut time

I'll show you how you can fly: think love-ly things and your world will have wings. Some-where up there in the

C♯m7 F♯7 D♯m7♭5 G♯7♭9
sky, I know you can
Fm7 B♭7 D♯7 G♯7♭9
fly. So can
C♯maj7 G♯7♭9 C♯maj7 G♯7♭9 C♯maj7 G♯7♭9
I. Why not try, don't be shy, come on,
C♯maj7 C♯m7/F♯ F♯7♭9
try!
3

Bm7
E7
Bm7
High a - bove a wor - ried world, we'll fly to my un -
E7
C♯m7
hur - ried world to - geth - er.
C♯m7/F♯
F♯7
B13
(♩=♩)
E9
D7♭5
Way a - bove the
C♯m7
F♯7♭9
Bm7
Bm7/A
G♯m7♭5
C♯7
weath - er, you can kiss your cares good -

bye. Life is nev-er quite the same a-gain when you can fly, fly, fly, fly, fly, fly, fly, fly, fly.

We did-n't know we could fly.

We used to stay on the

ground ev-'ry day. Now we can play in the sky. I'm glad we can fly! So am I, so am I, so am

Lyrics: Farther than the eye can see, beyond where even I can see, we're going. Knowing me, it's

gon - na be a treat you won't de-ny. Knowing Pe - ter, we will eat a sweet - er piece of pie. Life is nev - er quite the same a - gain when you can fly, fly, fly, fly, fly, fly, fly, fly, fly.

C-I-N-C-I-N-N-A-T-I
from the television production of *Babes In Toyland*

Words and Music by
Leslie Bricusse

Moderately bright cut time

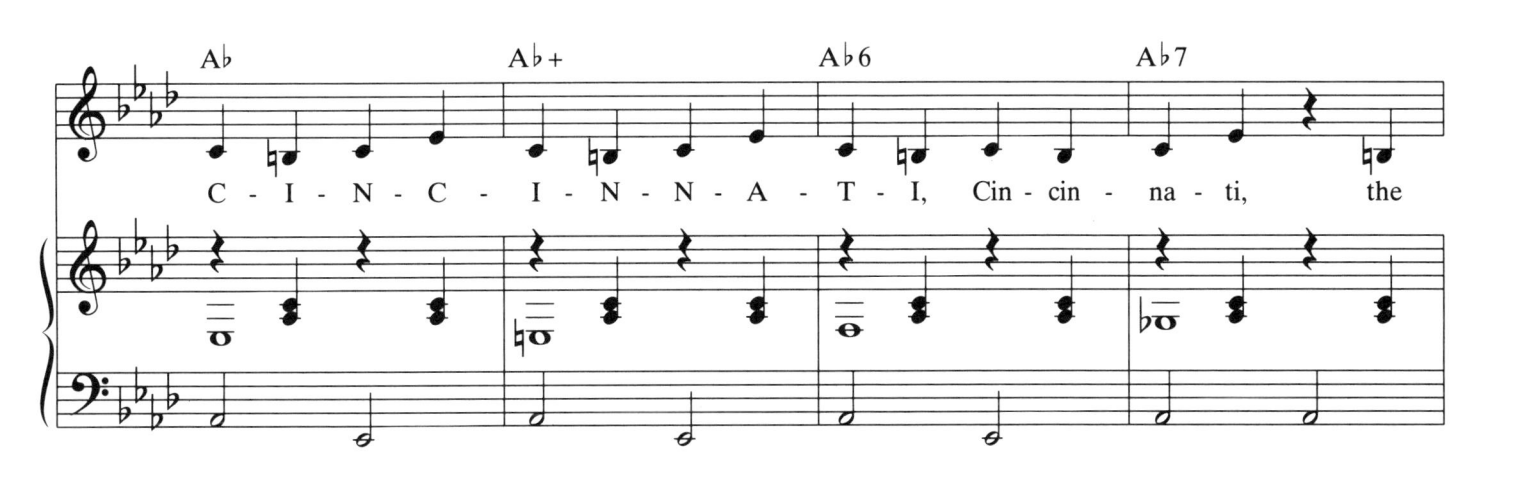

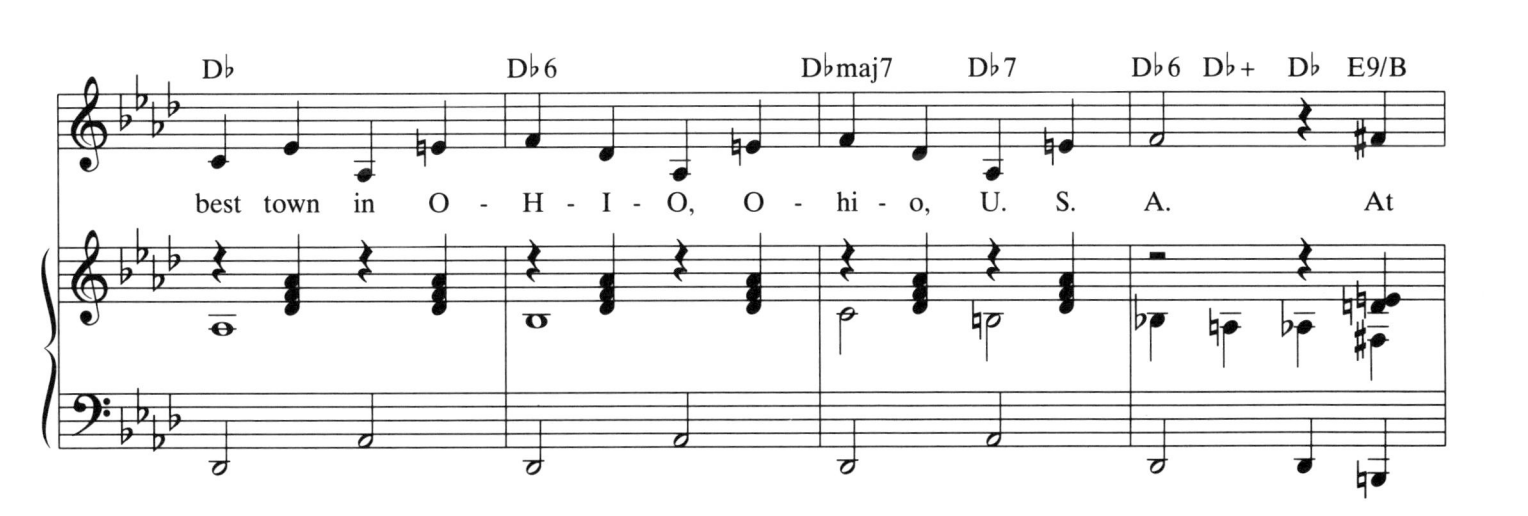

I come from C-I-N-C-I-N-N-A-T-I, Cincinnati, the best town in O-H-I-O, O-hi-o, U.S.A. At

Copyright © 1986 William Finnegan Productions (BMI)
International Copyright Secured All Rights Reserved

first they called it Cin - ci, but since Cin - ci is so nat - ty, they named it Cin - cin - na - ti, so they say. Hey, the girls are pret - ty pret - ty in this grit - ty lit - tle cit - y; the fell - ers are the feis - ti - est I've seen. And

when it comes to ball teams, the Red and the Bengals maul teams. They knock the socks off all teams on the green. I mean to argue's indefensible, the facts are common sensible. Since Cinci is invincible, ya know what I mean. Cinci's more than mere-ly nat-ty, she's O-hi-o's Ma-se-ra-ti. Cin-ci-na-ti's at the cen-ter of the scene. I mean to ar-gue's in-de-fen-si-ble, the facts are com-mon sen-si-ble. Since Cin-ci is in-vin-ci-ble, ya

know what I mean. Cin - ci's more than mere - ly nat - ty, she's O -
hi - o's Ma - se - ra - ti. Cin - ci - na - ti's at the
cen - ter of the scene.

THROUGH THE EYES OF A CHILD

from the television production of *Babes In Toyland*

Words and Music by
Leslie Bricusse

al - ways be free to be be - guiled. If you can think with the mind of a child, be - lieve and be lost in fan - ta - sy, be - lieve you me, that's more pre - cious than gold; you will al - ways hold in your child - like mind pre - cious dreams oth - er folks don't find. If you, like me, can think and see through the wan-d'ring won-dr'ing eyes and mind of a child.

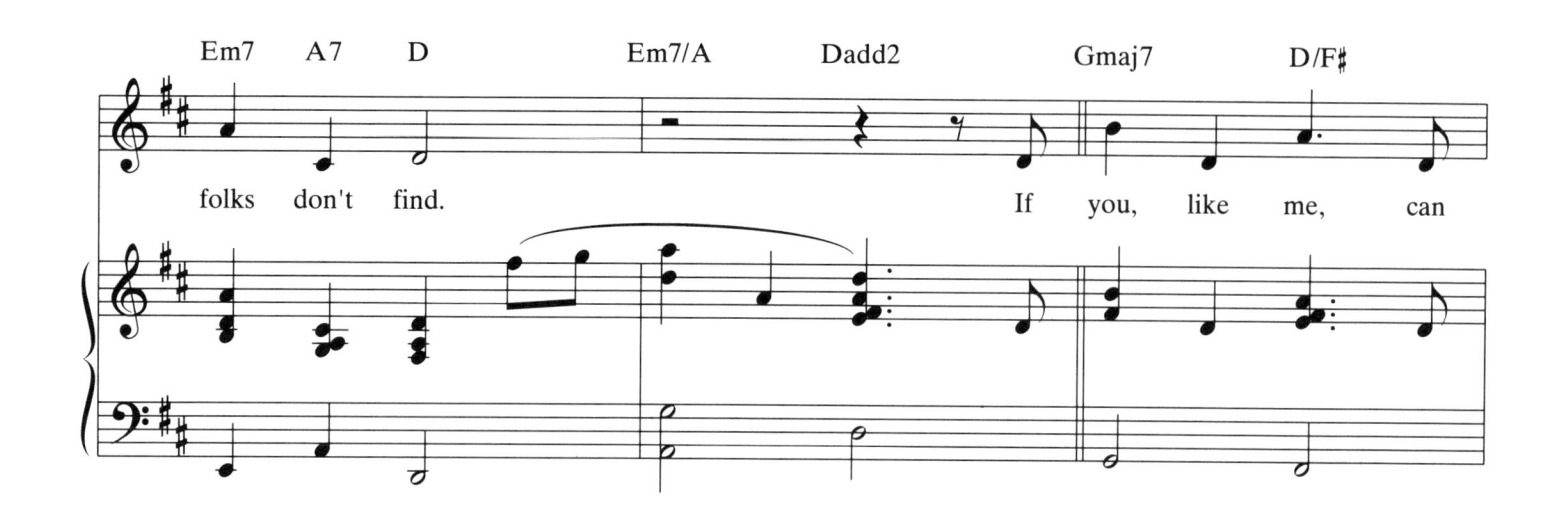

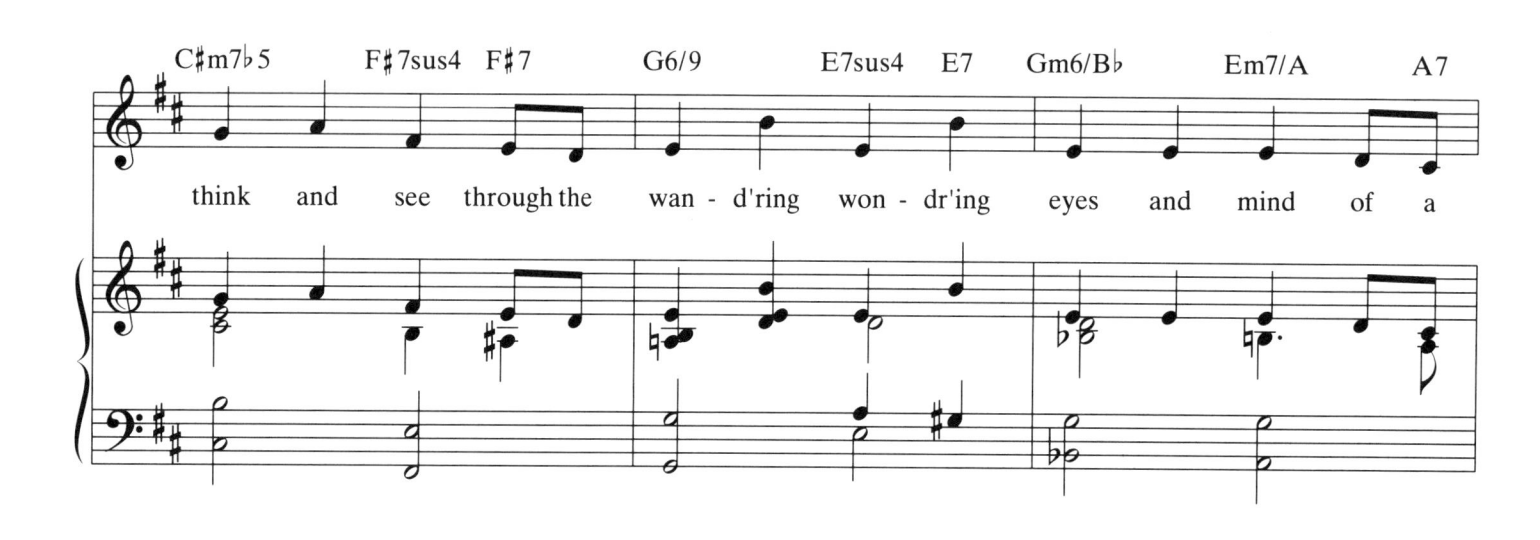

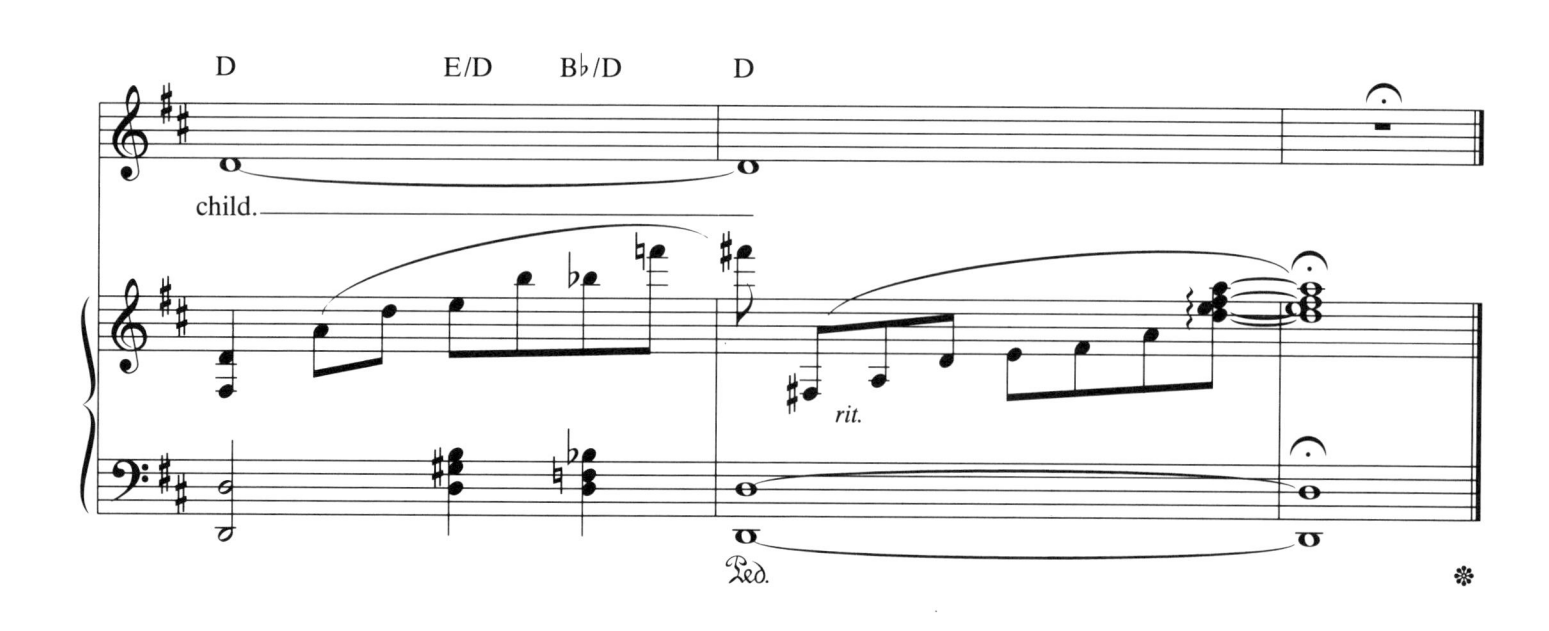

Music From The Stage

The Roar Of The Greasepaint—The Smell Of The Crowd (1964-6)

The writing of *The Roar of the Greasepaint* was spread over three years—from 1962 to 1965. We started early in 1962, while Newley was still in *Stop the World* in London, but the pressures of performing the hugely demanding role of Littlechap eight times a week, especially on Broadway (in 1962-3 and 1964), meant that we did not return to the project again until the spring of 1964.

After three years of *Stop the World*, Newley understandably had no desire to leap straight back into an eight-shows-a-week existence. So we took the project to Rex Harrison and Norman Wisdom to play Sir and Cocky—respectively the grand, arrogant, bullying 'Have' and the down-trodden, put-upon little 'Have-Not,' who were the central characters of the story. We got one and not the other.

Mr. Harrison eventually decided to play Pope Julius II to Charlton Heston's Michelangelo in *The Agony and the Ecstasy* instead. As it turned out, that wouldn't have been a bad title for *The Roar of the Greasepaint*, either.

Norman Wisdom said yes. He had been for over a decade England's most adored clown, with a succession of money-making movies and huge theatre box-office successes to his credit. He was perfect casting for the character of Cocky, and he knew it—and he accepted the role. We were clearly on our way to another major box-office hit. Wrong!

Six months later, the loudest sound in the auditorium came from the slapping of abandoned seats as disillusioned customers departed. This was not the Norman Wisdom they knew and loved.

Suddenly, at the darkest hour, like Robin Hood (we were in Nottingham, remember) arrived David Merrick. His words, verbatim, were these: "You don't go to London. You close in Manchester. Newley plays Cocky, and I'll give you another hit on Broadway."

We closed the show. To this day, London has never seen it. There are Liverpudlians who might well say, "Lucky old London!"

And so early in 1965, back to New York we went. And Merrick was right. Newley and Cyril Richard were both splendid, and sang the songs to a fare-thee-well. Tony Bennett had a big hit single with "Who Can I Turn To," and the song became a standard.

The audiences loved it. And when Newley and I were elected to the Songwriters Hall of Fame in New York in the spring of 1989 I believe in my heart that, more than any others, it was those early songs from *Stop the World* and *Greasepaint* that got us there!

The Good Old Bad Old Days (1972-3)

In 1971, after *Willy Wonka*, Tony Newley and I decided it was time to go back to the boards. I had come up with the basic idea for our next show—a modest little concept about the history of the world. God decides he's had enough of Man and wants to destroy the world. The Devil, to protect his job, tries to talk him out of it, so they re-run history to decide whether Man deserves one more chance.

As always, Tony and I had great fun writing it. As always, too, the book was very hard work and the songs came easily.

But we persevered, and a short time later I found myself in the London office of our good old, loyal old first producer, Bernard Delfont. Bernie gave us the Prince of Wales Theatre and carte blanche to go ahead, and go ahead we swiftly did.

The show ran for a year at the Prince of Wales. I still think it's one of our two best scores. It contains my favourite of all our songs—"The Good Things In Life." But the weekly break-even figure was about the same as World War II, so the show never made the large profit that it would have made had it been in the simple style of its predecessors. It would probably still be running!

Ondine

"Ondine" is the Jean Giraudoux play in which Audrey Hepburn achieved Broadway stardom and a Tony Award for Best Actress in the early 1950's. It is the story of Neptune's teenage granddaughter, the willful and totally enchanting sea-sprite Ondine, who ignores Neptune's stern warnings to stay away from the world of faithless men, and promptly proceeds to fall in love with a handsome medieval knight.

Originally proposed to me as a stage musical in the late 1960's, the elusive sea-sprite surfaced again as a possible film vehicle in the mid-1970's.

By now I so loved the piece that I wrote a 14-song score to it. Nothing happened, probably because I have never been able to find an appropriately breathtaking Ondine, and so I am still waiting for her to make a magical unscheduled appearance and immortalize my songs.

So, as a tiny token of my ongoing love for the lady, I felt that any anthology of children's songs I might ever assemble should include one song at least related to her. As seen through Ondine's eyes, "The World Is Beautiful."

THE ABC SONG

from the musical *Stop The World—I Want To Get Off*

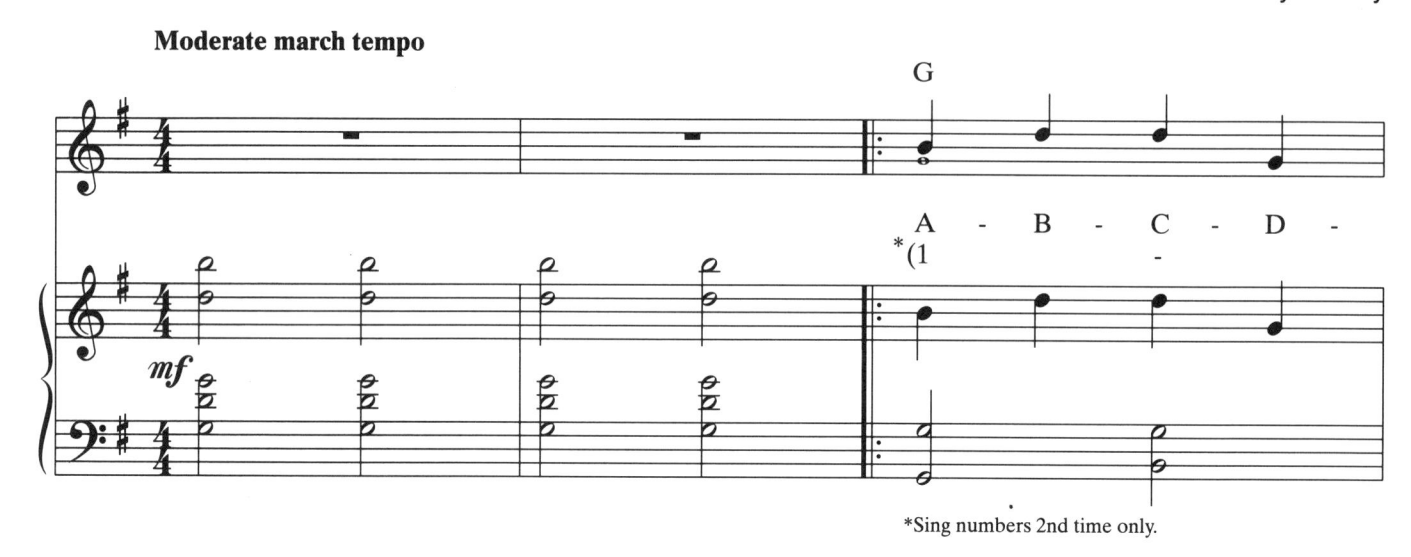

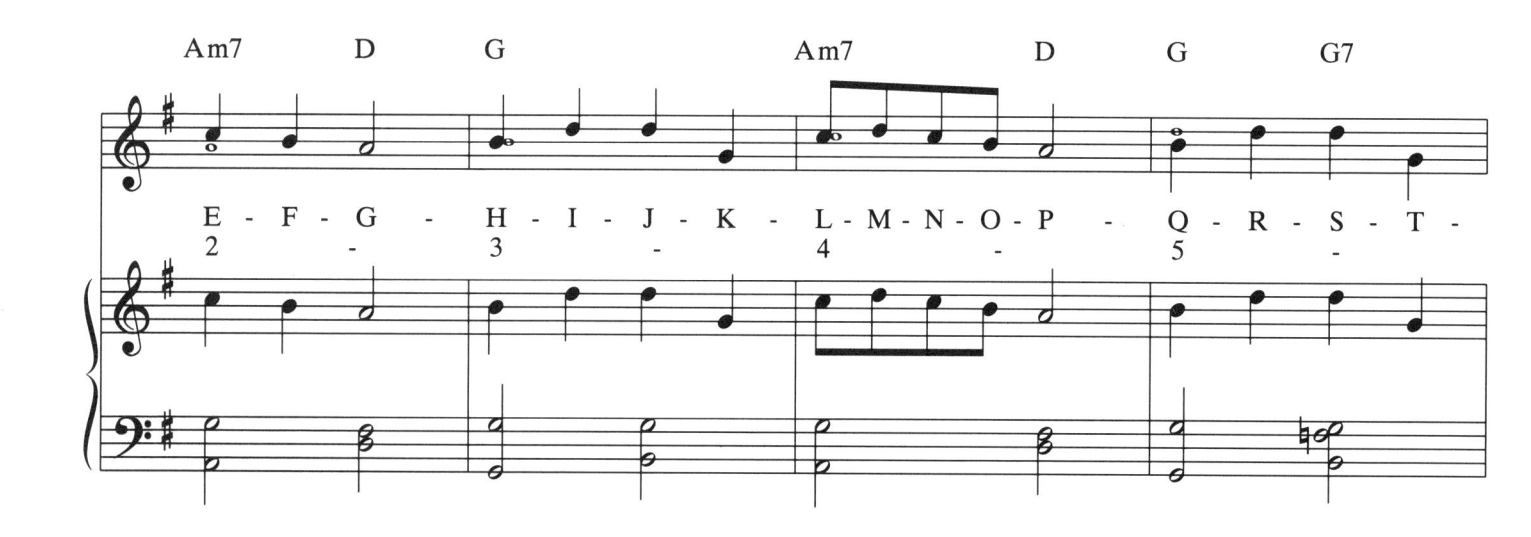

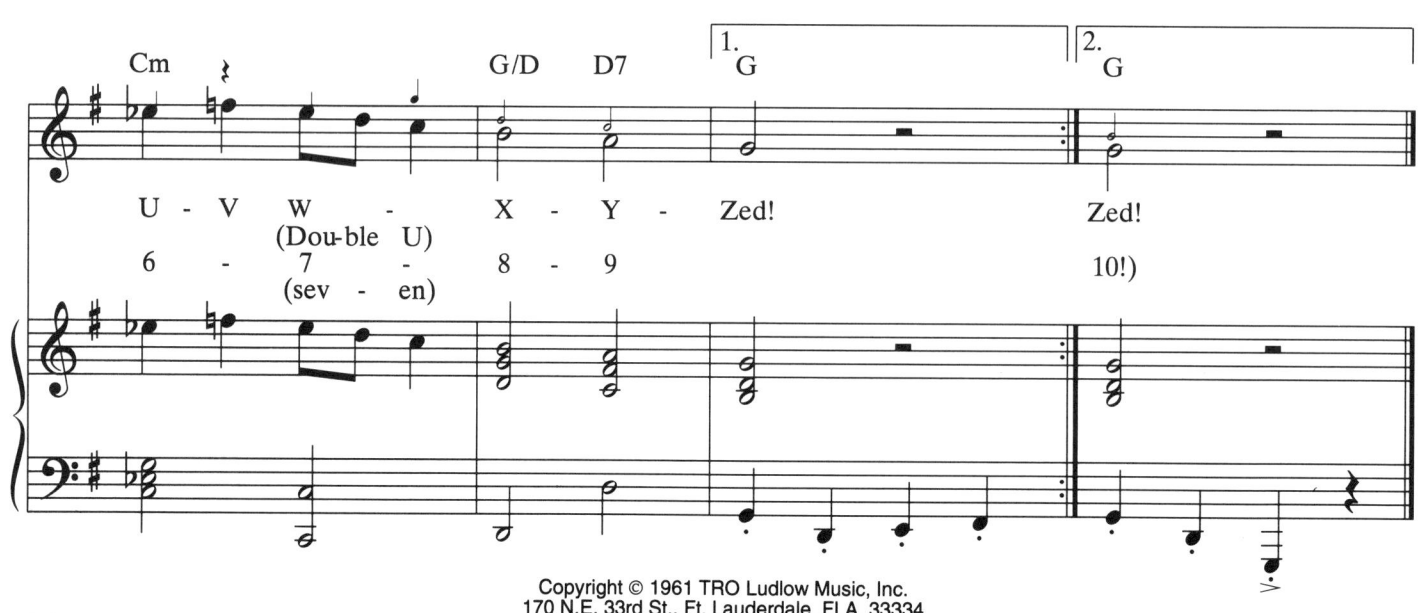

Words and Music by
Leslie Bricusse and Anthony Newley

Moderate march tempo

A - B - C - D -
*(1

*Sing numbers 2nd time only.

E - F - G - H - I - J - K - L - M - N - O - P - Q - R - S - T -
2 - 3 - 4 - 5

U - V - W - X - Y - Zed! | Zed!
(Dou-ble U)
6 - 7 - 8 - 9 | 10!)
(sev - en)

Copyright © 1961 TRO Ludlow Music, Inc.
170 N.E. 33rd St., Ft. Lauderdale, FLA. 33334
International Copyright Secured All Rights Reserved

THE BEAUTIFUL LAND

from the musical *The Roar Of The Greasepaint–The Smell Of The Crowd*

Words and Music by
Leslie Bricusse and Anthony Newley

Blue is the col-or of the sky in sum-mer-time; in-di-go is a Si-a-mese cat's eyes. Vio-let's the col-or of a pret-ty lit-tle flow'r; these are the col-ors of the rain-bow skies.

B♭ Cm7 B♭ E♭m F6 Gm7
There is a beau - ti - ful land where all your dreams come
mp-mf
C7 C9 F7 F/E♭ B♭ Gm7
true; it's all tied up in a rain - bow, all
Cm7 F9 B♭maj7 B♭6 F7 F/E♭
shin - y and new. But it's not eas - y to
B♭ Gm7 C7 Cm7/F F7
find, no mat - ter what you do. It's

not on top of a moun-tain, or be-neath the deep blue sea, or in Lon-don Zoo, or in Tim-buk-tu, or in Tim-buk-three. And if you trav-eled the world from Chi-na to Pe-ru, there's no beau - ti - ful land on the chart.___ An ex-plor-er could not be - gin to dis - cov - er its or - i - gin, for the beau - ti - ful land is in your heart.___ heart.___

LOOK AT THAT FACE

from the musical *The Roar Of The Greasepaint–The Smell Of The Crowd*

Words and Music by
Leslie Bricusse and Anthony Newley

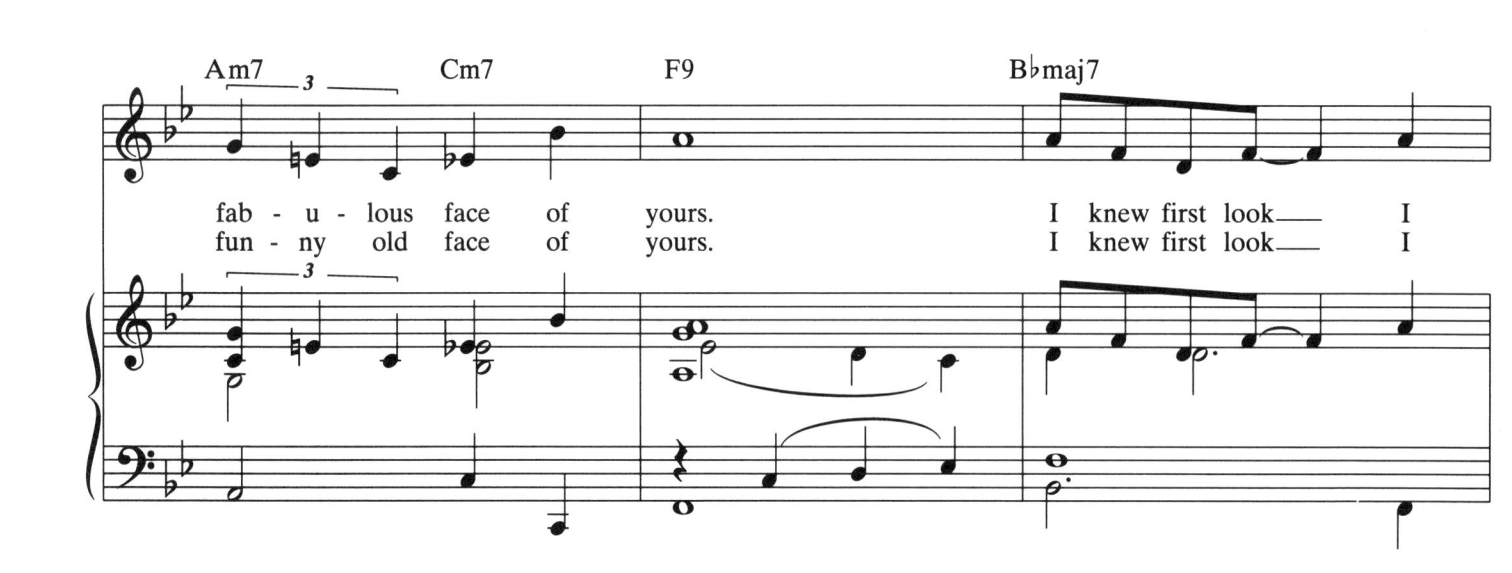

Moderately

Look at that face,— just look at it. Look at that
Look at that face,— just look at it. Look at that

fab - u - lous face of yours. I knew first look— I
fun - ny old face of yours. I knew first look— I

Copyright © 1965 TRO Musical Comedy Productions
170 N.E. 33rd. St., Ft. Lauderdale, FLA. 33334
International Copyright Secured All Rights Reserved

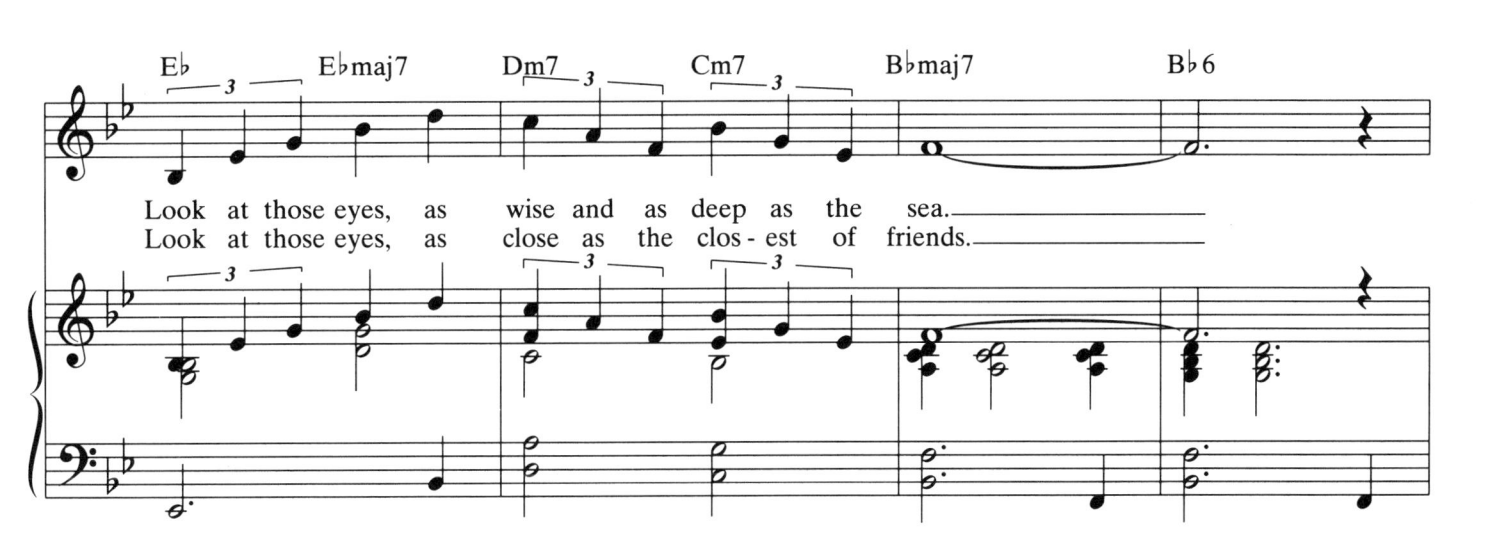

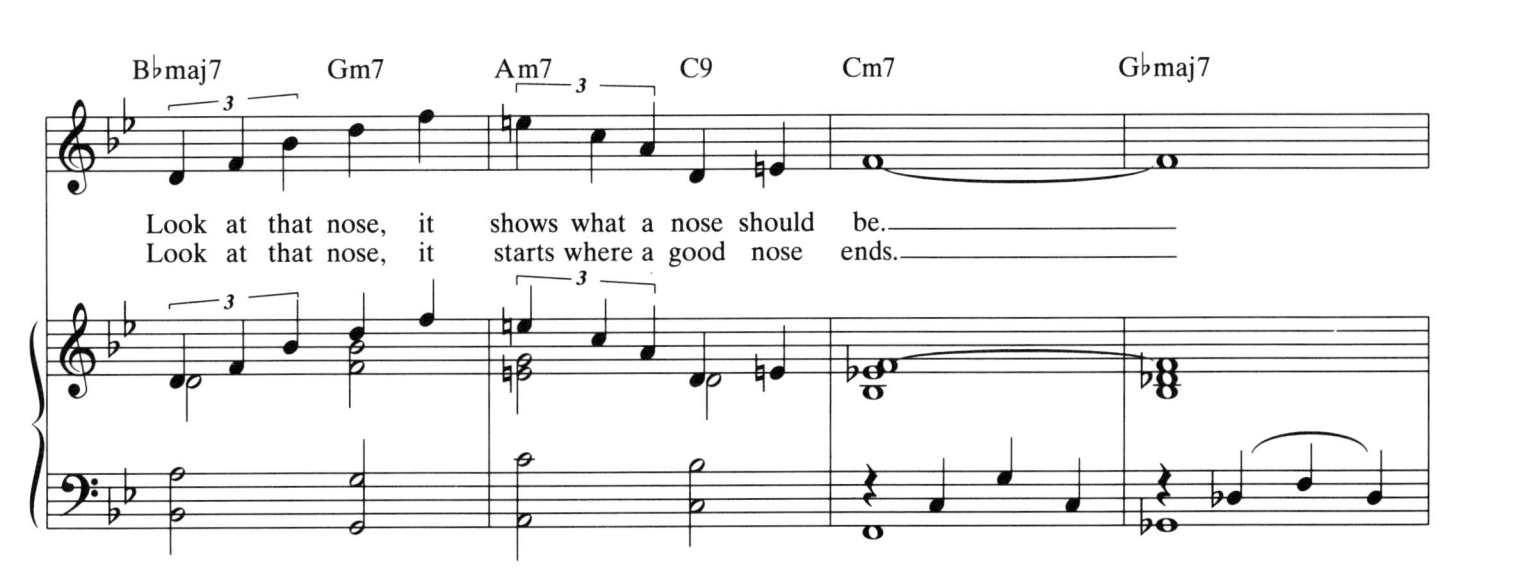

took at it, this was the face that the world a - dores.
took at it, you've got a face like a kitch - en door's

Look at those eyes, as wise and as deep as the sea.
Look at those eyes, as close as the clos - est of friends.

Look at that nose, it shows what a nose should be.
Look at that nose, it starts where a good nose ends.

Fmaj7 Gm7 Am7 Cm7
3
As for your smile, it's lyr - i - cal, friend - ly and warm as a sum - mer's
As for your smile, spec - tac - u - lar! One grin would fright - en the birds a -
F9 B♭maj7 Cm7
day. That face is just a mir - a - cle, where could I
way. You've got a face like Drac - u - la! And I mean
Dm7 Fm7 B♭9 E♭maj7 E♭6
ev - er find words to say the way that it makes me
that in the nic - est way. To say that there's no one

hap - py, what - ev - er the time or place? I'll
like you would not e - ven state the case. No

find in no book what I find when I look at that face.
won - der I shook when I first took a look at that

face.

THAT'S WHAT IT IS TO BE YOUNG

from the musical *The Roar Of The Greasepaint–The Smell Of The Crowd*

Words and Music by
Leslie Bricusse and Anthony Newley

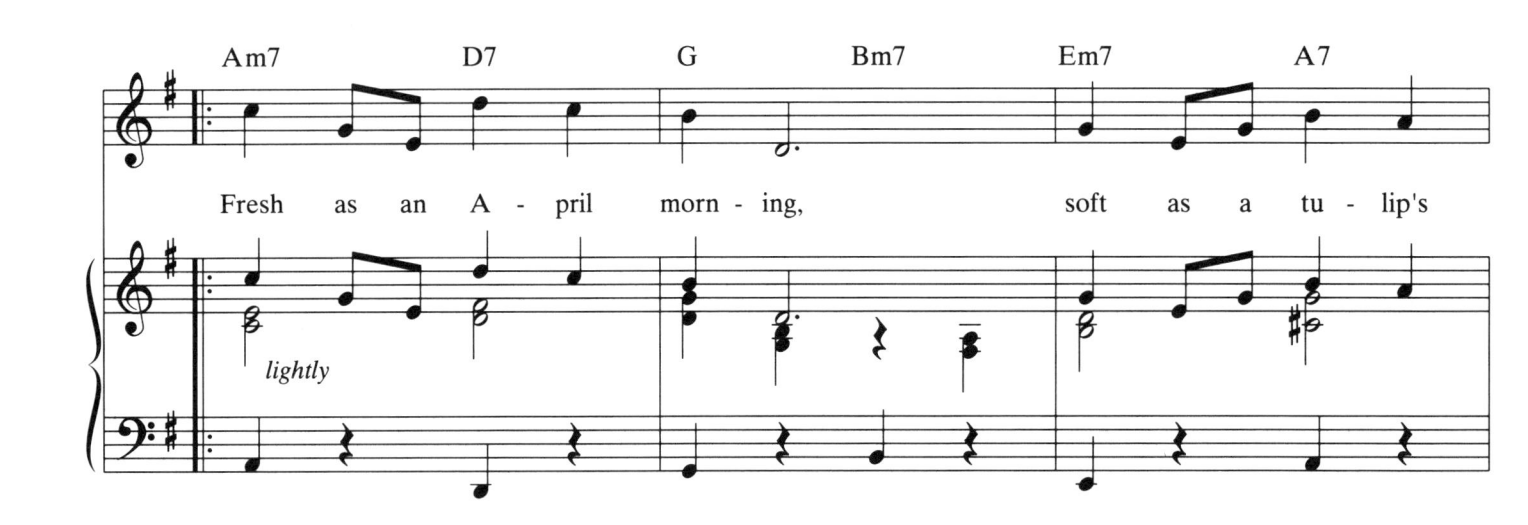

Am7 D7 B7♯5 B7 E7♭9 E7 Am7 D7
that's what it is to be young. Warm as a sum - mer
G Bm7 Em7 A7 D7
sun - rise, sweet as an eve - ning breeze.
C♯m7♭5 C6 G E9 E7♭9 Am D7
Pure as a note from a song bird's throat, rich as the green of the
G E♭ G
trees. Strong as the bite of a frost - y night,

E♭ G C
bold as a big brass band. Keen as a bean or a
Bm Em A7 D G♯°7
young sar - dine, not ver - y keen to be canned.
Am7 D7 G Bm7 Em7 A7
Bright as a new - born blue - bell, new as a song un -
D7 C♯m7♭5 C6 G B♭°7
sung. Live as a lamb who's the big "I am," as

soon as spring has sprung. Free as the breeze on the

sev-en seas, that's what it is_____ to be

1. young._____

2. young._____

THINGS TO REMEMBER

from the musical *The Roar Of The Greasepaint—The Smell Of The Crowd*

Words and Music by
Leslie Bricusse and Anthony Newley

Moderate Waltz tempo

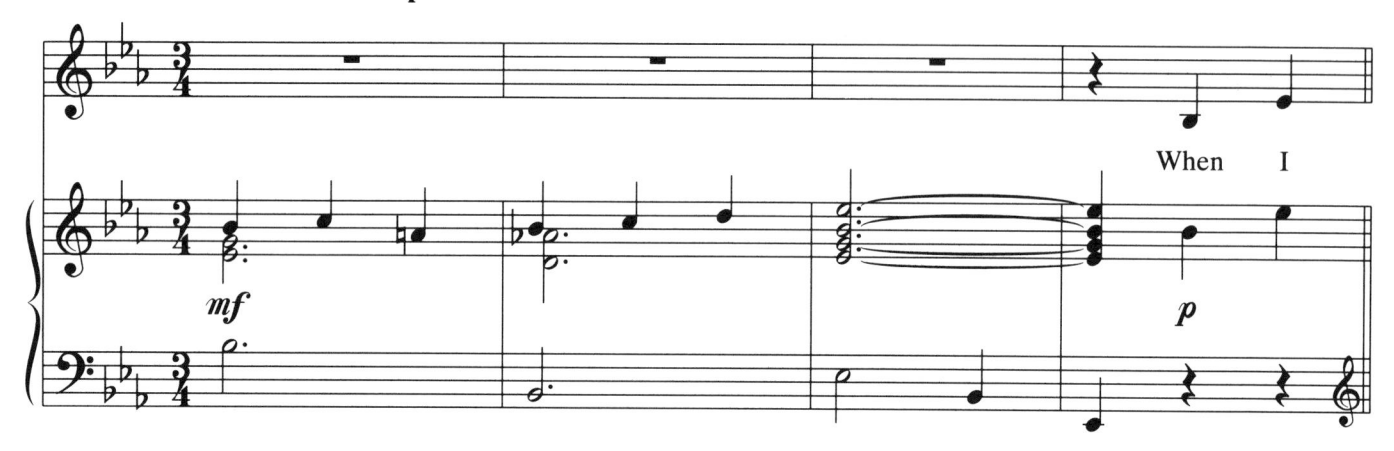

When I think of the good things that life has to give, I'm reluctantly forced to agree_____ that the

Copyright © 1965 TRO Musical Comedy Productions
170 N.E. 33rd St., Ft. Lauderdale, FLA. 33334
International Copyright Secured All Rights Reserved

216

number of people who know how to live is restricted, quite simply, to me. For life is like cricket, we play by the rules. And the secret, which few people know, which

keeps men of class well a-part from the fools____ is to
think up the rules as you go.____ There are
so man-y things to re-mem-ber____ as you
mem-ber your grand-moth-er's birth-day, and be
trav-el the high-way of life,____ like
proud of the flag at all times.____ Stand

al - ways be kind to your hus - band or,
up for the Na - tion - al An - them, sit
if you're a man, to your wife. You should
down to re - cite dirt - y rhymes. Al - ways
nev - er shoot trout in Sep - tem - ber. You should
hon - or your debts when you have to, and be
nev - er feed ba - bies on gin. Don't
hon - est un - less there's no need. Spend

B♭7 E♭ B7♭5
ev - er play po - ker on Sun - day un -
two hours a day with the Good Book, if
E♭ E♭m B♭m7 E♭7
less you are cer - tain to win! Don't go
you've noth - ing bet - ter to read. You must
A♭ A♭m6 E♭ Cm7
out of your way seek - ing dan - ger. Nev - er
al - ways be pa - tient with chil - dren, though they
Fm7 B♭7 E♭
stand on a croc - o - dile's tail. Nev - er
jan - gle your nerves, it is true. If a

buy Lon - don Bridge from a stran - ger, un -
child is a pres - ent from heav - en, thank

less you can make a few bob on the sale. Don't waste
God there aren't too man - y pres - ents like you! Don't drink

time on the friends that re - pel you, and don't
cham - pagne from sog - gy old slip - pers, though this

ev - er drink soup with a knife. Don't
bar - bar - ic cus - tom is rife. Don't

buy what those gyp - sy girls sell you, and
lift up a whale by its flip - pers, and

1.
if you re - mem - ber these things that I tell you, then

well, you'll do well all your life. Please re -

2.
on - ly buy clar - et from cer - ti - fied ship - pers. A -

void eat-ing gou-lash with ice cream and kip-pers. Re-
mem-ber these things, you ob-nox-ious young nip-pers, and

cresc. poco a poco

you will do well all your life! So cheers, me

dears, and here's to life!

IT'S A MUSICAL WORLD
from the musical *The Good Old Bad Old Days*

Words and Music by
Leslie Bricusse and Anthony Newley

Bb
World!
Ab
Bb (Ab bass)
Lis - ten to the rhy - thm of a
Lis - ten to the mu - sic of a
Gm7 Cm7 Abmaj7 Bb (Ab bass) Gm7 Eb
storm in sum - mer! Hear the mel - low mel - o - dy when church bells chime!
lone - ly sea shore! Hear the sad ca - coph - o - ny of sea - gull songs!
Db Eb (Db bass) Ab (C bass) Ab G C (G bass)
Is - n't that as mag - i - cal as once up - on a time?
Na - ture has an or - ches - tra where ev - ery sound be - longs!
G C7 (G bass) G C (G bass) G Ab Fm7 Bb Eb (Bb bass)
It's A Mu - si - cal World! Such a beau - ti - ful world!

Bb7
Eb
Gb
Eb
Abmaj7 Ab
Ding dong! Sing a song of spring and sum - mer!
Eb
Gb
Eb
Abmaj7
Eb
Gb
Eb
Absus9 Ab6
Spring song, sum-mer song and en - tre - nous, I love mu-sic, and I know that you do,
G
C (G bass)
G
C7 (G bass)
G
C (G bass)
G
Ab
Fm7
To Coda
too! It's A Mu - si - cal World! Such a beau - ti - ful
Gb
Bb
Eb (Bb bass)
Bb
world! The
D.S. al Coda

Coda

world! Ding Dong! Sing a song of spring and sum-mer!

Spring song, sum-mer song and en - tre - nous, I love mu-sic, and I know that you do,

too! It's A Mu-si-cal

World!

FAITH IN THE FUTURE
from the musical *Noah's Ark*

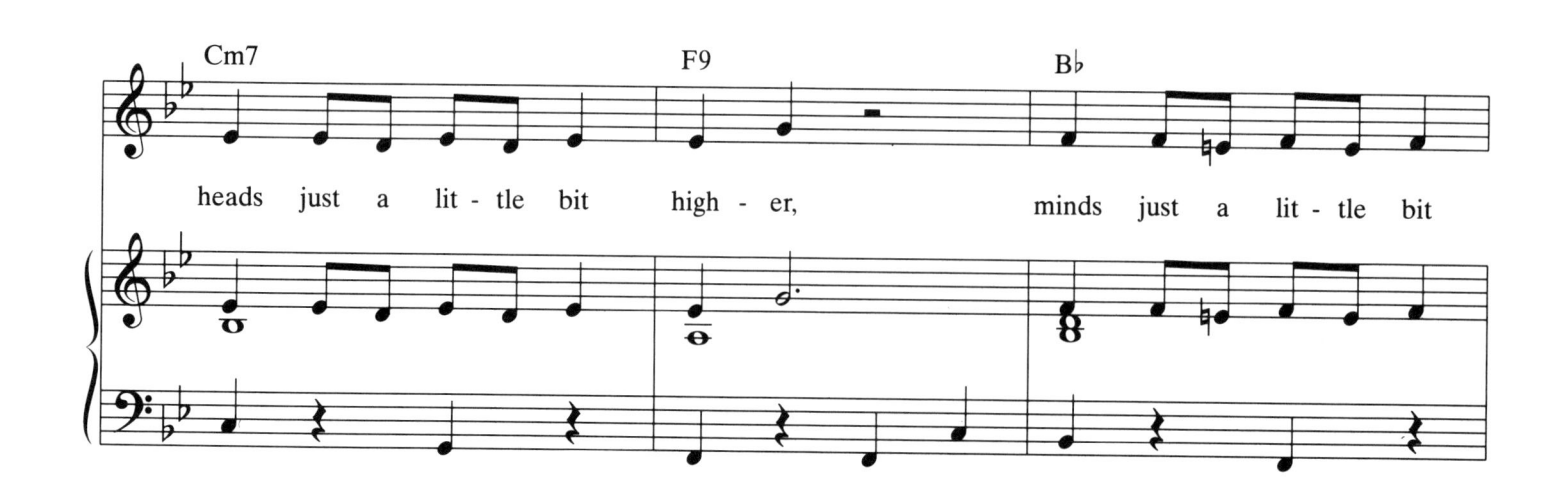

Words and Music by
Leslie Bricusse

Moderately fast

So, my friends, it seems we must be patient a little while longer, heads just a little bit higher, minds just a little bit strong - er. Eyes a lit - tle bright - er, hearts a lit - tle light - er, be a bit po - lit - er if we can. Belts a lit - tle tight - er, show 'em you're a fight - er, show that you are quite a man, or po - lar bear, or pel - i - can. We must have

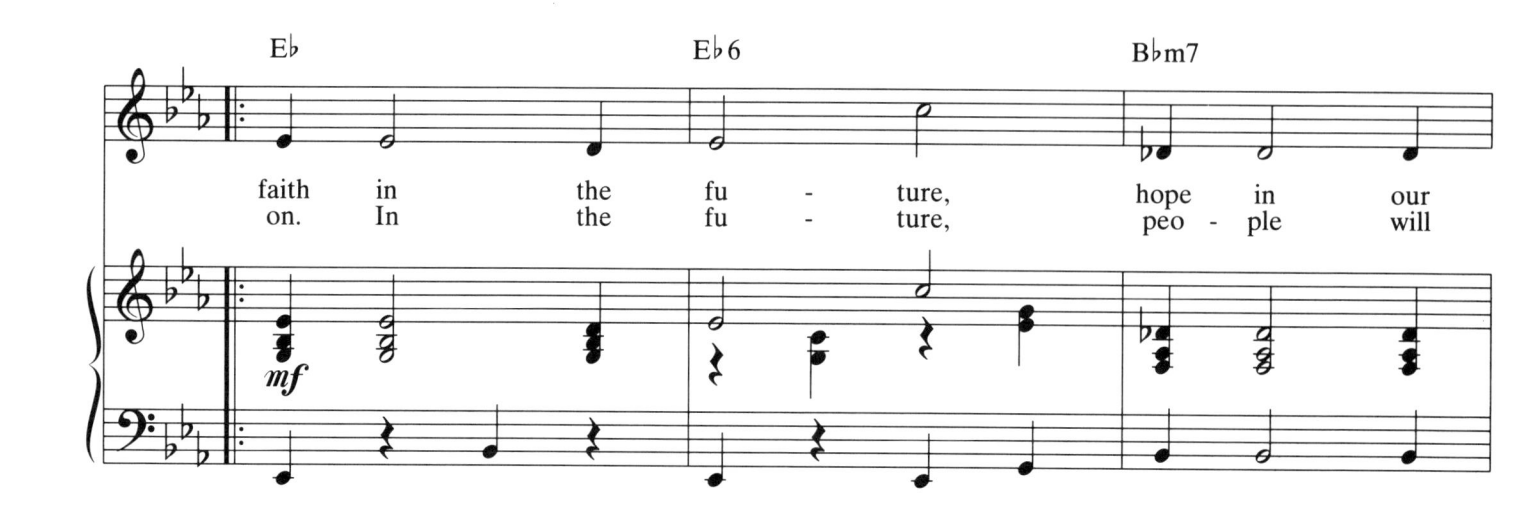

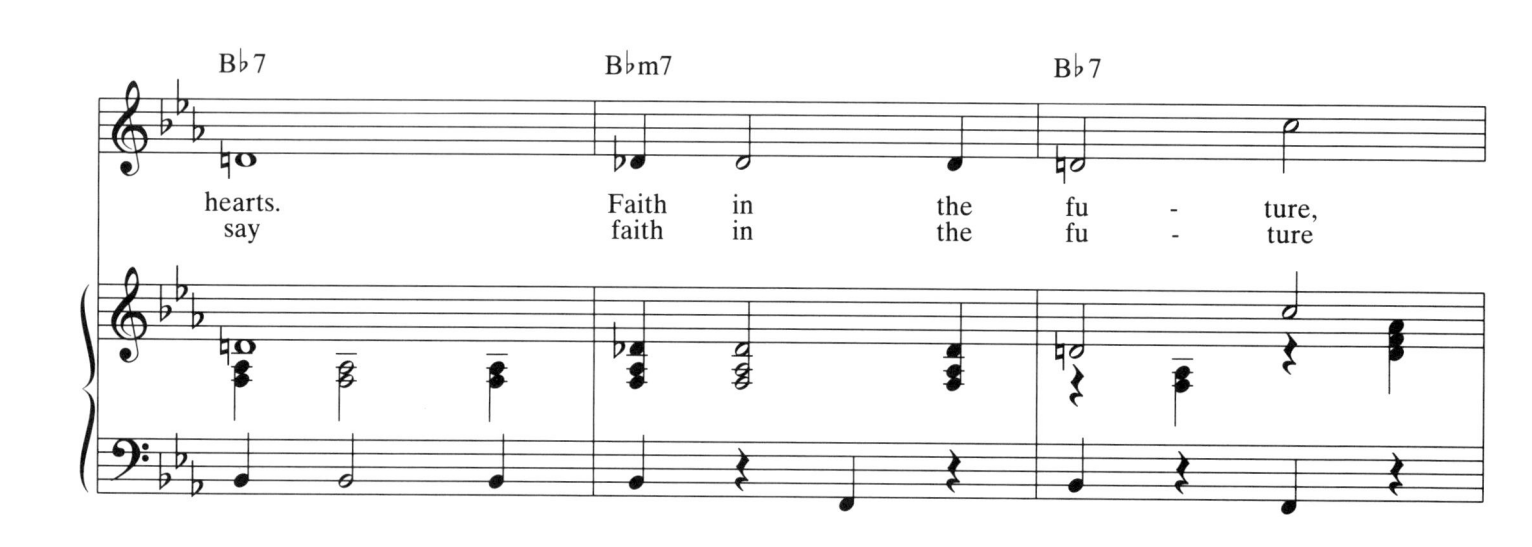

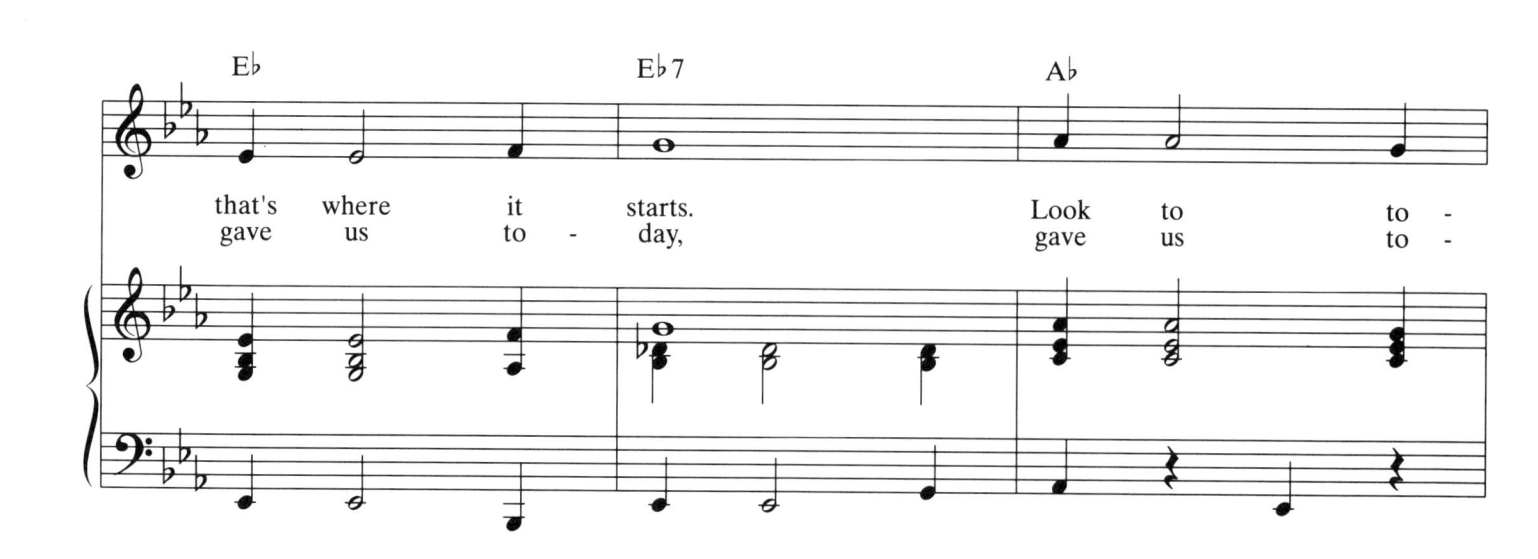

faith in the fu - ture, hope in our
on. In the fu - ture, peo - ple will

hearts. Faith in the fu - ture,
say faith in the fu - ture

that's where it starts. Look to to -
gave us to - day, gave us to -

1.
A♭m
E♭°
E♭
Gm7
Cm7
mor - row, yes - ter - day's gone.
mor - row, that's why we
F7
B♭
A♭
B♭7
What's past is past, but the world goes on and on and on and
2.
Gm7
B♭7
E♭
Fm7
Gm7
know our faith in the fu - ture will
A♭
Gm7
F7
E7
E♭6/9
grow and grow and grow.
rit.

THE WORLD IS BEAUTIFUL
from *Ondine**

Words and Music by
Leslie Bricusse

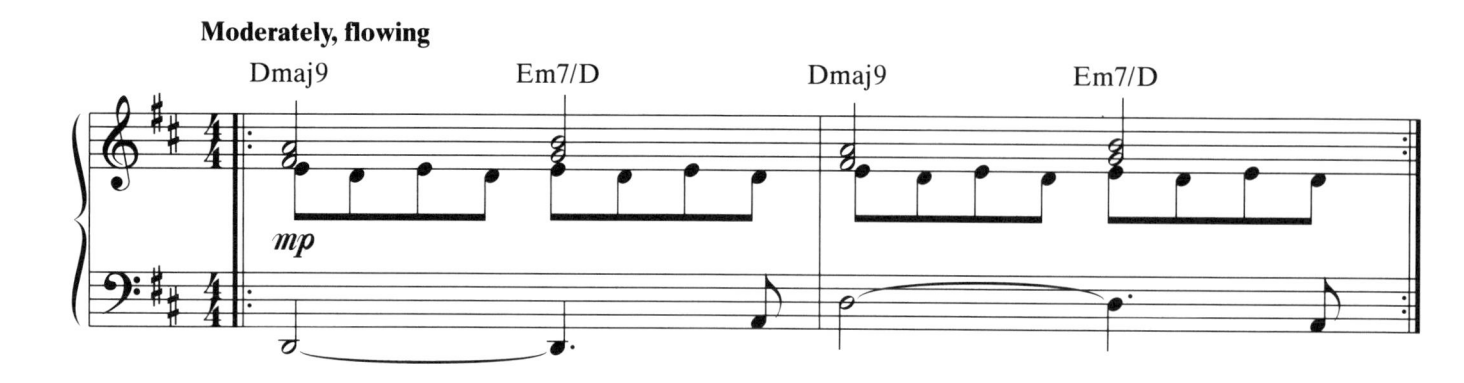

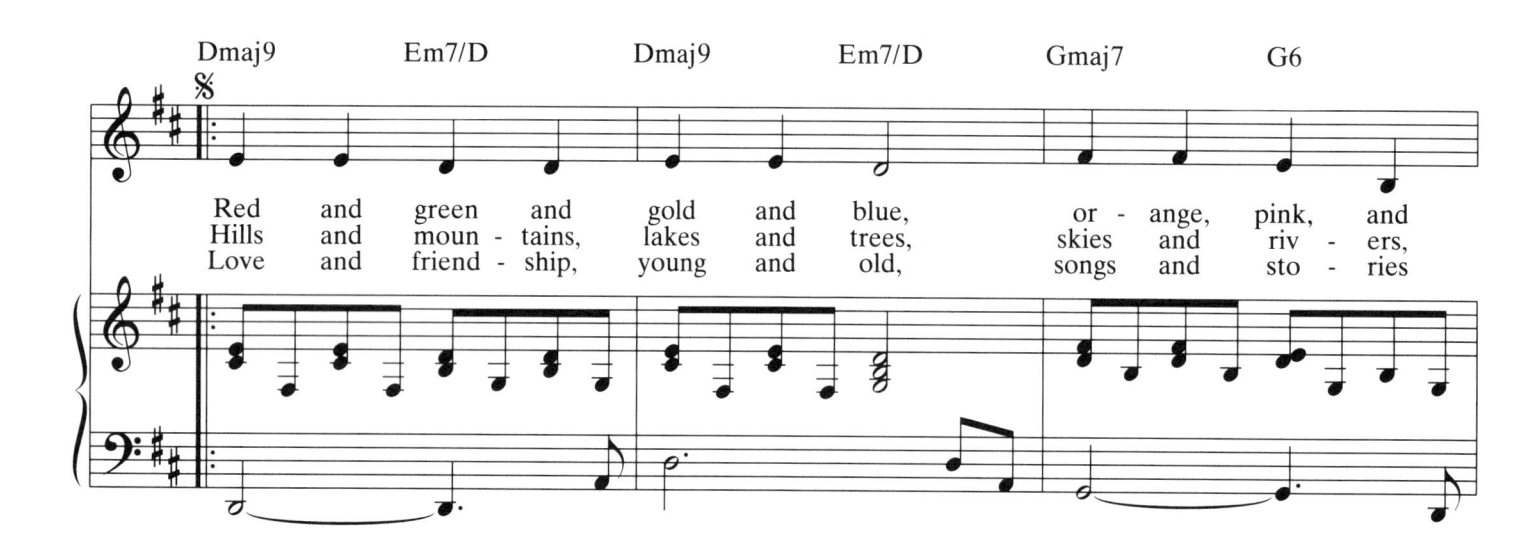

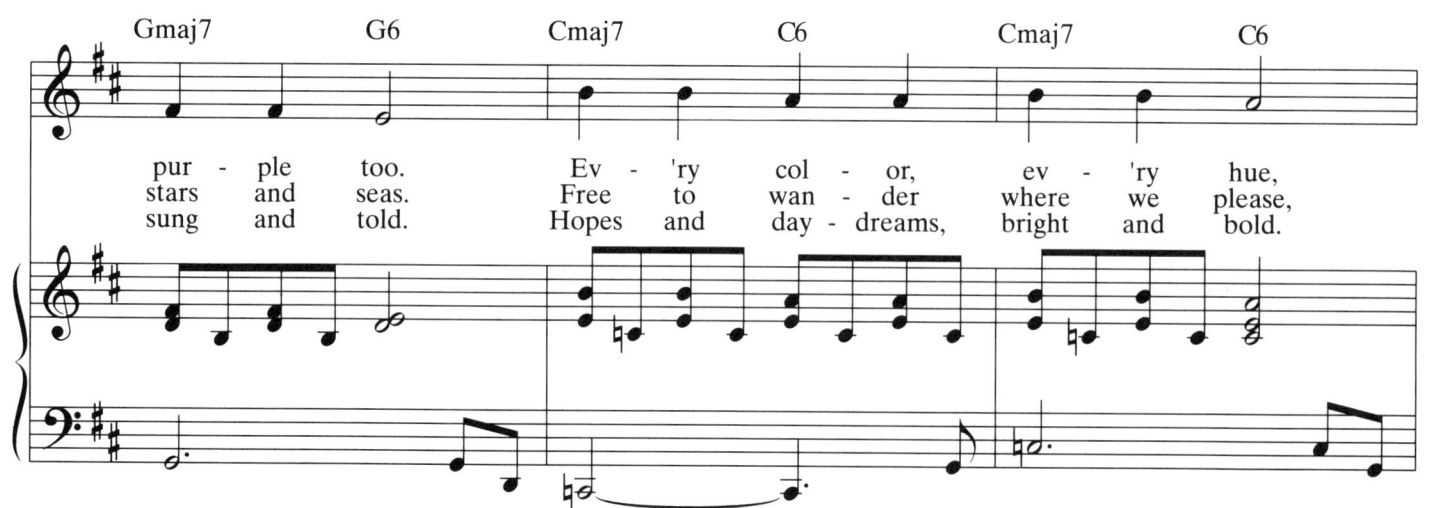

Moderately, flowing

Red and green and gold and blue, or - ange, pink, and
Hills and moun - tains, lakes and trees, skies and riv - ers,
Love and friend - ship, young and old, songs and sto - ries

pur - ple too. Ev - 'ry col - or, ev - 'ry hue,
stars and seas. Free to wan - der where we please,
sung and told. Hopes and day - dreams, bright and bold.

* Unproduced; see *Reflections*, p. 201.

Copyright © 1973 by Stage & Screen Music, Inc.
Worldwide Rights Administered by Cherry River Music (BMI)
International Copyright Secured All Rights Reserved

| Bbmaj7 | Bb6 | Bbmaj7 | Bb6 | F#7b9 F#7b9#5 F#m7/B B7 |

ev - er chang - ing, ev - er new. Just for me and
rain and sun - shine, mist and breeze. Dusk and dawn and
Win - ter morn - ings, crisp and cold. Sum - mer eve - nings,

| Cm6 | F#m7/B B7 | E13 Em7 A7b9 Dmaj9 | Em7/D |

To Coda

just for you.
times like these. } The world is beau - ti - ful.
soft and gold.

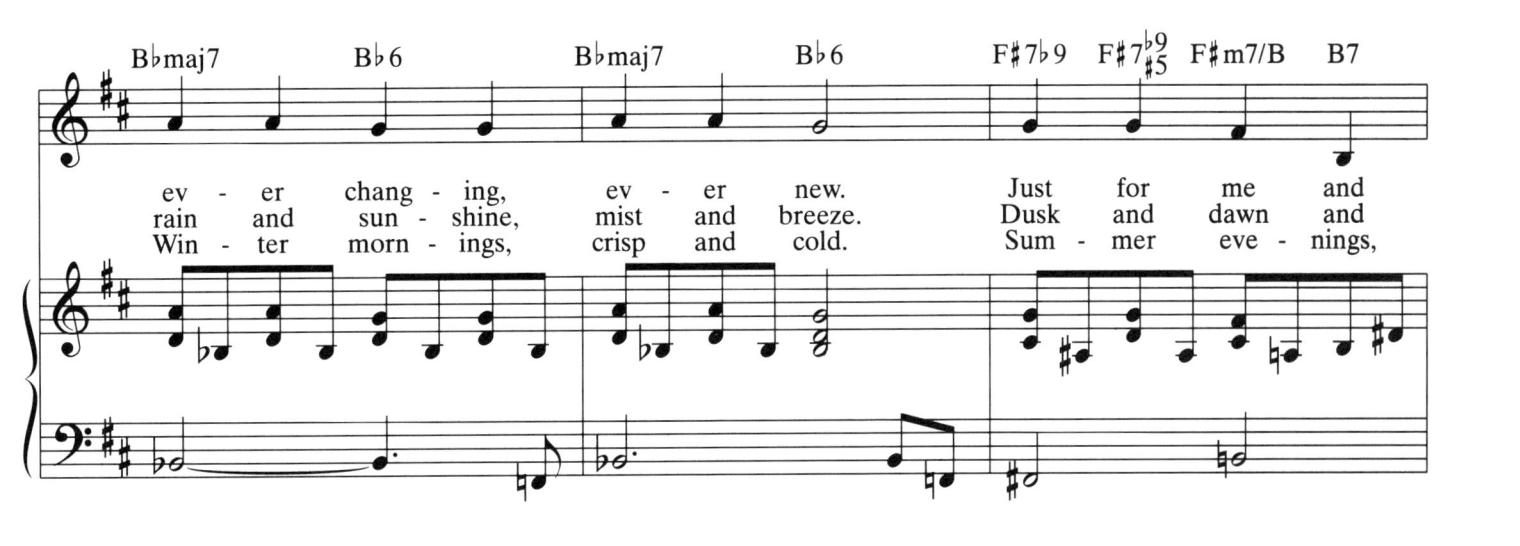

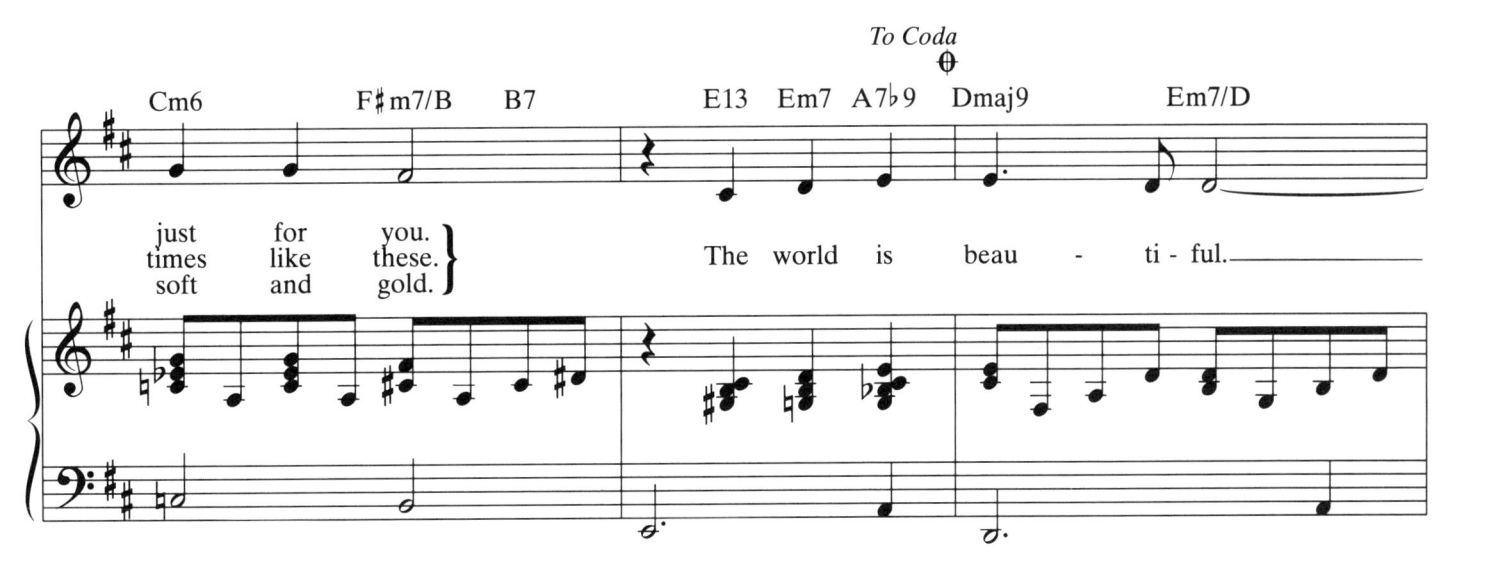

1. Dmaj9 Em7/D **2.** Dmaj9 Em7/D | Am9 D9

Kings and cas - tles,

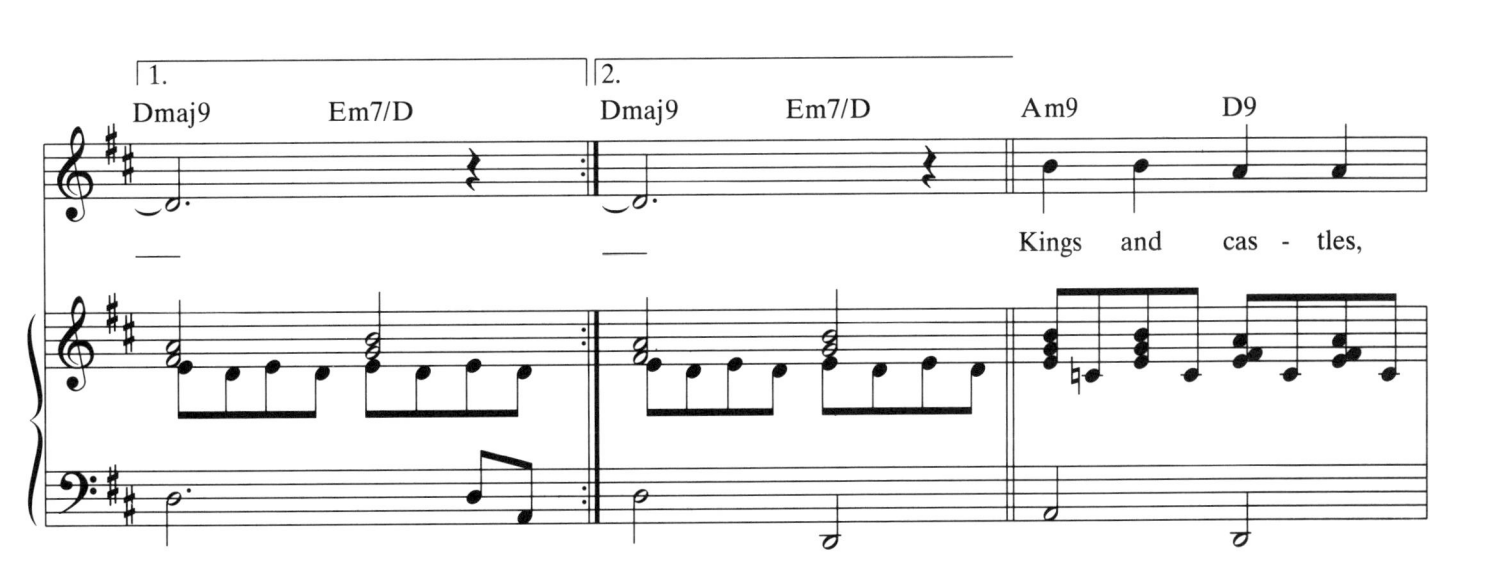

233

Am9 D9 Gmaj7 G6 Gmaj7 G6
spires and tow'rs, tales and leg - ends, mag - ic pow'rs.
Bm9 E7 Bm9 E7 Em7/A A13 Em7/G
Fate and for - tune, storms and show'rs, and fields of
F♯m7 B7 Em7add4
D.S. al Coda
flow'rs. All these are ours.
mf

Coda
Dmaj9 Bm7 Em7
beau - ti - ful, tru - ly.
E13 Em7/A A7♭9 Dmaj9 D6
The world is beau - ti - ful,
Cmaj7 C6 Fmaj7 Dmaj9 D6
tru - ly beau - ti - ful.
Dmaj9 D6 Dmaj9 D6 Dmaj9 D6 Dmaj9
rit.
8

Just For Fun

Amy Rainbow

Amy Rainbow was the title of the first children's book that Evie ever illustrated, back in 1980. Her author-collaborator was her lifelong frien the prolific British children's bookwriter, Nanette Newman, wife of my lifelong friend, the equally prolific screenwriter, novelist and fil director, Bryan Forbes.

I was enchanted by the name Amy Rainbow. It sounded as though it ought to be a song title, so I decided to make it one, based on th character of the delicious little girl that Evie and "Newman," as we call her, had created. At the time, I was working with that most wonder of singers, Andy Williams.

It occurred to my evil, scheming mind that Andy's uniquely dulcet tones would bring to the little song all the great charm it required, ar I must have convinced Andy, too, because a few days later, in a small London studio, the dulcet tones duly delivered the definitive versic of the song. The book and the song, together and separately, enjoyed what we all dubbed a "family success," since we all had a part in

From that day to this, I have derived enormous pleasure from writing little poems, verses and lyrics for many of Evie's illustrations, so is highly appropriate that "Amy Rainbow" should have her place in this book, where Evie has returned the compliment by creating origin illustrations for my songs. After all, in this particular genre, "Amy" was our first-born.

Tumbarumba

When Evie and I got married, we were very young, and had very little money, so we decided to spend six months going around the wor on our honeymoon—and we *did*!

We had an unimaginably wonderful time, traveling from London to Paris to New York, Toronto, Vancouver, San Francisco, Hawaii, F Sri Lanka, India, Egypt, Greece and on and on and on. But above all, Australia! You can't really say you've been around the world unle you go to Australia on the way.

We saw a lot of Australia—Sydney and Melbourne, Canberra and Adelaide, and across to Perth and Fremantle.

One day, planning our journey, I noticed these wonderful place-names dotted all over the map—great-sounding, lilting, lyrical names aboriginal origin (aboriginal *means* "from the beginning or origin.") I was so intrigued by their beauty, I started to list all the four-syllat names and then to find pairs that matched or rhymed. It was a simple process, and from the list I picked the most musical sounding name "Tumbarumba"—as the title for what I knew was a song—which I gave to Evie as a honeymoon souvenir of Australia.

AMY RAINBOW

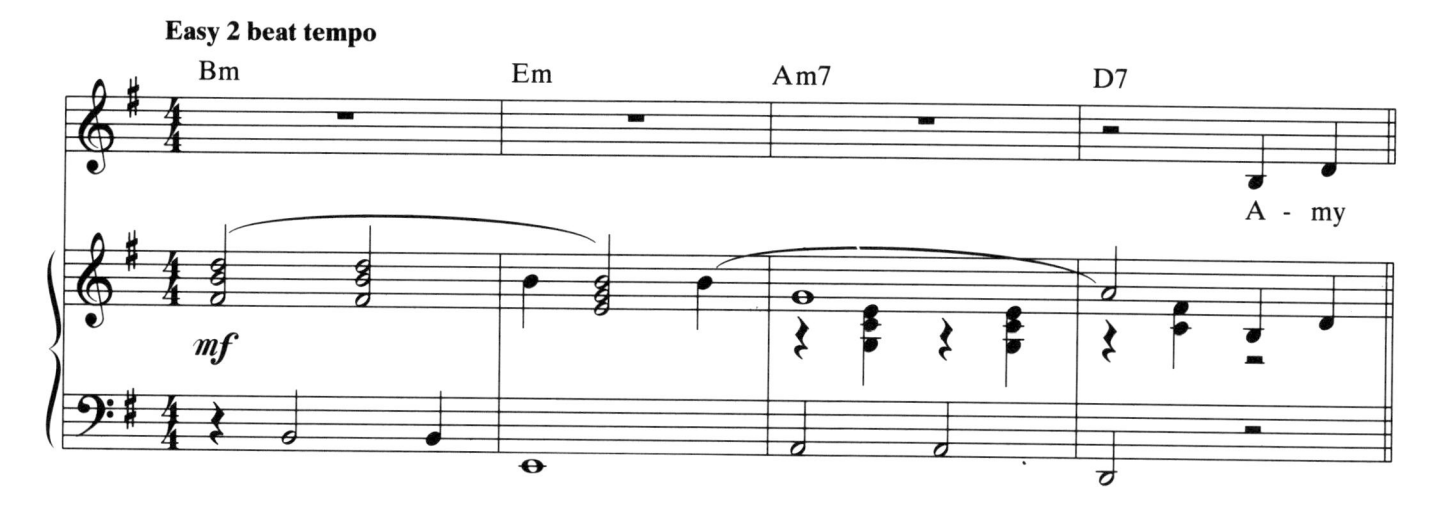

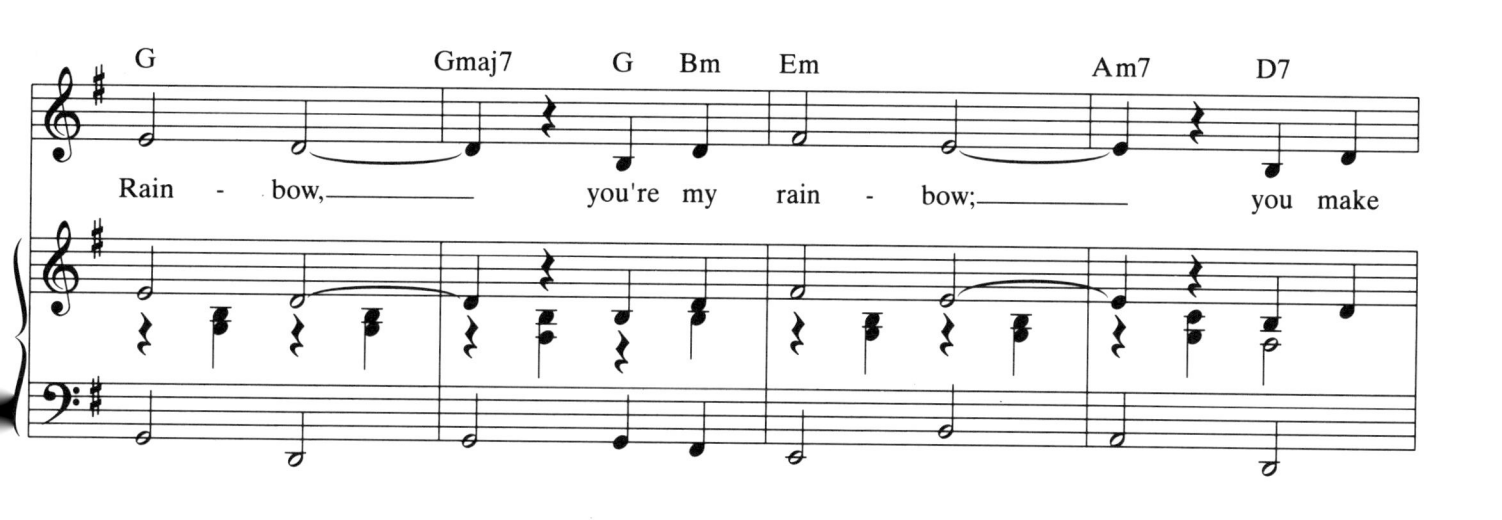

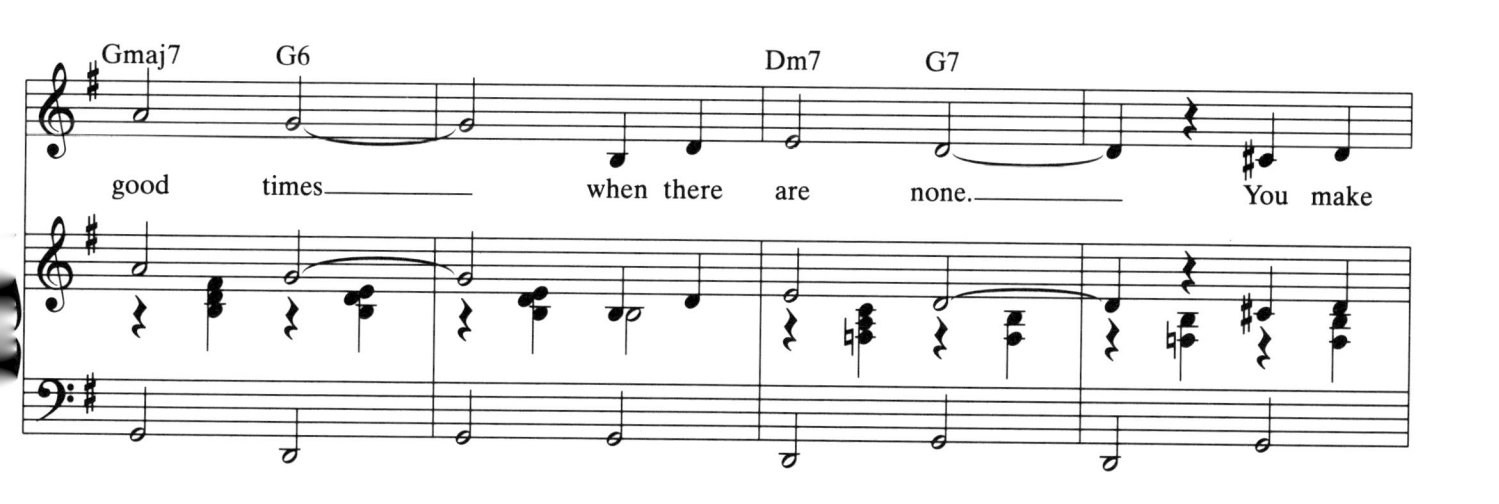

Words and Music by
Leslie Bricusse

Copyright © 1980 by Stage & Screen Music, Inc.
Worldwide Rights Administered by Cherry River Music (BMI)
International Copyright Secured All Rights Reserved

sun - shine_____ out of show - ers;_____ you make rain - bows,_____ 'cause you are one._____ You are child - hood,_____ you are flow - ers._____ You are mag - ic,_____ you have mag - ic pow - ers. There is

Christ-mas all a-round you; I'm so hap-py, A-my Rain-bow, that I found you.

I just could-n't care what to-mor-row brings, e-ven though it may dis-may me. Long as we can share the to-mor-row things, long as I can be with

C♯7/D D7 C♯7/D D7 C♯9 D9
A - my, my A - my, my rain - bow.
Am7/D Am7 Am7/D Gm(maj7)♭5 Am7 D9
You are
G Gmaj7 G Bm Em
spring time, you are laugh - ter.
Am7 D7 Dm7 G7 Cmaj7 C6
You are hap - py, you are ev - er

af - ter and a bright star shines a - bove you.

Have I told you, A - my Rain - bow, that I love you?

I love you. I

love you.

TUMBARUMBA

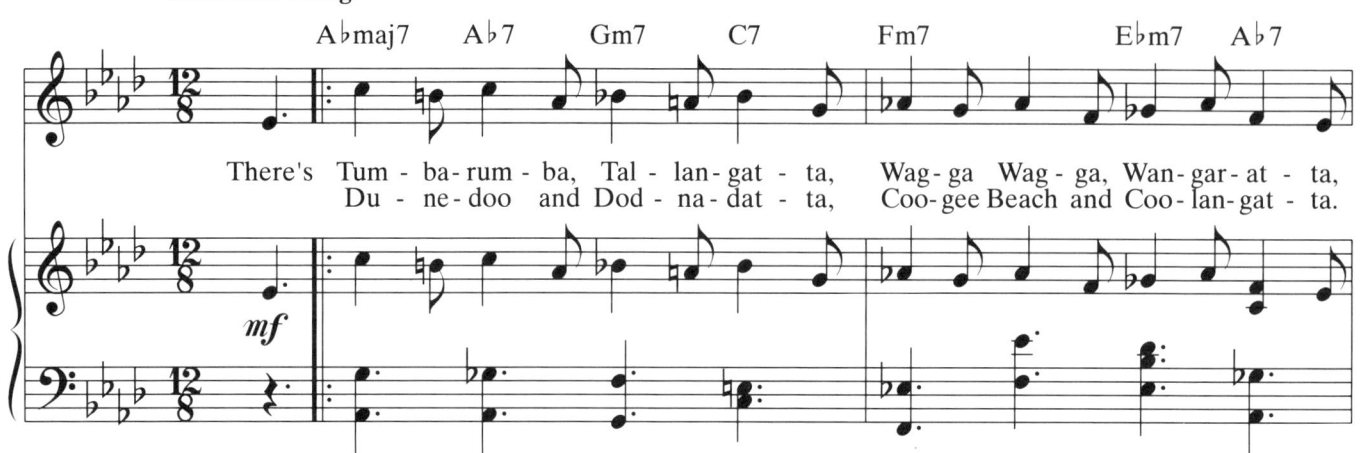

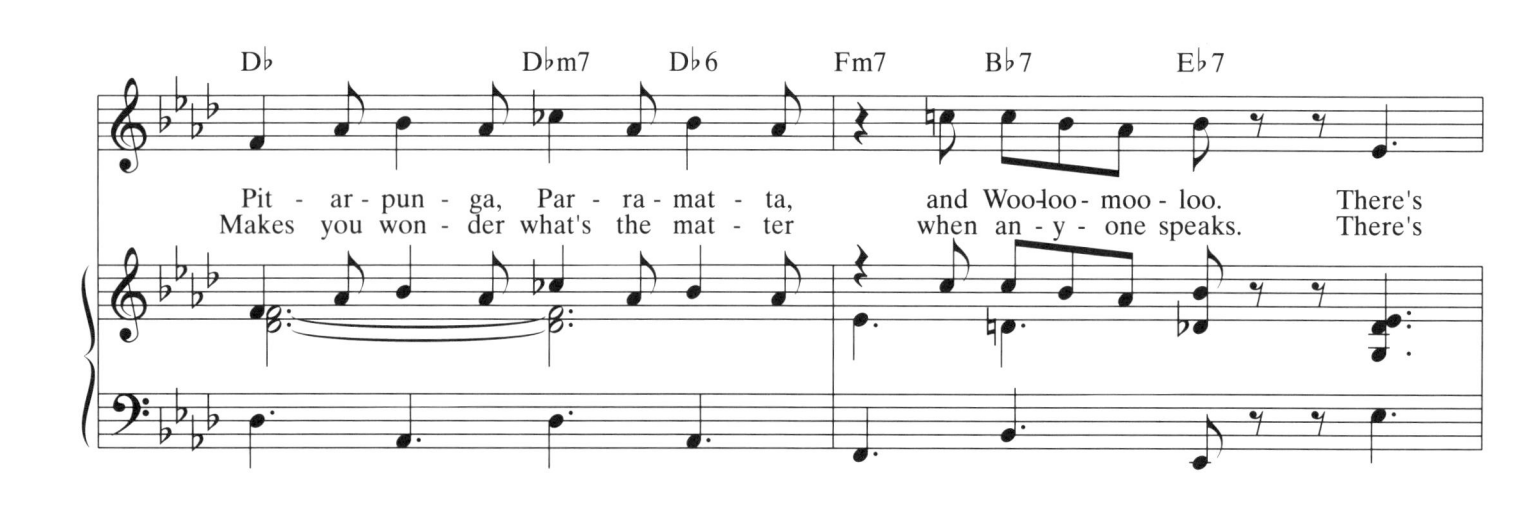

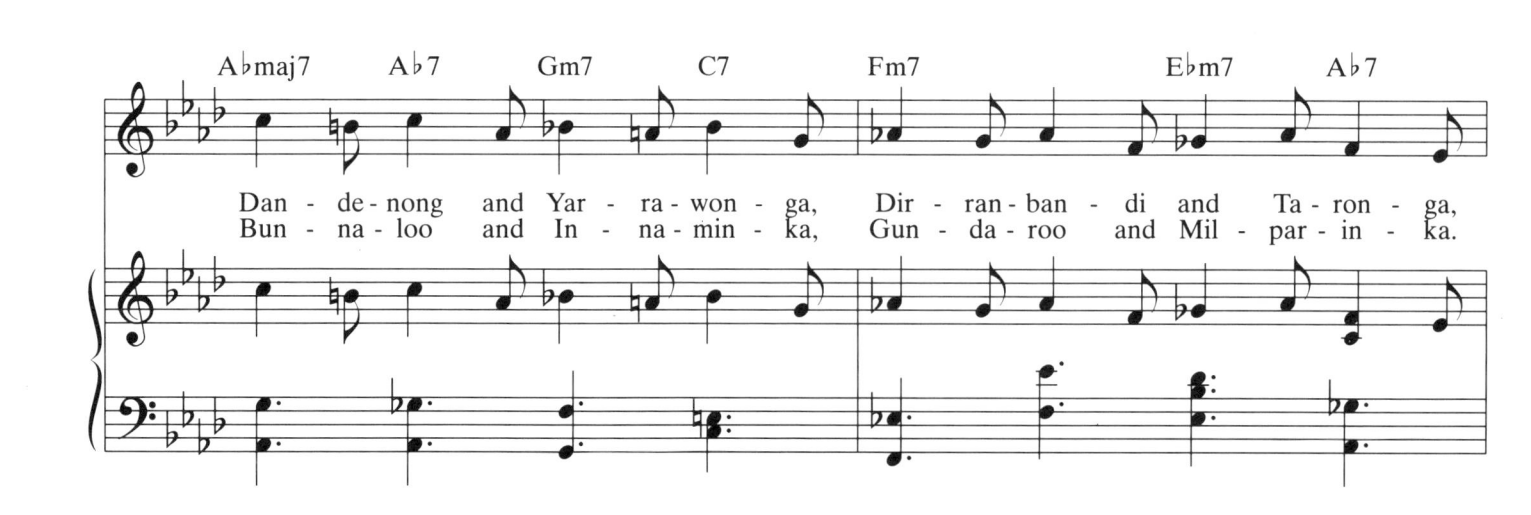

Words and Music by
Leslie Bricusse

Moderate swing

There's Tumbarumba, Tallangatta, Wagga Wagga, Wangaratta,
Dunedoo and Dodnadatta, Coogee Beach and Coolangatta.
Pitarpunga, Paramatta, and Woolloomooloo. There's
Makes you wonder what's the matter when anyone speaks. There's

Dandenong and Yarrawonga, Diranbandi and Taronga,
Bunaloo and Innaminka, Gundaroo and Milparinka.

Copyright © 1991 Stage & Screen Music, Inc.
Worldwide Rights Administered by Cherry River Music (BMI)
International Copyright Secured All Rights Reserved

Goon-di-win-di and Wo-don-ga, and Woo-mer-a-too. In case these words to you are a-lien, worse than words in Shaw's Pygmalion, I'll explain: they're all Australian cities and towns, the prettiest sounds. There's

Fun-ny names that make you think-a you're talk-ing to freaks. In case you think my English pi-geon-al, let me say these most o-rig-i-nal names are simp-ly ab-o-rig-i-nal cities and towns, the prettiest sounds. Like

A♭maj7 A♭7 Gm7 C7 Fm7 E♭m7 A♭7
Mit - ta - gong and Bil - la - bong, and Wool - lon - gong and Goo - loo - gong. So
D♭ C7♯5 C7 C7♭9 F7
sing a song with me to - day a -
B♭m7 E9♭5 B♭m7/E♭ E♭7
bout Aus - tray - li -
1.
A♭ Fm7
ay.
B♭m7 B♭m7/E♭ E♭7
There's
2.
A♭ E♭7 A♭
ay.

COMPLETE LYRICS
Illustrated by Evie Bricusse

Lyric Contents

Doctor Dolittle	Beautiful Things	251
	Doctor Dolittle	249
	Fabulous Places	251
	I've Never Seen Anything Like It	248
	My Friend The Doctor	249
	Talk To The Animals	247
Goodbye, Mr. Chips	Day Has A Hundred Pockets, A	257
	Fill The World With Love	255
	Schooldays	252
	That's A Boy!	256
	When I Am Older	253
	Where Did My Childhood Go?	255
Scrooge	Beautiful Day, The	259
	Christmas Carol, A	257
	Christmas Children	260
	Father Christmas	259
	Good Times	262
	I Like Life	261
	Minister's Cat, The	261
	Thank You Very Much	258
Willy Wonka & The Chocolate Factory	Candy Man, The	262
	Cheer Up, Charlie	263
	I've Got A Golden Ticket	264
	Oompa-Loompa Doompadee-Doo	263
	Pure Imagination	264
Santa Claus: The Movie	Thank You, Santa!	265
Home Alone	Somewhere In My Memory	265
	Star Of Bethlehem	265
Peter Pan	Growing Up	266
	House On Happiness Hill, The	272
	I'm Better With You	266
	Little Darlings	269
	Never-Never Land	270
	Once Upon A Bedtime	268
	Peter Pan	267
	Pretending	268
	Song Called Love, A	270
	You Can Fly	272
Babes In Toyland	C-I-N-C-I-N-N-A-T-I	274
	Through The Eyes Of A Child	273
Stop The World—I Want To Get Off	ABC Song, The	274
The Roar Of The Greasepaint—The Smell Of The Crowd	Beautiful Land, The	276
	Look At That Face	274
	That's What It Is To Be Young	277
	Things To Remember	278
Noah's Ark	Faith In The Future	278
The Good Old Bad Old Days	It's A Musical World	279
Ondine	World Is Beautiful, The	280
Just For Fun	Amy Rainbow	281
	Tumbarumba	282

This special lyric section represents the most complete and up-to-date versions, as edited by Leslie Bricusse.

Talk To The Animals
from the motion picture *Doctor Dolittle*

Words and Music by
Leslie Bricusse

If I could talk to the animals,
Just imagine it—
Chatting to a chimp in chimpanzee.
Imagine talking to a tiger—
Chatting to a cheetah—
What a neat achievement it would be!

If we could talk to the animals—
Learn their languages—
Maybe take an animal degree—
I'd study elephant and eagle—
Buffalo and beagle—
Alligator, guinea pig and flea!

I would converse in polar bear and python,
And I would curse in fluent kangaroo.
If people asked me
"Can you speak rhinoceros?"
I'd say, "Of courseros!—
Can't *you*?"

If I conferred with our furry friends—
Man to animal—
Think of the amazing repartee—
If I could walk with the animals—
Talk with the animals—
Grunt and squeak and squawk with the animals—
And they could talk to me!

If I consulted with quadrupeds,
Think what fun we'd have
Asking over crocodiles for tea!
Or maybe lunch with two or three lions—
Walruses and sea-lions—
What a lovely place the world would be!

If I spoke slang to orangutangs—
The advantages—
Any fool on earth can plainly see!—
Discussing eastern art and dramas
With intellectual llamas—
That's a big step forward, you'll agree!

I'd learn to speak in antelope and turtle—
My Pekingese would be extremely good!
If I were asked to sing in hippopotamus
I'd say "Why notamus?"—
And *would*!

If I could parley with pachyderms,
It's a fairy tale
Worthy of Hans Anderson or Grimm!—
A man who walks with the animals—
Talks with the animals—
Grunts and squeaks and squawks with the animals—
And they could talk to him!

I'd study every living creature's language—
So I could speak to all of them on sight.
If friends said, "Can he talk in crab or pelican?"
You'd say, "Like Helican!"—
And you'd be *right*!

And if you just stop and think a bit,
There's no doubt of it—
I would win a place in history!—
If I could walk with the animals—
Talk with the animals—
Grunt and squeak and squawk with the animals—
And they could squeak and squawk
And speak
And talk
To me.

Copyright © 1967 20th Century Music Corp.
All Rights Controlled by Hastings Music Corporation,
1350 Ave. Of Americas, New York, NY 10019
International Copyright Secured All Rights Reserved

I've Never Seen Anything Like It
from the motion picture *Doctor Dolittle*

Words and Music by
Leslie Bricusse

I've seen the world.
I've been around.
I could tell you stories
That would quite astound you.
I'm not a fool.
I went to school.
I've been from Liverpool to Istanbul!
Istanbul.
I'm no fool!

And anyone will tell you
That I'm sharper than a knife.
But I've never seen anything like it
In my life!

No, I've never seen anything like it!
Never seen anything like it!
I've never seen anything like it
In my life!

I thought I'd seen every wonder in the world!
I've seen the Coliseum in Rome—
And the Acropolis!
I made the biggest blunder in the world—
Because I've never seen anything quite like this!

I mean, I know the game.
I've seen 'em all.
I could tell you stories
That would quite enthrall you.
I know me job—
Pleasing the mob.
I give 'em what they want for just two bob!
Just two bob.
That's my job!

But this is so fantastic
I can't wait to tell the wife.
'Cause I've never seen anything like it
In my life!

No, I've never seen anything like it!
Never seen anything like it!
I've never seen anything like it
In my life!

I thought I'd seen
Every miracle on earth!
I've seen the leaning Tower of Pisa
And the Pyramids.
They're not worth
Half what the pushmi-pullyu's worth!—
Because they
Really don't have an appeal for kids!

I mean,
I'm down to earth.
I'll tell you straight—
I could tell you stories
That would fascinate you.
I know the trade.
I know the tricks.
Once bought an elephant
For two pound six.
Two pound six.
Taught it tricks.

But for a pushmi-pullyu
I'd pay three pounds ... four pounds ... five!
'Cause I've never seen anything like it
That's alive!

No, I've never seen anything like it!
There's never been anything like it!
I've never seen anything like it
In all my life!

Copyright © 1967 20th Century Music Corp.
All Rights Controlled by Hastings Music Corporation,
1350 Ave. Of Americas, New York, NY 10019
International Copyright Secured   All Rights Reserved

Doctor Dolittle

from the motion picture *Doctor Dolittle*

Words and Music by
Leslie Bricusse

This is the world of Doctor Dolittle.
The wonderful world of Doctor Dolittle.
Where crocodiles talk
And elephants sing,
And animals do most any old thing—
Where polar bears wear top hats,
And leopards with spots wear spats.

Well, that's life in the world of Doctor Dolittle.
Doves start to coo when they see Dolittle.
He has a profound philosophy.
If animals can be friends, says he,
Well then, why can't we?

Say how d'you do to Doctor Dolittle.
Life is a zoo to Doctor Dolittle—
Where antelopes lope
And ostriches fan—
And kangaroos do what kangaroos can
To make the hyenas laugh—
As long as a long giraffe.

Every calf starts to moo when they see Dolittle—
Even the few who used to moo little.
For all of the birds and beasts agree
He has a profound philosophy—
And so why can't we
Do-little things to help them?....
Why can't we?

Copyright © 1967 20th Century Music Corp.
All Rights Controlled by Hastings Music Corporation, New York, NY 10019
International Copyright Secured All Rights Reserved

My Friend The Doctor

from the motion picture *Doctor Dolittle*

Words and Music by
Leslie Bricusse

Now any man who understands The Irish
Can't be reckoned altogether bad.
The same way that a lunatic
Whose patron saint is Patterick
Can't be reckoned altogether mad.

The doctor's very smart—
An Irishman at heart!
His favourite colour, sure it must be green.
And also he's a man
Who'll blarney when he can—
Let me explain the sort of thing I mean.

My friend the doctor says
The moon is made of apple pie—
And once a month it's eaten by the sun.
And that is why,
Up in the sky,
You'll find, as every month goes by,
Somebody in the sky's making another one.

My friend the doctor says
The sun is made of cheddar cheese—
The doctor even knows the reason why!
The facts are these—
Try, if you please,
Pretending you're a lonely cheese—
Wouldn't you want to try finding an apple pie?

Maybe what the doctor tells me
Isn't altogether true.
But I love every tale he tells me—
I don't know any better ones, do you?

My friend the doctor says
The world is full of fantasy—
And who are you and I to disagree?
Let's hope and pray
That is the way
The life we love will always stay
For my friend the doctor
And me!

My friend the doctor says
The stars are made of lemon drops.
The bigger ones are lollipops and ice.
The clouds have shops
Up on the tops
That sell you sweets and soda pops—
What do they call the place—isn't it paradise?

My friend the doctor says
That every time it starts to rain,
And people run indoors again in swarms,
If you remain
Out in the rain,
You'll think you're drinking pink champagne—
And you will spend your life praying for thunderstorms.

Maybe what the doctor tells me
Isn't altogether true.
But I love every tale he tells me—
I don't know any better ones—do you?

My friend the doctor says
The world is full of fantasy—
And who are you and I to disagree?
Let's hope and pray
That is the way
The life we love will always stay
For my friend the doctor
And me.
My friend the doctor
And me!

Copyright © 1967 20th Century Music Corp.
All Rights Controlled by Hastings Music Corporation,
1350 Ave. Of Americas, New York, NY 10019
International Copyright Secured All Rights Reserved

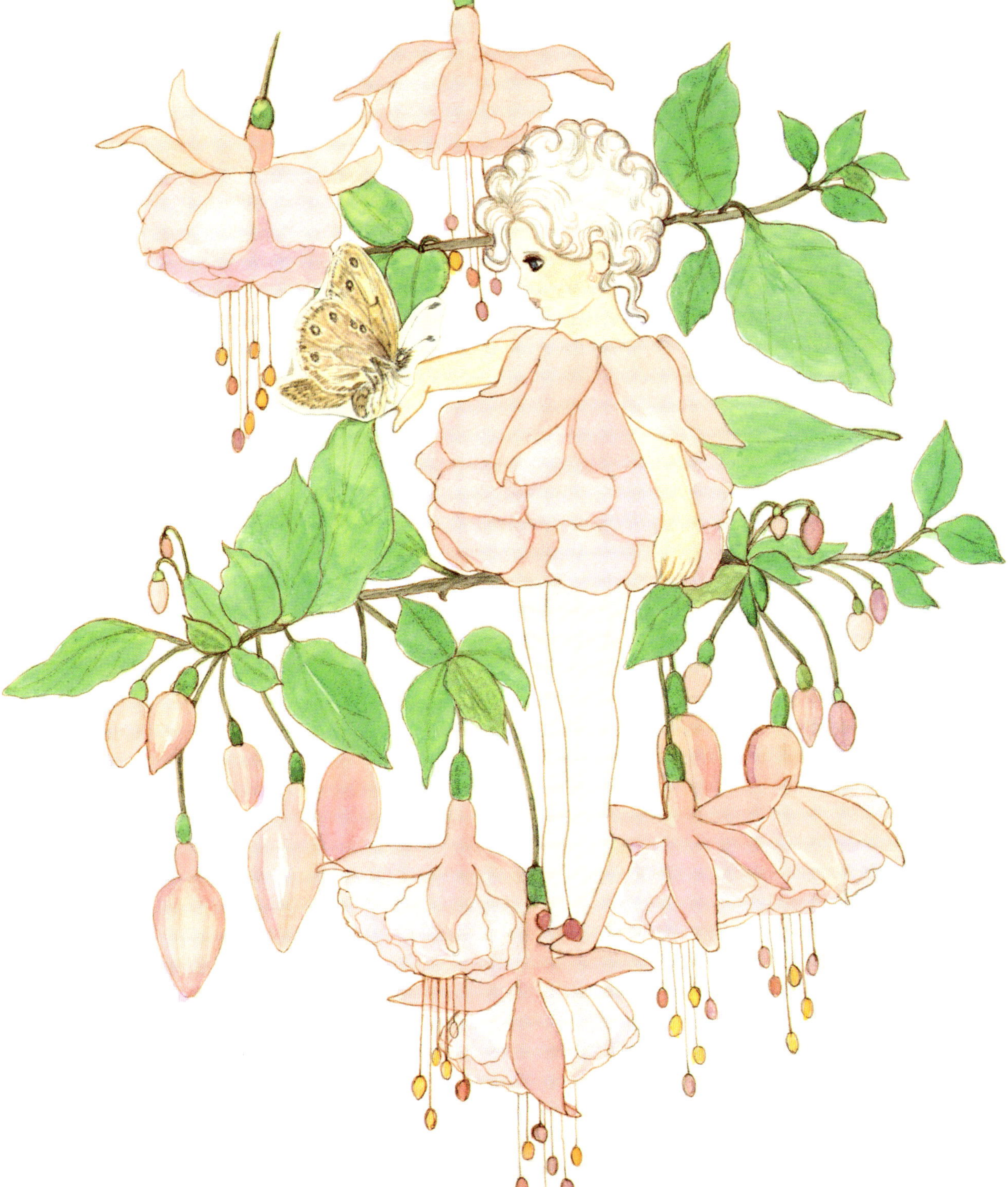

Beautiful Things

from the motion picture *Doctor Dolittle*

Words and Music by
Leslie Bricusse

The world is full of beautiful things—
Butterfly wings—
Fairy-tale kings.
And each new day undoubtedly brings
Still more beautiful things.

The world abounds with many delights—
Magical sights—
Fanciful flights—
And those who dream on beautiful nights
Dream of beautiful things.

Beautiful days for sunshine lazin'—
Beautiful skies and shores.
Beautiful days when I can gaze in
Beautiful eyes like yours.

You wonder why the nightingale sings—
Lovers have wings—
People wear rings.
The world is full of beautiful things—
Beautiful people, too!—
Beautiful people
Like you!

The world is full of beautiful things—
Daffodil springs—
Children on swings—
And each new day undoubtedly brings
Still more beautiful things.

The world is dipped in delicate dreams—
Sparkling streams—
Lullaby themes—
Where every flight of fantasy seems
Filled with beautiful things.

Beautiful days of sunkissed flowers—
Beautiful sea-kissed breeze.
Beautiful nights of moon-kissed hours—
Beautiful dreams like these.

Our lives tick by like pendulum swings—
Poor little things—
Puppets on strings—
But life is full of beautiful things—
Beautiful people, too!
Beautiful people
Like you!

Copyright © 1967 20th Century Music Corp.
All Rights Controlled by Hastings Music Corporation,
1350 Ave. Of Americas, New York, NY 10019
International Copyright Secured All Rights Reserved

Fabulous Places

from the motion picture *Doctor Dolittle*

Words and Music by
Leslie Bricusse

There are so many fabulous faraway places to see—
Such as Mexico, Sweden, Hawaii, Japan and Capri.
There's so many exciting and wonderful places—
Much more inviting than desert oases.
Pleasant as home is,
It isn't what Rome is—
So why stay there?

When there are so many fabulous faraway places to see?—
Why should Spain and Tahiti and Rio
Just be only names to you and me?
I feel certain there are people
We'd be glad to know there—
So tell me why don't we get up and go there?—
Go to those fabulous places where we long to be?
Go to Bangkok and Hong Kong
And Paris and Venice—
Tokyo and Cairo
And Lisbon and London—
Wonderful fabulous places we're longing to see!

There are so many simply incredible places to see—
When I think of the warm Caribbean
I see a new world for you and me!
I'd give anything
Just to have one single day there!—
And once we get there,
I know that we'll stay there!—
Stay in those fabulous places
Where we long to be!—
Such as Siam, Sienna, Vienna, Verona—
Java, Jamaica, Bombay, Barcelona—
Show me those fabulous places
We're longing to see.

Copyright © 1967 20th Century Music Corp.
All Rights Controlled by Hastings Music Corporation,
1350 Ave. Of Americas, New York, NY 10019

Schooldays

from the motion picture *Goodbye, Mr. Chips*

Words and Music by
Leslie Bricusse

Schooldays, so they tell us,
Are the most sublime of our lives.
We'll have the time of our lives.
It's the absolute prime of our lives.
They tell us schooldays are golden.
In the olden days
It might have been true.
But in the olden days
They like torture and slavery, too!
What are you going to do?

Schooldays, so we gather,
Are the sweetest days that we'll know,
And if that really is so,
Well, it comes as a bit of a blow.
I mean,
If Schooldays are the best of our lives,
Imagine the rest of our lives!
Schooldays, schooldays—
Never let me go!

Schooldays—
Are sublime!

We're in the thick of them!—
And we are sick of them!
You can take your pick of them!

Schooldays—
What a time!

Schooldays—
How divine!

Schooldays—
They're so fine!

Schooldays—
They're the best!

Schooldays—
That's the test!

Have you guessed
That I'll miss
My schooldays?
My Tom Brown's
Tom Fool days!
Schooldays, Schooldays—
Never let me go!

Working for scholarships.
Similar to prison ships.
Talk about dictatorships!

Studying Ancient Greek
All the week.
Latin is all we speak.

Class at nine—
Rain or shine!
You can have all of mine!

Oh, what a pain they are!
Think of the strain they are!
Cruel and inhumane they are!
Slightly insane they are!
Isn't it plain they are!

Funny days!
Sunny days!
Jolly days!
Holidays!
Schooldays, Schooldays—

Copyright © 1968, 1969 Metro-Goldwyn-Mayer Inc., New York, NY
Rights Throughout the World Controlled by Hastings Music Corporation, New York, NY
International Copyright Secured All Rights Reserved

When I Am Older

from the motion picture *Goodbye, Mr. Chips*

Words and Music by
Leslie Bricusse

Seven weeks of home sweet home are over—
They're over!
Seven weeks of mother's cooking—
Mother's love and mother's looking after—
And laughter—
And living in clover
Are over!

Moreover,
Fourteen weeks of Michaelmas term
Stretch endlessly ahead!—
Fourteen weeks of nameless horror
Wait to be unfurled!—
Fourteen weeks of Latin verbs—
I wish that I was dead!
Fourteen weeks of schoolcap tipping—
Filthy food and Mister Chipping.
Fourteen weeks in the dungeon
Of a schoolboy's world!
But one day...
One day...

When I am older,
I'll be the President of Peru.
I'll own an emerald mine or two.
I'll swim for England
In the next Olympic Games.

I'm gonna be a playboy farmer.
I'm gonna be a lady charmer.
I'm gonna be a knight in armor.
Find a damsel and disarm her.

When I am older,
I'll be the multiest millionaire.
I'll be the fellow beyond compare.
I'll be the hero
That the populace acclaims.

I'm gonna carve the world in pieces.
I'm gonna be as rich as Croesus.
Think of the mighty empire
I shall rule!—
When I am older,
Wiser and bolder—
On the day that I get out of school!

When I am older,
I'll be the novelist of the year.
I'll be an eminent engineer.
I'll be the actor
That the audience applauds.

I'm gonna be a fine musician.
I'm gonna be a rich physician.
I'm gonna be a politician.
I shall be an obstetrician.
I'll achieve my great ambition.

When I am older,
I'll be the fellow who makes the rules.
I will abolish our public schools.
I'll be the chairman
Of at least a hundred boards.

I'll run a fleet of ocean tankers.
I'll buy a street of merchant bankers.
I'll be the greatest man
You've ever seen!—
When I am older,
Wiser and bolder—
Just as soon as I am seventeen!

Copyright © 1968, 1969 Metro-Goldwyn-Mayer Inc., New York, NY
Rights Throughout the World Controlled by Hastings Music Corporation, New York, NY
International Copyright Secured All Rights Reserved

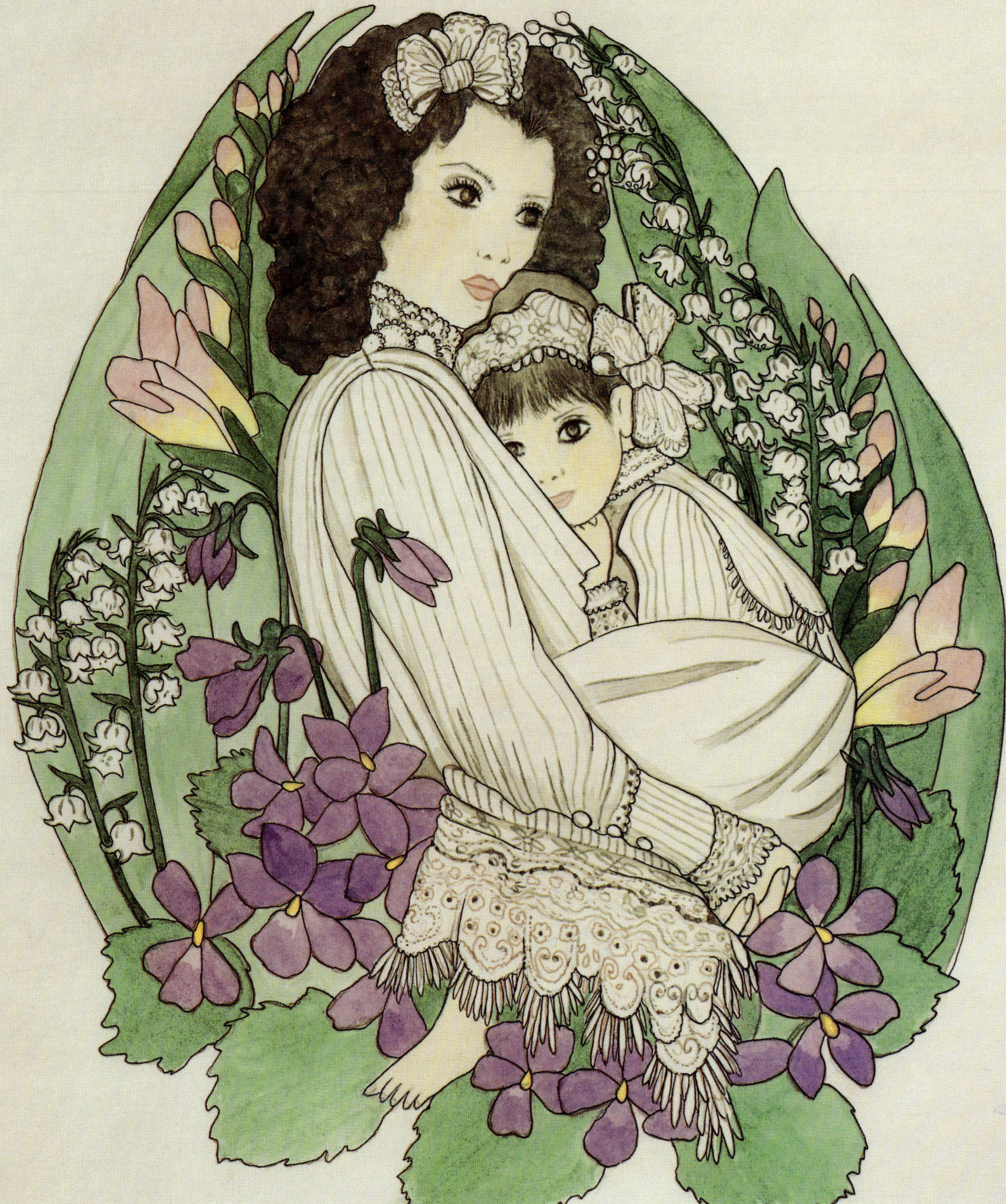

Fill The World With Love
from the motion picture *Goodbye, Mr. Chips*

Words and Music by
Leslie Bricusse

In the morning of my life
I shall look to the sunrise—
At a moment in my life
When the world is new—
And the blessing I shall ask
Is that God will grant me
To be brave and strong and true—
And to fill the world with love
My whole life through.

And to fill the world with love—
And to fill the world with love—
And to fill the world with love—
My whole life through.

In the noon-time of my life
I shall look to the sunshine—
At a moment in my life
When the sky is blue—
And the blessing I shall ask
Will remain unchanging—
To be brave and strong and true—
And to fill the world with love
My whole life through.

And to fill the world with love—
And to fill the world with love—
And to fill the world with love—
My whole life through

In the evening of my life
I shall look to the sunset—
At a moment in my life
When the night is due—
And the question I shall ask
Only I can answer—
Was I brave and strong and true?
Did I fill the world with love
My whole life through?

Did I fill the world with love?—
Did I fill the world with love?—
Did I fill the world with love
My whole life through?

Copyright © 1968, 1969 Metro-Goldwyn-Mayer Inc., New York, NY
Rights Throughout the World Controlled by Hastings Music Corporation, New York, NY
International Copyright Secured All Rights Reserved

Where Did My Childhood Go?
from the motion picture *Goodbye, Mr. Chips*

Words and Music by
Leslie Bricusse

They think I do not understand them.
They think I do not hear or see.
I only wish they knew
That I do understand them.
I only wish they understood me.

Yesterday I was their age.
Tomorrow they'll be my age.
Sooner, much sooner than they know.
And suddenly they will ask
What every child must ask—
'Where did my childhood go?'

Where did my childhood go?
When did my youth, so sweet and free,
Suddenly slip away from me?
Was it so long ago?
Where did my childhood go?

Where did the magic end?
When did the future meet the past?—
Ending a dream too good to last—
Taking away a friend—
When did my childhood end?

Was it that day
In early spring that lingers on?—
When somehow I knew
This precious time would soon be gone.

What does the future show?
Spring will return again next year.
And when she does, she'll find me here
Wondering still, I know,
Where did my childhood go?

Yesterday I was their age.
Tomorrow they'll be my age.
Sooner, much sooner than they know.
And suddenly they will ask
What every man must ask—
Where did my childhood go?

Copyright © 1968, 1969 Metro-Goldwyn-Mayer Inc., New York, NY
Rights Throughout the World Controlled by Hastings Music Corporation, New York, NY
International Copyright Secured All Rights Reserved

That's A Boy!

from the stage production of *Goodbye, Mr. Chips*

Words and Music by
Leslie Bricusse

How much easier it would be
To teach them football
Or cricket!
It's tricky teaching classics—
You're on such a sticky wicket!
If all we taught was games
I know they'd all be thrilled to see us!
But Heaven help the Classics master
Offering them Aeneas!

Boys are venomous with Virgil!
Horrified by Homer!
Cicero in Verrem
Throws them all into a coma!
And Pindar's very name
Is like some terrible aroma!
The expressions on their faces—
You should see!
But Max, I can't blame Pindar!—
I blame *me*!

What is a boy?
A boy is a thing
With string in its pocket
And a grin on its face—
Racing round like a rocket—
Spreading dirt around the place.
An absolute disgrace—
That's a boy!

Why does a boy
Rampage like a fool
Through school and through college—
With a great deal of noise
And a vast lack of knowledge—
And a total lack of poise?
P'raps that's what he enjoys!
That's a boy!

Regardless of climate or season,
Boys are born to defile and destroy.
Yet for some inexplicable reason,
To their mothers they're a fountain
Of infinite joy!
It's sickening!—
The devastating tricks
They employ!

I mean, why should it be
To me they're a curse?
Their nursemaid-cum-father—
That's the job that I've got!
There are times
When I'd rather like to drown the bloody lot!
No, now I'm talking rot!—
No, I'm *not*!

I'm an expert on Troy.
I can speak fluent Greek.
But there's one thing
That mystifies me
Seven days a week—
That's a boy!

I am bound to admit
That the future is his....
But I still don't know
What a boy *is*!

How can a boy
Retain any hope
To cope as a scholar
When there's mud in his brain—
And there's blood on his collar?—
It can drive a man insane!
The answer's very plain!—
That's a boy!

We're told boys are delicate creatures—
To be handled with limitless care.
I've observed all their delicate features—
They're as delicate
As some kind of small grizzly bear!
They're elephants! Rhinoceroses!—
Look over there!

Ah well, all I can say
Is maybe a boy
Is more than we reckon.
He is not just a lout.
He's aware fate will beckon,
And he knows what he's about!—
But that I greatly doubt!
Max, look out!

Youth's a thing to enjoy,
For, like faith, it's a gift.
They say faith can move mountains—
But there's one thing it can't shift—
That's a boy!

And I refuse to believe
That will grow up to be
A mature human being
Like me!

Copyright © 1981 Stage And Screen Music Inc.
Worldwide Rights Administered by Cherry River Music (BMI)
International Copyright Secured All Rights Reserved

A Day Has A Hundred Pockets

from the stage production of *Goodbye, Mr. Chips*

Words and Music by
Leslie Bricusse

A day has a hundred pockets—
If you know what to put inside!
If you've got enough schemes—
And you've got enough dreams—
You can fill 'em
Until they burst their seams!
I know! I've tried!

Each one of the hundred pockets
Can be squeezed into every day.
You can fill the day up
Like a bottomless cup.
If you're clever,
You'll never spill a drop!
Or so they say!

There's a pocket for hope—
And a pocket for rope—
And a pocket for odds and ends.
There's a pocket for plans—
And a couple for hands—
And a beautiful pocket
Full of friends!
It all depends!

We all have a hundred pockets.
Only we know what they should hold.
When you're planning your day,
You should plan in a way
That the day becomes big and bold.
A hundred pockets
Improve a day
A hundredfold!

A day has a hundred pockets
If you know what to put inside!
If you've got enough schemes—
And you've got enough dreams—
You can fill 'em
Until they burst their seams!
I know! I've tried!

There's a pocket for fears—
And a pocket for tears—
And a pocket for storing sun.
There's a pocket for glad—
And a pocket for sad—
And a wonderful pocket just for fun!—
My favorite one!

We all have a hundred pockets—
Only we know what they should hold.
When you're planning your day,
You should plan in a way
That the day becomes big and bold.
A hundred pockets
Improve a day
A hundredfold!

A hundred pockets
Improve a day
A hundredfold!

Copyright © 1981 Stage And Screen Music, Inc.
Worldwide Rights Administered by Cherry River Music (BMI)
International Copyright Secured All Rights Reserved

A Christmas Carol

from the motion picture *Scrooge*

Words and Music by
Leslie Bricusse

Sing a song of gladness and cheer!—
For the time of Christmas is here!
Look around about you and see
What a world of wonder
This world can be!

Sing a Christmas carol—
Sing a Christmas carol—
Sing a Christmas carol—
Like the children do!

And enjoy the beauty—
All the joy and beauty—
That a Merry Christmas
Can bring to you!

Copyright © 1970 by Stage And Screen Music, Inc.
Worldwide Rights Administered by Cherry River Music (BMI)
International Copyright Secured All Rights Reserved

Thank You Very Much
from the motion picture *Scrooge*

Words and Music by
Leslie Bricusse

On behalf of all the people
Who have assembled here,
I would merely like to mention, if I may,
That our unanimous attitude
Is one of lasting gratitude
For what our friend
Has done for us today!
And therefore I would simply like to say...

Thank you very much!
Thank you very much!
That's the nicest thing
That anyone's ever done for me!
It may sound double Dutch,
But my delight is such
I feel as if a losing war's
Been won for me!

And if I had a flag
I'd hang my flag out—
To add a sort of final victory touch!
But since I left my flag at home
I'll simply have to say
Thank you very, very, very much!

Thank you very much!
Thank you very much!
That's the nicest thing
That anyone's ever done for me!
It sounds a bit bizarre—
But things the way they are,
I feel as if
Another life's begun for me!

And if I had a cannon
I would fire it—
To add a sort of celebration touch!
But since I left my cannon at home
I'll simply have to say
Thank you very, very, very much!

Thank you very much!
Thank you very much!
That's the nicest thing
That anyone's ever done for me!
It isn't every day
Good fortune comes my way—
I never thought the future
Would be fun for me!

And if I had a bugle
I would blow it—
To add a sort of how's your father touch!
But since I left my bugle at home
I'll simply have to say
Thank you very, very, very much!

Thank you very much!
Thank you very much!
That's the nicest thing
That anyone's ever done for me!
The future looks all right!
In fact it looks so bright,
I feel as if
They're polishing the sun for me!

And if I had a drum
I'd have to bang it!—
To add a sort of rumpty-tumpty touch!
But since I left my drummer at home
I'll simply have to say
Thank you very, very, very much!
Thank you very, very, very much!

Copyright © 1970 by Stage And Screen Music, Inc.
Worldwide Rights by Administered by Cherry River Music (BMI)
International Copyright Secured All Rights Reserved

Father Christmas

from the motion picture *Scrooge*

Words and Music by
Leslie Bricusse

1st Version (in praise of Santa Claus)
Father Christmas! Father Christmas!
He's the greatest man
In the whole wide world!
In the whole wide world!
And he knows it!

Every Christmas,
Father Christmas
Puts a great big sack
On his dear old back,
'Cause he loves us all—
And he shows it!

And he goes
For a sleighride,
If it snows
Then he may ride all night!—
But that's all right!

In the morning—
Christmas morning—
If you lift your eyes,
There's a big surprise—
On your bed you'll see
There's a gift from Father Christmas!—
That's how Christmas ought to be!

Father Christmas! Father Christmas!
He's a dear old gent—
He was Heaven-sent—
It would not be Christmas
Without him!

He's a sweetheart!
He's a darling!
He's an "astocrat!"
He's a pussy cat!
We'd be foolish
Ever to doubt him!

He's got style!—
Such a manner!
And his smile
Is a banner of joy
You can't destroy!

Merry Christmas,
Father Christmas!—
For it's thanks to you—
And the things you do—
That the likes of me
Think the world of Father Christmas!—
Who makes all our dreams come true!

2nd Version (Anti-Santa)
Father Christmas! Father Christmas!
He's the meanest man
In the whole wide world!
In the whole wide world!
You can feel it!

He's a miser!
He's a skinflint!
He's a stingy lout!
Leave your stocking out
For your Christmas gift
And he'll steal it!

It's a shame!
He's a villain!
What a game
For a villain to play
On Christmas Day!

After Christmas,
Father Christmas
Will be just as mean
As he's ever been,
And I'm here to say
We should all send Father Christmas
On his Merry Christmas way!

Copyright © 1970 by Stage And Screen Music, Inc.
Worldwide Rights Administered by Cherry River Music (BMI)
International Copyright Secured All Rights Reserved

The Beautiful Day

from the motion picture *Scrooge*

Words and Music by
Leslie Bricusse

On a beautiful day
That I dream about—
In a world I would love to see—

Is a beautiful place
Where the sun comes out—
And it shines in the sky for me.

On this beautiful winter's morning,
If my wish could come true
Somehow,

Then the beautiful day
That I dream about
Would be here
And now.

Copyright © 1970 by Stage And Screen Music, Inc.
Worldwide Rights Administered by Cherry River Music (BMI)
International Copyright Secured All Rights Reserved

Christmas Children

from the motion picture *Scrooge*

Words and Music by
Leslie Bricusse

Christmas children peep into Christmas windows—
See a world as pretty as a dream—
Christmas trees and toys—
Christmas hopes and joys—
Christmas puddings rich with Christmas cream.

Christmas presents shine in the Christmas windows—
Christmas boxes tied with pretty bows.
Wonder what's inside—
What delights they hide—
But till Christmas morning no one knows!
Won't it be exciting if it snows?

I suppose
That children everywhere
Will say a Christmas prayer
Till Santa brings
Their Christmas things.

Christmas children hunger for Christmas morning.
Christmas day's a wonder to behold!
Wondrous things to eat!
Every Christmas treat!
I believe that story we've been told—
Christmas is for children, young and old!

Copyright © 1970 by Stage And Screen Music, Inc.
Worldwide Rights Administered by Cherry River Music (BMI)
International Copyright Secured All Rights Reserved

I Like Life

from the motion picture *Scrooge*

Words and Music by
Leslie Bricusse

Ebenezer Scrooge,
The sins of man are huge.
A never-ending symphony
Of villainy and infamy—
Duplicity, deceit and subterfuge.
And no one's worse
Than Ebenezer Scrooge!

Though man's a handy candidate for Hell,
I must admit
Life sometimes has
Its brighter side as well!

I like life! Life likes me!
Life and I fairly fully agree
Life is fine! Life is good!
'Specially mine,
Which is just as it should be!

I like pouring the wine,
And why not?
Life's a pleasure
That I deny not!

I like life! Here and now!
Life and I made a mutual vow!
Till I die,
Life and I
We'll both try to be better somehow!

And if life were a woman,
She would be my wife!
Why?
Because I
Like life!

I like life! Life likes me!
I make life a perpetual spree,
Eating food, drinking wine,
Thinking who'd
Like the privilege to dine me.

I like living the life
Of pleasure,
Pausing only
To take my leisure

I like songs! I like dance!
I hear music and I'm in a trance.
Tra-la-la
Oom-pah-pah,
Chances are I shall get up and prance.

Where there's music and laughter,
Happiness is rife!—
Why?
Because I
Like life!

Copyright © 1970 by Stage And Screen Music, Inc.
Worldwide Rights Administered by Cherry River Music (BMI)
International Copyright Secured All Rights Reserved

The Minister's Cat

from the stage production of *Scrooge*

Words and Music
by Leslie Bricusse

The minister's cat is an affable cat—
The minister's cat is a boring cat—
The minister's cat is a charming cat—
At one o'clock on a Monday!

The minister's cat is a darling cat—
The minister's cat is an evil cat—
The minister's cat is a frightful cat—
At two o'clock on a Tuesday!

The minister's cat is a grumpy cat—
The minister's cat is a hungry cat—
The minister's cat is an idiot cat—
At three o'clock on a Wednesday!

The minister's cat is a jealous cat—
The minister's cat is a kindly cat—
The minister's cat is a lonely cat—
At four o'clock on a Thursday!

The minister's cat is a monster cat—
The minister's cat is a naughty cat—
The minister's cat is an oval cat—
At five o'clock on a Friday!

The minister's cat is a perfect cat—
The minister's cat is a quirky cat—
The minister's cat is a reverent cat—
At six o'clock on a Saturday!

The minister's cat is a silky cat—
The minister's cat is a tiresome cat—
The minister's cat is a useless cat—
At seven o'clock on a Sunday!

The minister's cat is a vicious cat—
The minister's cat is a wise old cat—
The minister's cat's an extraord'n'ry cat—
A yellow-eyed cat—
A zippy zany Zanzibar cat!—

And what do you make of all of that?—
I'll tell you what we make of that!—
The minister truly, truly has
An absolutely, most remarkable cat!

Copyright © 1982 by Stage And Screen Music, Inc.
Worldwide Rights Administered by Cherry River Music (BMI)
International Copyright Secured All Rights Reserved

Good Times
from the stage production of *Scrooge*

Words and Music by
Leslie Bricusse

Some days are up days,
Some days are down days.
Some days are golden,
Some dark brown days.
I never mind when we have blue days—
They're always followed by "we've come through" days.

We've had good times before,
And we'll have good times again.
Whatever we've done,
We've made life fun.
And when things were bad,
And bad times we've had,
We've fought and we've won—
One for all, all for one.

So if today things get rough,
Then we've just gotta get tough.
We're made of the stuff
That makes men men.
We're gonna come through,
And, kids, when we do,
We'll only know good times again.

We've had good times before,
And we'll have good times again.
Whatever we've done,
We've made life fun.
And when things were bad,
And bad times we've had,
We've fought and we've won—
One for all, all for one.

So if today things get rough,
Then we've just gotta get tough.
We're made of the stuff
That makes men men.
We're gonna come through,
And, kids, when we do,
We'll never know bad times—
Goodbye to the sad times—
We'll only know good times again!

Copyright © 1977 Stage And Screen Music Inc.
Worldwide Rights Administered by Cherry River Music (BMI)
International Copyright Secured All Rights Reserved

The Candy Man
from the motion picture
Willy Wonka & The Chocolate Factory

Words and Music by
Leslie Bricusse and Anthony Newley

I can't stop eating sweets!
All those wonderful Willy Wonka treats!
You can keep the others—
'Cause me, I'm a Wonkerer.
When it comes to candy,
Willy's the conquerer!

Who can take a sunrise—
Sprinkle it with dew?
Cover it in chocolate
And a miracle or two?
The Candy Man—
The Candy Man can.

The Candy Man can—
'Cos he mixes it with love
And makes the world taste good.

Who can take a rainbow—
Wrap it in a sigh—
Soak it in the sun
And make a strawberry lemon pie?
The Candy Man
The Candy Man can.

The Candy Man can—
'Cos he mixes it with love
And makes the world taste good.

The Candy Man makes
Everything he bakes
Satisfying and delicious!
Talk about your childhood wishes!
You can even eat the dishes!

Who can take tommorrow—
Dip it in a dream—
Separate the sorrow and collect up all the cream?
The Candy Man—
The Candy Man can.

The Candy Man can—
'Cos he mixes it with love
And makes the world taste good.

And the world tastes good
'Cos The Candy Man
Thinks it should.

Copyright © 1970, 1971 by Taradam Music
International Copyright Secured All Rights Reserved

Oompa-Loompa Doompadee-Doo

from the motion picture
Willy Wonka & The Chocolate Factory

Words and Music by
Leslie Bricusse and Anthony Newley

1. Oompa-Loompa, Doompadee-Doo!
   I've got a perfect puzzle for you!
   Oompa-Loompa, Doompadee-Dee!
   If you are wise, you'll listen to me!

   What do you get when you guzzle down sweets?
   Eating as much as an elephant eats?
   What are you at, getting terribly fat?
   What do you think will come of that?
   (I don't like the look of it!)

   Oompa-Loompa, Doompadee-Da!
   If you're not greedy, you will go far!
   You will live in happiness, too!
   Like the Oompa-Loompa, Doompadee-Doo!

2. Oompa-Loompa, Doompadee-Doo!
   I've got another puzzle for you!
   Oompa-Loompa, Doompadee-Dee!
   If you are wise, you'll listen to me!

   What do you get when your manners are bad?
   Why are you rude to your mother and dad?
   What do you gain driving people insane?
   I should have thought the answer's plain!
   (You don't gain anything!)

   Oompa-Loompa, Doompadee-Da!
   Given good manners, you will go far!
   You will live in happiness, too!
   Like the Oompa-Loompa, Doompadee-Doo!

3. Oompa-Loompa, Doompadee-Doo!
   I've got another puzzle for you!
   Oompa-Loompa, Doompadee-Dee!
   If you are wise, you'll listen to me!

   Who do you blame when a kid is a brat?—
   Pampered and spoiled, like a Siamese cat?
   What can you say when a kid is a curse?
   The parents are usually ten times worse!
   (Or haven't you noticed?)

   Oompa-Loompa, Doompadee-Da!
   If you're not spoiled, then you will go far!
   You will live in happiness, too!
   Like the Oompa-Loompa, Doompadee-Doo!

4. Oompa-Loompa, Doompadee-Doo!
   I've got a final puzzle for you!
   Oompa-Loompa, Doompadee-Dee!
   If you are wise, you'll listen to me!

   What do you get from a glut of TV?
   A pain in the neck and an I.Q. of three!
   Why don't you try simply reading a book?
   Or could you just not bear to look?
   (You'll get no commercials!)

   Oompa-Loompa, Doompadee-Da!
   Do as I say, and you will go far!
   You will live in happiness, too!
   Like the Oompa-Loompa, Doompadee-Doo!

Copyright © 1970, 1971 Taradam Music
International Copyright Secured All Rights Reserved

Cheer Up, Charlie

from the motion picture
Willy Wonka & The Chocolate Factory

Words and Music by
Leslie Bricusse and Anthony Newley

You get blue, like everyone—
But me and Grandpa Joe
Can make your troubles go away...
Blow away ... There they go.

Cheer up, Charlie—
Give me a smile.
What happened to that smile
I used to know?
Don't you know your grin
Has always been my sunshine?
Let that sunshine show!

Come on, Charlie—
No need to frown.
Deep down you know
Tomorrow is your toy.
When the world gets heavy,
Never pit-a-pat 'em!
Up and at 'em, boy!

Some day, sweet as a song,
Charlie's lucky day will come along.
Till that day you gotta stay in strong,
Charlie.
Up on top is right where you belong.

Look up, Charlie—
You'll see a star.
Just follow it
And keep your dreams in view.
Pretty soon the skies
Are gonna clear up, Charlie
Cheer up, Charlie, do.
Cheer up, Charlie—
Just be glad you're you.

Copyright © 1970, 1971 by Taradam Music
International Copyright Secured All Rights Reserved

I've Got A Golden Ticket

from the motion picture
Willy Wonka & The Chocolate Factory

Words and Music by
Leslie Bricusse and Anthony Newley

I never thought my life could be
Anything but catastrophe!
But suddenly I begin to see
A bit of good luck for me!
'Cause I've got a golden ticket!
I've got a golden twinkle in my eye!

I never had a chance to shine—
Never a happy song to sing.
But suddenly half the world is mine—
What an amazing thing!
'Cause I've got a golden ticket!
I've got a golden sun up in my sky!

I never thought I'd see the day
When I would face the world and say
"Good morning! - Look at the sun!"
I never thought that I would be
Slap in the lap of luxury!
'Cause I'd have said
It couldn't be done!
But it *can* be done!

I never dreamed that I could climb
Over the moon in ecstasy.
But nevertheless it's there that I'm
Shortly about to be!
'Cause I've got a golden ticket!
I've got a golden chance
To make my way!
And with a golden ticket,
It's a golden day!

Copyright © 1970, 1971 Taradam Music
International Copyright Secured All Rights Reserved

Pure Imagination

from the motion picture
Willy Wonka & The Chocolate Factory

Words and Music by
Leslie Bricusse and Anthony Newley

Come with me and you'll be
In a world of pure imagination!
Take a look and you'll see
Into your imagination!

We'll begin with a spin
Traveling in the world of my creation!
What we'll see
Will defy explanation!

If you want to view paradise,
Simply look around and view it!
Anything you want to, do it!
Want to change the world?
There's nothing to it!

There is no life I know
To compare with pure imagination!
Living there, you'll be free—
If you truly wish to be!

You will find in your mind
There's a world of endless fascination.
No more fun place to be
Than in your imagination!

You can dream any dream,
You can savor every situation!
Life in there's
A sensational sensation!

If you want to see magic lands,
Close your eyes and you will see one!
Wanna be a dreamer? Be one!
Any time you please—
And please save me one!

There is no place to go
To compare with your imagination!
So go there to be free—
If you truly wish to be!

Copyright © 1970, 1971 Taradam Music
International Copyright Secured All Rights Reserved

Thank You, Santa!
from the motion picture *Santa Claus: The Movie*

Words by Leslie Bricusse
Music by Henry Mancini

Christmas is the best of days!—
Who's the happy cause?
It's our favorite person—
Mine and yours—
Santa Claus!

Santa gives to all of us
All he has to give.
Santa really knows
The way to live!

Thank you, Santa!—
Thank you, Santa!—
When it snows,
We know you're near!

We wanta
Thank you, Santa!
Thank you, Santa!
'S nice to know you're coming back
Next year!

He belongs to everyone—
Him we share for sure!
Santa is forever
Everywhere, evermore!

Santa Claus is ours because
He's a friend in need!
Santa is our friend—
In word and deed!

Thank you, Santa!—
Thank you, Santa!—
You bring
All the world good cheer!

We're here ta
Thank you, Santa!
Frankly, Santa,
We'd like Christmas
Twenty times a year!

We wanta
Thank you, Santa!—
Thank you, Santa!—
You bring all the world
Good cheer!
We're here ta
Thank you, Santa!—
Thank you, Santa!—
'S nice to know you're coming back
Next year!

Copyright © 1985 Calash Corporation N.V.
International Copyright Secured All Rights Reserved

Somewhere In My Memory
from the motion picture *Home Alone*

Words by Leslie Bricusse
Music by John Williams

Candles in the window—
Shadows painting the ceiling—
Gazing at the fire-glow—
Feeling that "gingerbread" feeling.

Precious moments, special people—
Happy faces I can see.

Somewhere in my mem'ry,
Christmas joys all around me—
Living in my mem'ry—
All of the music—
All of the magic—
All of the family
Home here with me!

Copyright © 1990 Fox Film Music Corporation
International Copyright Secured All Rights Reserved

Star Of Bethlehem
from the motion picture *Home Alone*

Words by Leslie Bricusse
Music by John Williams

Star of Bethlehem, shining bright—
Bathing the world in heavenly light—
Let the glow of your distant glory
Fill us with hope this Christmas night!

Star of innocence, star of goodness—
Gazing down since time began—
You who've lived through endless ages,
View with love the age of man!

Star of beauty, hear our plea—
Whisper your wisdom tenderly.
Star of Bethlehem, set us free—
Make us a world we long to see!

Star of Bethlehem, shining bright—
Bathing the world in heav'nly light—
Let your luminous light from heaven
Enter our hearts and make us fly!

Star of happiness, star of wonder,
You see everything from afar.
Cast your eye upon the future—
Make us wiser than we are!

Star of gentleness, hear our plea—
Whisper your wisdom tenderly.
Star of Bethlehem, set us free—
Make us a world we long to see!

Copyright © 1990 Fox Film Music Corporation
International Copyright Secured All Rights Reserved

I'm Better With You
from the television production of *Peter Pan*

Words and Music by
Leslie Bricusse and Anthony Newley

I'm better with you
Than without—
Without a doubt,
I've found that out
About you.

When you're here,
I see good an' clearly—
Get to do
A lotta things I've got to do!
When you're not,
Dunno what to do!—
Fretting and getting upset
And forgetting
The sorta things I oughta not to!

When you're gone,
It's as though the sun had never shone—
Life's bouquet goes—
And the day goes
On and on and on!

And so you see
It's clear to me
That we should be together,
Now and always—
Big and small ways—
Ballrooooms and hallways—
You're what my life's about!
I am better with you
Than without!

Copyright © 1975 Taradam Music, Inc.
International Copyright Secured All Rights Reserved

Growing Up
from the television production of *Peter Pan*

Words and Music by
Leslie Bricusse and Anthony Newley

The trouble with growing up
Is seeing a dream blow up!—
Giving away your childhood!

The feeling of being free—
As only a child can be—
Living the life a child should.

I don't see why
I've got to say goodbye
To my childhood.
Let them take their closed-up world
And leave me an open sky,
Here in my childhood!

I've got no time for growing up!
When you've got time,
Don't waste it!
Taste it—
Each and any way you choose!
Use each lovely moment—
Youth is too good to lose!

Raise your voice—
And make your choice!
If you've got youth, rejoice!

Growing up
Is going up a hill
You ought to be going down!
I think growing up
Is slowing up a dream
That doesn't need slowing down!
Growing up
Is throwing up a challenge
You should be throwing down!

And I've got no time for growing up!—
Ever!

They take away all the sun!—
And take away all the fun!—
Do things because they've got to!

They wouldn't know blue from green!—
They live in a dull routine!—
They wouldn't know how not to!

And that's why I'm not growing up!-
Never ever!
Never ever!
Never!

Copyright © 1975 Taradam Music Inc.
International Copyright Secured All Rights Reserved

Peter Pan
from the television production of *Peter Pan*

Words and Music by
Leslie Bricusse and Anthony Newley

Who can catch a shooting star?—
Throw it with the moon among his toys?
Keep a sunbeam in a jar?
Peter Pan—
The king of boys!

Who can fling a rainbow round the sun?—
And make life fun?
Sweet Peter can!

Who can tie a tincan to the wind?—
And grin with joy?
Only one boy can—
Peter Pan!

Who has never read a book?
But could rook the Emperor of Japan?
Who's a match for Captain Hook?—
Or any man?
Sweet Peter Pan!

Who is music?
Who is panache?
Who is as quick
As a lightning flash?—
Whizz-bang-crash!
It's me!—
Peter Pan!
Catch me if you can!—
But no man can!

Who has never been to school?—
But can rule the greatest land there is?
Make the wisest man a fool?
Peter Pan—
The world is his!

Copyright © 1975 Taradam Music, Inc.
International Copyright Secured All Rights Reserved

Once Upon A Bedtime

from the television production of *Peter Pan*

Words and Music by
Leslie Bricusse and Anthony Newley

Once upon a time—
Words we love so well—
Storytellers tell,
In words with wings,
Of knaves and kings,
And wondrous things.

Like a nursery rhyme—
Like a magic spell—
Every dream we weave
Is make-believe
That tugs the sleeve
Of time.

Tales we're told—
Bold and true.
Though we all grow old,
Stories never do.
I know why
Stories never die—
They just wait for children
Passing by.

Time to go to sleep—
Count your pretty sheep—
Dream a dream to keep
Tomorrow new!
Happy endings, too!—
Hope your dreams come true.
Once upon a bedtime story,
They do!

Copyright © 1975 Taradam Music, Inc.
International Copyright Secured All Rights Reserved

Pretending

from the television production of *Peter Pan*

Words and Music by
Leslie Bricusse and Anthony Newley

Pretending is only a game!—
But it's a lovely game!—
One everyone in the world can play!
All that you do is to make a wish—
And you're a fish!—
Or you can be
A king or a flea—
By pretending!

Depending on who might be there,
You can go anywhere—
Anywhere fancy you care to find!—
And since it's all in your mind,
You'll find fantasies
That are never-ending!

Close your eyes—
The sky's the limit!—
Now you've found the magic potion—
If the ocean's wide, just swim it!
Nothing you can't do!—
Just pretend it's true!

Pretending you're mending the moon—
Putting the world in tune—
Make every day an unending spree!—
Anything splendid you long to be—
Mimic or mime—
Just do it—
Like I'm recommending!

Then your world
Will grow—
When pretending
Makes it so!

Copyright © 1975 Taradam Music Inc.
International Copyright Secured All Rights Reserved

Little Darlings

from the television production of *Peter Pan*

Words and Music by
Leslie Bricusse and Anthony Newley

Little Jesus—
Gentle Jesus—
Be with me tonight.
Pray for mama—
Pray for papa—
Till we see the daylight.

Pray for John—
And pray for Wendy—
Pray for Michael, too!
Little Jesus—
Gentle Jesus—
Keep me safe with you.

Little light,
Burning bright—
Bid the night welcome.

Spread your glow
Soft and low,
So she'll know
She's welcome.

Sleep, my sleepyheads,
In your baby beds—
Send the world away
'Till there's a brand-new day.

Friendly light—

Burning bright—

Be the night's

Eyesight.

Guard my
Children's
Dreams until,
By-and-by,
Day draws nigh.
Hush-a-bye,
Little
Darlings.

Little Jesus—
Gentle Jesus—
Be with me tonight.
Pray for mama—

Pray for papa—
Till we see the daylight.

Pray for John—
And pray for Wendy—
Pray for Michael, too!
Little Jesus—
Gentle Jesus—
Keep me safe with you.

Amen.

Copyright © 1975 Taradam Music Inc.
International Copyright Secured All Rights Reserved

A Song Called Love

from the television production of *Peter Pan*

Words and Music by
Leslie Bricusse and Anthony Newley

There is a thing
I wish I could sing of.
But it's a thing
I don't know a thing of.
If I were king,
It's what I'd be king of.
Love.

If I could build a world of my own,
The world would never be lonely.
On a golden day that would never end,
Everybody would be my friend—
And the world I would build
Would be called Love.

If I could have a dream of my own,
The night would never be lonely.
I would dream of moments I've never known—
Warm and cozy, but not alone—
And the dream I would dream
Would be called Love.

For of all the people
That I recall,
No one knows who I am
At all.

If I could sing a song of my own,
My heart would never be lonely.
I would sing of days that I hope to see—
Days I hope you will spend with me—
And the song I would sing
Would be called Love.

Copyright © 1975 Taradam Music, Inc.
International Copyright Secured All Rights Reserved

Never-Never Land

from the television production of *Peter Pan*

Words and Music by
Leslie Bricusse and Anthony Newley

Never-never land—
My forever land—
Let me stay on your shores.
Every childhood dream I ever had
Was yours—
The most lovely land
That was ever planned—
Where my mind still explores—
Still explores....

For to understand
Life in Never-land
You must know where to go—
To that part of children's minds
They never show.
Every fantasy
Children plan to see
It is here. It will grow.
It will grow....

Tigers and blue-eyed elephants—
Bits off a falling star!—
If ever you eyed elephants,
Here's where they are!

Monkeys and gray-nosed porcupines—
Flunkies in purple coats!—
Children have seen those porcupines—
Sailing in boats—
Beautiful boats....

Never-never land—
You're a clever land,
For you hold in your hand
Every precious secret
Children understand.
In whatever land
We may ever land,
Only here can we live
What we dream—
And we dream
That we live
Here in Never-land!

Copyright © 1975 Taradam Music Inc.
International Copyright Secured All Rights Reserved

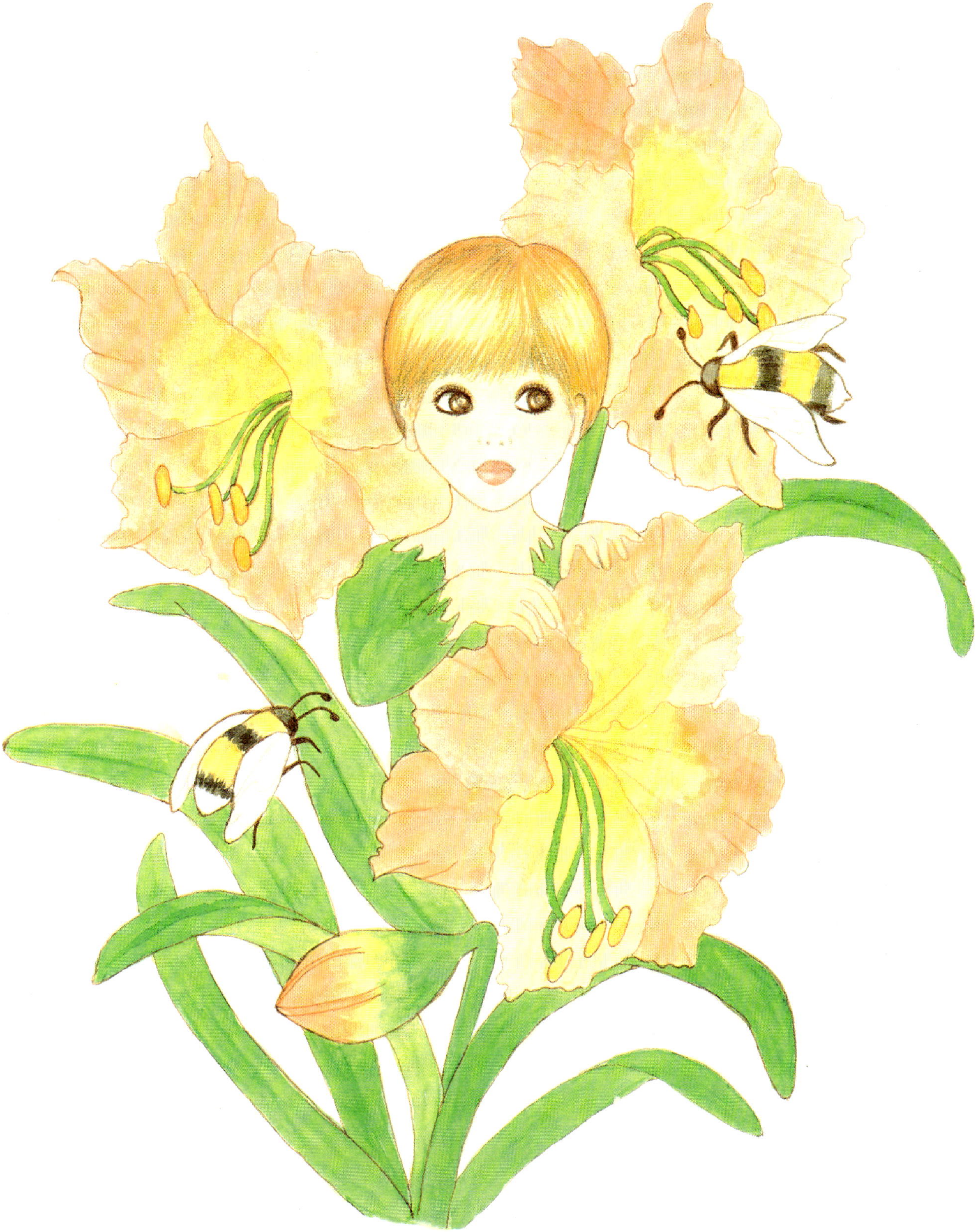

You Can Fly
from the television production of *Peter Pan*

Words and Music by
Leslie Bricusse and Anthony Newley

I'll show you how you can fly!
Think lovely things—
And the world will have wings—
Somewhere up there in the sky!
I know you can fly!—
So can I!
Why not try?
Don't be shy!...
Come on, try!

High above a worried world,
We'll fly to my unhurried world
Together!
Way above the weather,
You can kiss your cares goodbye!
Life is never quite the same again
When you can fly!
Fly! Fly! Fly! Fly!
Fly! Fly! Fly! Fly!
Fly!

We didn't know we could fly!
We used to stay
On the ground every day!—
Now we can play in the sky!
I'm glad we can fly!
So am I!
So am I!
So am I!

Farther than the eye can see!—
Beyond where even I can see!—
We're going!
Knowing me,
It's gonna be a treat,
You won't deny!—
Knowing Peter,
We will eat a sweeter piece of pie!

Life is never quite the same again
When you can fly!
Fly! Fly! Fly! Fly!
Fly! Fly! Fly! Fly!
Fly!

Copyright © 1975 Taradam Music Inc.
International Copyright Secured All Rights Reserved

The House On Happiness Hill
from the television production of *Peter Pan*

Words and Music by
Leslie Bricusse and Anthony Newley

Building a house—
How do you begin it?
What must you do
To be happy in it?

I know a hill—
One with the sun on its face.
Happiness Hill—
It's a good place.

This house needs love and care—
There's someone special living there.
We'll use contentment for
The floor of it!—
And welcome for
The door of it!—
There's more of it!

Windows of hope—
Looking out at rainbows.
Straight down the slope
Is where all the rain goes.

Friendship's the roof—
Peace is the key to the door—
If you need proof
What it's there for.

Live there in all goodwill—
As in my heart I know I will.
Love is a house—
High up on Happiness Hill!
Live there in love—
High up on Happiness Hill!

Copyright © 1975 Taradam Music Inc.
International Copyright Secured All Rights Reserved

Through The Eyes Of A Child

from the television production of *Babes In Toyland*

Words and Music by
Leslie Bricusse

If you can see
Through the eyes of a child
The wonderful world
That children see,
Believe you me,
You will never grow old—
You will always be free
To be beguiled.

If you can think
With the mind of a child—
Believe and be lost
In fantasy—
Believe you me,
That's more precious than gold—
You will always hold,
In your childlike mind,
Precious dreams
Other folk don't find.

If you, like me,
Can think and see
Through the wand'ring,
Wond'ring
Eyes and mind
Of a child.

Copyright © 1986 William Finnegan Productions (BMI)
International Copyright Secured   All Rights Reserved

C-I-N-C-I-N-N-A-T-I

from the television production of *Babes In Toyland*

Words and Music by
Leslie Bricusse

I come from
C-I-N-C-I-N-N-A-T-I—
Cincinnati!
The best town in O-H-I-O—
Ohio, U.S.A.!

At first they called it Cinci,
But since Cinci is so natty,
They named it Cincinnati,
So they say!

Hey, the girls are pretty pretty
In this gritty little city—
And the fellers
Are the feistiest I've seen!

And when it comes to ball teams,
The Reds and The Bengals maul teams!—
They knock the socks off all teams
On the green!

I mean,
To argue's indefensible—
The facts are common-sensible—
Since Cinci is invincible—
Ya know what I mean?

Cinci's more than merely natty!—
She's Ohio's Maserati!—
Cincinnati's
At the centre of the scene!

Copyright © 1986 William Finnegan Productions (BMI)
International Copyright Secured All Rights Reserved

The ABC Song

from the musical *Stop The World—I Want To Get Off*

Words and Music by Leslie Bricusse
and Anthony Newley

A-B-C-D-	1-
E-F-G-	2-
H-I-J-K-	3-
L-M-N-O-P-	4-
Q-R-S-T-	5-
U-V-W-	6-7-
X-Y-	8-9-
Zed!	10!

Copyright © 1961 TRO Ludlow Music, Inc.
170 N.E. 33rd St., Ft. Lauderdale, FLA 33334
International Copyright Secured All Rights Reserved

Look At That Face

from the musical *The Roar Of The Greasepaint—
The Smell Of The Crowd*

Words and Music by
Leslie Bricusse and Anthony Newley

1st Chorus (flattering)
Look at that face—
Just look at it!
Look at that fabulous face
Of yours!

I knew
First look I took at it,
This was the face
That the world adores!

Look at those eyes—
As wise and as deep as the sea.
Look at that nose—
It shows what a nose should be!

As for your smile,
It's lyrical—
Friendly and warm as a summer's day.
That face
Is just a miracle!—
Where could I ever find words to say
The way
That it makes me happy—
Whatever the time or place?
I'll find in no book
What I find when I look
At that face!

2nd Chorus (unflattering)
Look at that face—
Just look at it!
Look at that funny old face
Of yours!

I knew
First look I took at it,
You've got a face
Like a kitchen door's!

Look at those eyes—
As close as the closest of friends.
Look at that nose—
It starts where a good nose ends!

As for your smile—
Spectacular!
One grin would frighten the birds away!
You've got a face
Like Dracula!—
And I mean that in the nicest way!
To say
That there's noone like you
Would not even state the case!
No wonder I shook
When I first took a look
At that face!

Copyright © 1965 TRO Musical Comedy Productions
170 N.E. 33rd St., Ft. Lauderdale, FL 33334
International Copyright Secured All Rights Reserved

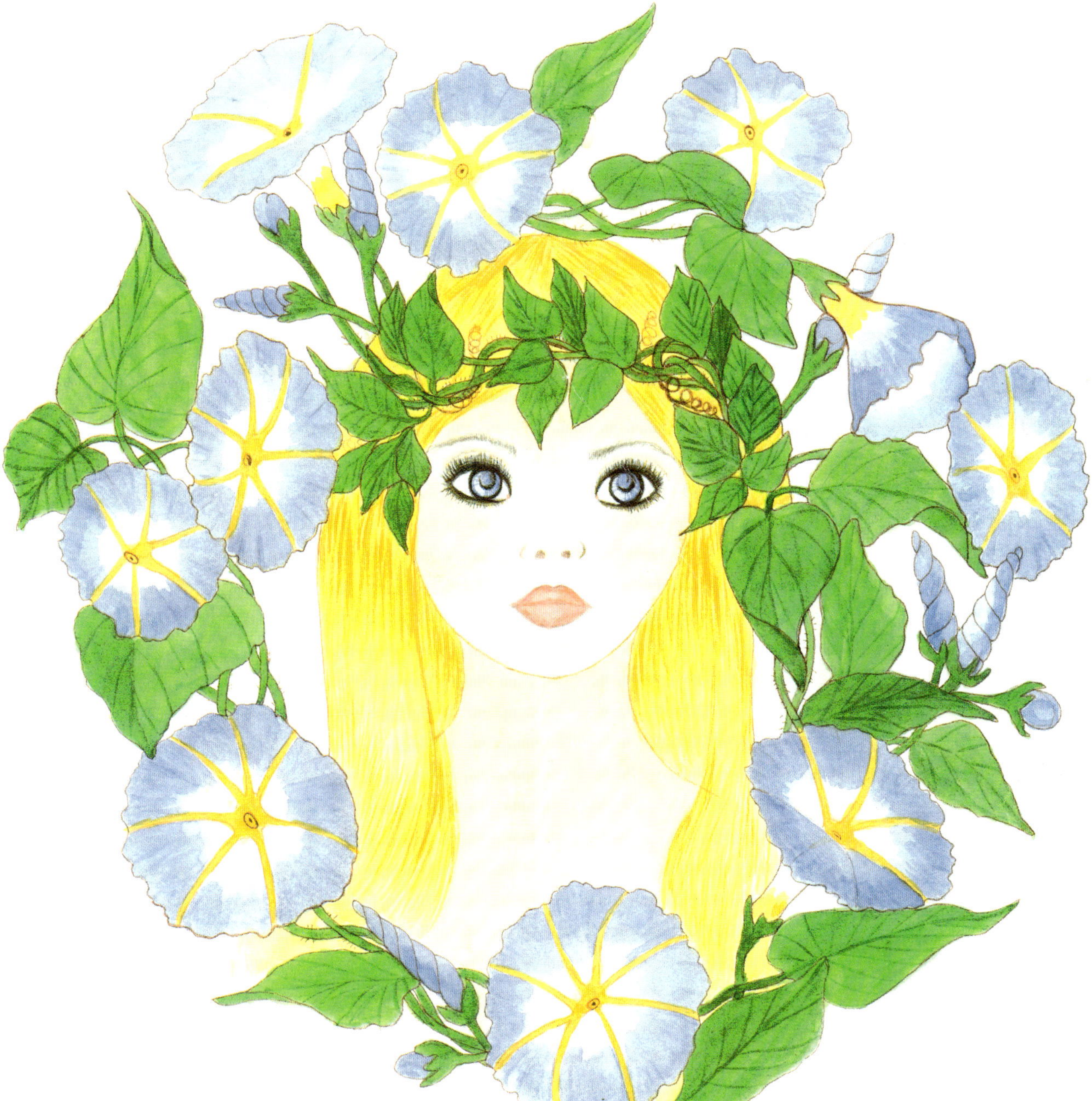

The Beautiful Land

from the musical *The Roar Of The Greasepaint—The Smell Of The Crowd*

Words and Music by
Leslie Bricusse and Anthony Newley

Red is the colour of a pretty pillar box.
Orange is any orange on a tree.
Yellow's the colour of a bag of lemon drops.
Green is a piece of seaweed in the sea.
Blue is the colour of the sky in summertime.
Indigo is a Siamese cat's eyes.
Violet's the colour of a pretty little flow'r.
These are the colours of the rainbow skies.

There is a beautiful land
Where all your dreams come true.
It's all tied up in a rainbow,
All shiny and new—
But it's not easy to find,
No matter what you do.

It's not on top of a mountain,
Or beneath the deep blue sea—
Or in London zoo—
Or in Timbuktu—
Or in Tim-buk-three!

And if you travelled the world
From China to Peru,
There's no beautiful land on the chart.
An explorer could not begin
To discover its origin—
For the beautiful land is in your heart!

Copyright © 1965 TRO Musical Comedy Productions
170 N.E. 33rd St., Ft. Lauderdale, FL 33334
International Copyright Secured All Rights Reserved

That's What It Is To Be Young
from the musical *The Roar Of The Greasepaint—The Smell Of The Crowd*

Words and Music by
Leslie Bricusse and Anthony Newley

Fresh as an April morning—
Soft as a tulip's tongue—
Clear as the gleam
Of a mountain stream—
That's what it is
To be young!

Warm as a summer sunrise—
Sweet as an evening breeze—
Pure as a note
From a song-bird's throat—
Rich as the green
Of the trees.

Strong as the bite
Of a frosty night—
Bold as a big brass band—
Keen as a bean—
Or a young sardine
Not very keen
To be canned!

Bright as a newborn bluebell—
New as a song unsung—
Live as a lamb
Who's the big 'I am'
As soon as Spring has sprung—

Free as the breeze
On the seven seas—
That's what it is
To be young!

Copyright © 1965 TRO Musical Comedy Productions
170 N.E. 33rd St., Ft. Lauderdale, FL 33334
International Copyright Secured All Rights Reserved

Things To Remember
from the musical *The Roar Of The Greasepaint—The Smell Of The Crowd*

Words and Music by
Leslie Bricusse and Anthony Newley

When I think of the good things that life has to give,
I'm reluctantly forced to agree
That the number of people who know how to live
Is restricted, quite simply, to me.

For life is like cricket—we play by the rules—
And the secret, which few people know,
Which keeps men of class
Well apart from the fools,
Is to think up the rules
As you go.

There are so many things to remember
As you travel the highway of life—
Like always be kind to your husband—
Or, if you're a man, to your wife.

You should never shoot trout in September.
You should never feed babies on gin.
Don't ever play poker on Sundays—
Unless you are certain to win!

Don't go out of your way seeking danger!—
Never stand on a crocodile's tail!
Never buy London Bridge from a stranger!—
Unless you can make a few bob on the sale!

Don't waste time on the friends that repel you—
And don't ever drink soup with a knife!
Don't buy what those gypsy girls sell you—
And if you remember these things that I tell you
By hell, you'll do well all your life!

Please remember your grandmother's birthday—
And be proud of the flag at all times!
Stand up for the National Anthem!—
Sit down to recite dirty rhymes!

Always honour your debts—when you have to!
And be honest—unless there's no need!
Spend two hours a day with the Good Book!—
If you've nothing better to read!

You must always be patient with children—
Though they jangle your nerves, it is true!
If a child is a present from Heaven,
Thank God there aren't too many presents like you!

Don't drink champagne from soggy old slippers,
Though this barbaric custom is rife!
Don't lift up a whale by its flippers!—
And only buy claret from certified shippers—
Avoid eating goulash with ice cream and kippers!—
Remember these things,
You obnoxious young nippers!—
And you will do well all your life!

So cheers, me dears—
And here's to life!

Copyright © 1965 TRO Musical Comedy Productions
170 N.E. 33rd St., Ft. Lauderdale, FL 33334
International Copyright Secured All Rights Reserved

Faith In The Future
from the musical *Noah's Ark*

Words and Music by
Leslie Bricusse

So, my friends,
It seems we must
Be patient a little while longer—
Heads just a little bit higher—
Minds just a little bit stronger—

Eyes a little brighter—
Hearts a little lighter—
Be a bit politer
If we can!
Belts a little tighter—
Show 'em you're a fighter—
Show 'em you are quite a man—
Or polar bear—
Or pelican!

We must have
Faith in the future—
Hope in our hearts.
Faith in the future—
That's where it starts.
Look to tomorrow—
Yesterday's gone.
What's past is past—
But the world goes on
And on and on—

And on in the future,
People will say
Faith in the future
Gave us today—
Gave us tomorrow—
That's why we know
Our faith in the future
Will grow and grow and grow!

Copyright © 1964 by Stage And Screen Music, Inc.
Worldwide Rights Administered by Cherry River Music (BMI)
International Copyright Secured All Rights Reserved

It's A Musical World

from the musical *The Good Old Bad Old Days*

Words and Music by
Leslie Bricusse and Anthony Newley

The world is made of music!
Never-ending symphonies
Of sound surround us!
Miracles of melody
Abound around us, too!
It's a musical world!
Such a beautiful world!

Listen to the rhythm
Of a storm in summer!
Hear the mellow melody
When church bells chime!
Isn't that as magical
As once upon a time?
It's a musical world!
Such a beautiful world!

Ding-dong!
Sing a song of Spring and Summer!
Spring song, Summer song
And entre nous,
I love music,
And I know that you do, too!
It's a musical world!
Such a beautiful world!

The world's a maze of music!
Everthing contributes
To the rare concerto!
Elephants and butterflies
Have their concerto, too!
It's a musical world!
Such a beautiful world!

Listen to the music
Of a lonely seashore!
Hear the sad cacophony
Of sea gull songs!
Nature has an orchestra
Where every sound belongs!
It's a musical world!
Such a beautiful world!

Ding-dong!
Sing a song of Spring and Summer!
Spring song, Summer song
And entre nous,
I love music
And I know that you do, too!
It's a musical world!
Such a beautiful world!

Ding-dong!
Sing a song of Spring and Summer!
Spring song, Summer song
And entre nous,
I love music
And I know that you do, too!
It's a musical world!

Copyright © 1971, 1972 by Taradam Music, Inc.
International Copyright Secured   All Rights Reserved

The World Is Beautiful
from *Ondine**

Words and Music by
Leslie Bricusse

Red and green and gold and blue.
Orange, pink and purple, too.
Every colour, every hue.
Ever-changing, ever-new.
Just for me and just for you.
The world is beautiful.

Hills and mountains, lakes and trees.
Skies and rivers, stars and seas.
Free to wander where we please.
Rain and sunshine, mist and breeze.
Dusk and dawn and times like these.
The world is beautiful.

Kings and castles, spires and towers.
Tales and legends, magic powers.
Fate and fortune, storms and showers.
And fields of flowers.
All these are ours.

Love and friendship, young and old.
Songs and stories, sung and told.
Hopes and daydreams, bright and bold.
Winter mornings, crisp and cold.
Summer evenings, soft and gold.
The world is beautiful.
Truly, the world is beautiful.
Truly beautiful.

*Unproduced; see Reflections, p. 201.

Copyright © 1973 by Stage And Screen Music, Inc.
Worldwide Rights Administered by Cherry River Music (BMI)
International Copyright Secured All Rights Reserved

Amy Rainbow

Words and Music by
Leslie Bricusse

Amy Rainbow
You're my rainbow!
You make good times
When there are none!—
You make sunshine
Out of showers—
You make rainbows—
'Cause you are one!

You are childhood—
You are flowers—
You are magic—
You have magic powers!
There is Christmas
All around you—
I'm so happy, Amy Rainbow,
That I found you!

I just couldn't care
What tomorrow brings—
Even though it may
Dismay me!
Long as we can share
The tomorrow things—
Long as I can be with
Amy, my Amy, my rainbow!

You are springtime—
You are laughter—
You are happy—
You are ever after!—
And a bright star
Shines above you—
Have I told you, Amy Rainbow,
That I love you?

Copyright © 1980 Stage And Screen Music, Inc.
Worldwide Rights Administered by Cherry River Music (BMI)
International Copyright Secured All Rights Reserved

Tumbarumba

Words and Music by
Leslie Bricusse

There's Tumbarumba, Tallangatta,
Wagga Wagga, Wangaratta,
Pitarpunga, Parramatta
And Wooloomooloo!

There's Dandenong and Yarrawonga,
Dirranbandi and Taronga,
Goondiwindi and Wodonga,
And Woomera, too!

In case these words to you are alien—
Worse than words in Shaw's Pygmalion—
I'll explain they're all Australian
Cities and towns—
The prettiest sounds!

There's Mittagong and Billabong
And Woollongong and Gooloogong—
So sing a song with me today
About Austray-li-ay!

There's Dunedoo and Doodnadatta,
Coogee Beach and Coolangatta—
Makes you wonder what's the matter
When anyone speaks!

There's Bunnaloo and Innaminka,
Gundaroo and Milparinka—
Funny names that make you thinka
You're talking to freaks!

In case you think my English pigeonal,
Let me say these most original
Names are simply aboriginal
Cities and towns—
The prettiest sounds!

Like Mittagong and Billabong,
And Woollongong and Gooloogong—
So sing a song with me today
About Austray-li-ay!

Copyright © 1991 Stage And Screen Music, Inc.
Worldwide Rights Administered by Cherry River Music (BMI) International Copyright
Secured All Rights Reserved

Where Did My Childhood Go?

from the motion picture *Goodbye, Mr. Chips*

Words and Music by
Leslie Bricusse

They think I do not understand them.
They think I do not hear or see.
I only wish they knew
That I do understand them.
I only wish they understood me.

Yesterday I was their age.
Tomorrow they'll be my age.
Sooner, much sooner than they know.
And suddenly they will ask
What every child must ask—
'Where did my childhood go?'

Where did my childhood go?
When did my youth, so sweet and free,
Suddenly slip away from me?
Was it so long ago?
Where did my childhood go?

Where did the magic end?
When did the future meet the past?—
Ending a dream too good to last—
Taking away a friend—
When did my childhood end?

Was it that day
In early spring that lingers on?—
When somehow I knew
This precious time would soon be gone.

What does the future show?
Spring will return again next year.
And when she does, she'll find me here
Wondering still, I know,
Where did my childhood go?

Yesterday I was their age.
Tomorrow they'll be my age.
Sooner, much sooner than they know.
And suddenly they will ask
What every man must ask—
Where did my childhood go?

Copyright © 1968, 1969 Metro-Goldwyn-Mayer Inc., New York, NY
Rights Throughout the World Controlled by Hastings Music Corporation, New York, NY
International Copyright Secured All Rights Reserved

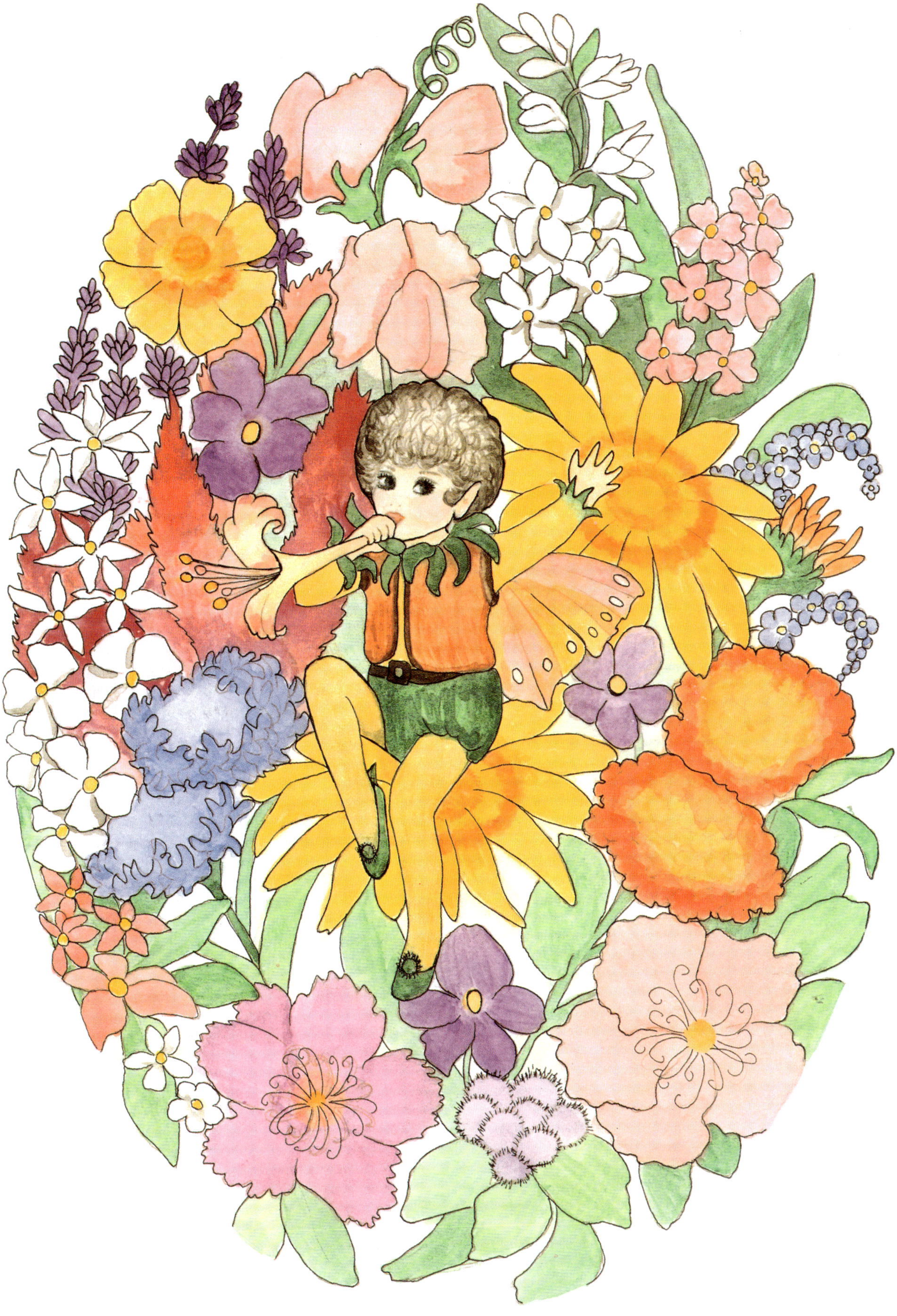

CHERRY LANE MUSIC:
THE PRINT COMPANY

EXECUTIVE: Michael Lefferts, President; Kathleen A. Maloney, Director of Customer Service; Len Handler, Creative Services Manager; Rock Stamberg, Advertising and Promotion Manager; Karen DeCrenza, Executive Secretary; Karen Carey, Division Secretary.
MUSIC: Mark Phillips, Director of Music; Jon Chappell, Associate Director of Music; Steve Gorenberg, Music Editor; Kerry O'Brien, Music Editor; Gordon Hallberg, Director, Music Engraving.
ART: Kerstin A. Fairbend, Art Director; Rosemary Cappa, Art Assistant.
PRODUCTION: Daniel Rosenbaum, Production Manager; James Piacentino, Production Coordinator.

9136018